releasing
THE CAPTIVE

REFLECTIONS FOR THE YEAR OF MARK

GEOFFREY PLANT

Published by
John Garratt Publishing
32 Glenvale Crescent
Mulgrave, Vic. 3170
www.johngarratt.com.au

Copyright ©2011 Geoffrey Plant

All rights reserved. Except as provided by the Australian copyright law, no part of this book may be reproduced in any way without permission in writing from the publisher.

Design and typesetting: Lucille Hughes
Text editing: Maryna Mews

Printed Coordinated by Advent Print Management

Cover image: www.thinkstockphotos.com.au/
ISBN: 9781921946134

Cataloguing in Publication information for this title is available from the National Library of Australia.
www.nla.gov.au

For Ronan Kilgannon, Peter McGrath ofm, Marie Willey, Val Willsteed, Frank Walter, Craig and Jackie Harrison, Bénédicte Cruysmans and Fedor Mediansky, Elizabeth Rieger, Wyn Jones, Greg and Liz Fitzgerald, and Richard and Annette Dobson, and in memory of Bronwyn Walter and Jimmy Willsteed

How can anyone tell how much he owes to the goodness of those who love him? If we knew what people in their love for us do to save us from damnation by the simple fact of their friendship for us, we would learn some humility.

Thomas Merton

CONTENTS

Introduction	ix
First Sunday of Advent	1
Second Sunday of Advent	7
Third Sunday of Advent	13
Fourth Sunday of Advent	20
Christmas Day	26
Solemnity of Mary, Mother of God	31
Feast of the Holy Family	37
Feast of the Epiphany	42
Ash Wednesday	48
First Sunday of Lent	54
Second Sunday of Lent	61
Third Sunday of Lent	66
Fourth Sunday of Lent	73
Fifth Sunday of Lent	80
Passion Sunday (Palm Sunday)	87
Mass of the Lord's Supper (Holy Thursday)	91
Good Friday	97
Easter Sunday	101
Second Sunday of Easter	106
Third Sunday of Easter	111
Fourth Sunday of Easter	117
Fifth Sunday of Easter	122
Sixth Sunday of Easter	127
Seventh Sunday of Easter	133
The Ascension of the Lord	138
Pentecost Sunday	144
Trinity Sunday	149

The Body and Blood of Christ	155
Australia Day	161
The Assumption of the Blessed Virgin Mary	167
Feast of All Saints	172
Feast of All Souls	177
Baptism of the Lord (First Sunday in Ordinary Time)	182
Second Sunday in Ordinary Time	189
Third Sunday in Ordinary Time	195
Fourth Sunday in Ordinary Time	202
Fifth Sunday in Ordinary Time	209
Sixth Sunday in Ordinary Time	215
Seventh Sunday in Ordinary Time	222
Eighth Sunday in Ordinary Time	227
Ninth Sunday in Ordinary Time	232
Tenth Sunday in Ordinary Time	239
Eleventh Sunday in Ordinary Time	245
Twelfth Sunday in Ordinary Time	251
Thirteenth Sunday in Ordinary Time	257
Fourteenth Sunday in Ordinary Time	263
Fifteenth Sunday in Ordinary Time	269
Sixteenth Sunday in Ordinary Time	275
Seventeenth Sunday in Ordinary Time	281
Eighteenth Sunday in Ordinary Time	287
Nineteenth Sunday in Ordinary Time	294
Twentieth Sunday in Ordinary Time	299
Twenty-First Sunday in Ordinary Time	305
Twenty-Second Sunday in Ordinary Time	310
Twenty-Third Sunday in Ordinary Time	316

Twenty-Fourth Sunday in Ordinary Time	322
Twenty-Fifth Sunday in Ordinary Time	328
Twenty-Sixth Sunday in Ordinary Time	334
Twenty-Seventh Sunday in Ordinary Time	339
Twenty-Eighth Sunday in Ordinary Time	346
Twenty-Ninth Sunday in Ordinary Time	351
Thirtieth Sunday in Ordinary Time	356
Thirty-First Sunday in Ordinary Time	363
Thirty-Second Sunday in Ordinary Time	368
Thirty-Third Sunday in Ordinary Time	373
Christ the King	378
Bibliography	383

INTRODUCTION

Releasing the Captive is a collection of reflections for Year B of the liturgical cycle, the year of Mark. It is a companion volume to *Ascending the Mountain* (Year A, the year of Matthew) and *Welcoming the Outsider* (Year C, the year of Luke). I have chosen the titles for these volumes to reflect the distinctive emphasis that each of the evangelists offers us on the life and ministry of Jesus. Matthew presents Jesus as the new Moses, while in the material unique to Luke's gospel we meet a Jesus who welcomes outsiders of one kind or another. I believe that an interpretative key to Mark's gospel can be found in the incident that he places at the beginning of Jesus' public ministry: an exorcism in the synagogue at Capernaum. We meet a man with symptoms that a modern reader might identify with epilepsy, and Jesus heals him. He has been set free, released from captivity, and that is what exorcism is all about. Despite supernatural horror movies like *The Exorcist* (1973) and *The Rite* (2011), exorcisms are not part of the world view of people living in the twenty-first century, at least in the Western world. But the reality behind demonic possession is very much with us today because we are held captive by forces over which we have little or no control, forces that rob us of freedom, alienate us from God and others, and stunt our human growth. A contemporary example of 'possession' is our addiction to possessions, described by Clive Hamilton and Richard Denniss by the coined word 'affluenza'. Affluenza is the 'bloated, sluggish and unfulfilled feeling that results from efforts to keep up with the Joneses'.[1] We are confused about what it takes to live a worthwhile life, and part of this confusion 'is a failure to distinguish between what we want and what we need'. For example, only 20 per cent of Americans said a second car was a 'necessity' in 1973; by 1996 that figure had risen to 37 per cent. In Australia, items that were once considered as luxuries have become necessities – items such as plasma-screen TVs, air conditioning, personal computers, second bathrooms and mobile phones, to name but a few.[2] (Reflection for the Thirty-Second Sunday in Ordinary Time).

World poverty is also an evil that holds millions of people in bondage. For that reason the work of people like David Bussau, founder of Opportunity International (Reflection for the Fourth Sunday in Ordinary Time), and Muhammad Yunus, founder of the Grameen Bank (Reflection for the Eleventh Sunday in Ordinary Time) could be described as exorcism because they are liberating people in Third

---

[1] Clive Hamilton and Richard Denniss, *Affluenza*, Allen & Unwin, Crows Nest, NSW, 2005, p. 3.
[2] Clive Hamilton and Richard Denniss, *Affluenza* p. 7.

World countries from poverty. But, sadly, we can resist the gracious invitation offered to us. The rich young man (Reflection for the Twenty-Eighth Sunday in Ordinary Time) who approached Jesus with the question 'What must I do to inherit eternal life?' is sincere in his quest. Jesus, we are told, 'looked steadily at him and loved him'. But he is beset with fear. Who would he be without his wealth? What friends would he have were he to give away all his possessions? It was a threshold he could not cross. Sadly, this man's many possessions held him captive.

We can also be held captive by our busyness, and this is a recurring theme in several of these homilies. The social commentator Hugh Mackay argues that we have become obsessed by the need to appear busy (Reflection for the First Sunday of Lent). 'Busy-busy' has become a kind of mantra in our lives.[3] And keeping busy is one sure way to avoid listening. Frantic busyness can be a wonderful hiding place. If you stay busy for long enough, you might never have time to listen, you might never have time 'to take a closer look at the things and people one would rather not see, to face situations one would rather avoid, to answer questions one would rather forget'.[4] Henri Nouwen writes that 'one of the most obvious characteristics of our daily lives is that we are busy. We experience our days as filled with things to do, people to meet, projects to finish, letters to write, calls to make, and appointments to keep. Our lives often seem like

---

3   Hugh Mackay, 'Flat out, but are we really doing anything?', *The Australian*, 1 April 1996.
4   Alessandro Pronzato, quoted in John Moses, *The Desert: An Anthology for Lent*, Canterbury Press, Norwich, 1977, p. 57.

over-packed suitcases bursting at the seams'[5] (Reflection for Ash Wednesday). Jesus invites us into the desert to confront the truth about our own lives and the choices we make, to make a personal stocktake.

An earlier version of some of these reflections appeared in the Australasian Catholic Record, and I am grateful to Fr Gerard Kelly for permission to reproduce them here. Once again I would like to express my gratitude to the parishioners of St Luke's, Revesby, who have sat through these when I gave them as homilies. Their encouragement and support has been a blessing over the years.

---

5. Henri Nouwen, *Making All Things New: An Introduction to the Spiritual Life*, Doubleday, New York, 1981, p. 23.

Reflections for the year of Mark

FIRST SUNDAY OF ADVENT

(YEAR B)

And what I say to you I say to all: Stay awake! (Mk 1:37)

The Second Coming may occur sooner than we think, if genetic technology continues to progress by leaps and bounds. In February 1997, scientists working at the Roslin Institute in Edinburgh, Scotland, created world news headlines by successfully creating a cloned sheep, subsequently named Dolly. This means that Dolly's genetic make-up is identical to the adult sheep from which it was cloned. Scientists are now suggesting that it won't be long before we have the expertise to clone extinct animals. The director of the Australian Museum, Dr Mike Archer, says that it's time to bring the Tasmanian tiger back to life. The last tiger died in Hobart Zoo in 1936, but the museum has the remains of a very young tiger, collected in 1866 and perfectly preserved since then in a bottle of alcohol.[6] Scientists would first have to harvest the tiger's DNA, its genetic blueprint, from the preserved specimen. The tiger's DNA would then be inserted into the egg of a host animal, making sure that all genetic material had been removed from the unfertilised

---

6   James Woodford, 'Baby tiger has power to revive species', *The Sydney Morning Herald*, 13 May 1999, p. 3.

egg.[7] But the Tasmanian tiger isn't the only extinct animal that may walk the earth yet again. Scientists are now attempting to clone a 20,000-year-old giant woolly mammoth excavated from permafrost in Siberia. The mammoth's DNA is to be inserted into the egg of an Asian elephant, an animal with greater biological similarities to the mammoth than to African elephants.[8]

But that isn't as easy as it sounds. We all start out as a fertilised egg, a zygote, which is a single cell. But when the embryo grows to eight or sixteen cells, the cells begin to differentiate. That is, they begin to take on specific roles; they become brain cells, liver cells, nerve cells, and so on. Each of the cells has the same DNA, but they activate different genes. DNA is like a piano with 100,000 keys, and each key represents a particular genetic trait. Once a cell has differentiated into, say a hair cell, only the keys controlling hair still work in that cell. The other keys no longer work. Once the DNA expresses a particular gene, there's no going back. Once a cell has become a hair cell, it can't become a blood cell.[9] The key to successful cloning lies in reversing the process of differentiation. Dolly was cloned from mammary cells of the parent sheep. Scientists had to break the genetic locks on the mammary cells to allow all the

---

7   Professor Ian Wilmut, creator of 'Dolly' believes that it would be virtually impossible to recreate the extinct Tasmanian tiger by cloning the thylacine pup preserved in alcohol since 1866. 'It's extraordinarily unlikely that the genetic information in that (preserved pup) is usable,' Professor Wilmut said in a recent interview. *The Age*, 28 September 1999.
8   Penny Fannin, 'Bid to clone woolly mammoth', *The Age*, 22 October, 1999.
9   Information on cell differentiation comes from John Case, *The Genesis Code*, Arrow Books, London, 1997, pp. 450-3.

genes to become functional. In other words, the entire genetic code had to be unlocked to create a cloned sheep. All the 'keys' on the genetic keyboard had to be activated. Despite technical difficulties and legal and ethical dilemmas, scientists have already commenced work on cloning human beings, a possibility anticipated years ago by science fiction writers. Ira Levin's 1976 novel *The Boys from Brazil*, subsequently made into a movie starring Gregory Peck and Laurence Olivier, tells the chilling story of Hitler clones created by Nazi war criminal Josef Mengele in an attempt to produce a new *führer*.

'The evil that men do lives after them,' Shakespeare tells us, 'The good is oft interred with their bones'[10] ... until now! What if it were possible to clone heroic figures from the past? What if scientists could resurrect the Messiah? Improbable as it might sound, that is the theme of two recent novels, *Honk if You Are Jesus*, by Peter Goldsworthy,[11] and *The Genesis Code*, by John Case. In each of these novels the DNA necessary for cloning is obtained from authenticated relics – unspecified relics of likely provenance in one story, and a crucifixion nail in the other. In both cases unsuspecting women are the recipients of a fertilised messianic ovum. And so it comes to pass, in Case's novel, that Marie gives birth to Jesse, while protected by Joe from villains attempting to destroy the unborn child. Sound vaguely familiar?

What would happen if scientists created a Jesus clone? Would the Messiah fare any better at his second coming? A prosperous farmer

---

10   *Julius Caesar*, 3, i, 76-7.
11   Peter Goldsworthy, *Honk if You Are Jesus*, Flamingo, London, 1992.

rushed into his house and cried out to his wife in an anguished voice, 'Rebecca, I have just heard a terrible rumour that is spreading through town like wildfire – the Messiah has come!' After thinking about what her husband had just said, Rebecca replied, 'What is so terrible about that? Why are you so upset?'

'I'm upset because after years of sweat and toil we have finally found prosperity. We have a thousand head of cattle, our barns are full to overflowing, and all our trees are heavily laden with fruit. What if the Messiah tells us to give it all away and follow him?'

'Calm down. We Jews have endured great suffering and hardship down through the ages. We have been enslaved by Egyptians, exiled by the Babylonians, slaughtered by the Romans, herded into ghettoes by Christians. We have endured the Holocaust and the vengeance of the Arab world, and yet we have survived. Just have faith, my dear husband. When the Messiah comes, we will find a way to deal with him!'[12]

In Dostoyevsky's nineteenth-century novel, *The Brothers Karamazov*, the Lord 'passes once more among men in that same human form in which for three years He walked among men 15 centuries earlier.'[13] He comes to Seville, just a day after one hundred heretics had been burnt all in one go, 'ad majorem gloriam Dei', to the greater glory of God. The 'sun of love burns in his heart' as he passes among people with 'a quiet smile of infinite compassion'. Everyone

---

[12] Adapted from Anthony de Mello, *The Prayer of the Frog, vol. 1*, Gujarat Sahitya Prakash, Anand, India, 1989, p. 71.
[13] Fyodor Dostoyevsky, *The Brothers Karamazov*, Penguin Classics, London, 1993, pp. 286ff.

recognises him; they weep and kiss the ground on which He walks. 'The children throw flowers in his path, singing and crying to Him: "Hosannah!"'

Jesus passes by the cathedral just as the coffin of a seventeen-year-old girl is borne inside. The mother of the dead girl throws herself at the feet of Jesus and beseeches him, 'If it is You, then raise up my child!' He gazes at the lifeless body with compassion, and softly pronounces the words 'Talitha cumi'. The girl rises in her coffin 'with astonished, wide-open eyes', a bouquet of white roses in her arms. Just at that moment the Cardinal Grand Inquisitor passes by the cathedral. 'He is an old man of almost ninety, tall and straight, with a withered face and sunken eyes, in which, however, there is still a fiery, spark-like gleam.' He wears only an 'old, coarse monkish cassock', not the resplendent cardinal's attire he had worn the day before when 'the enemies of the Roman faith were being burned.'

The Grand Inquisitor has witnessed the dead girl being raised to life, and he orders the guard to arrest Jesus. Later that night he confronts his prisoner, the two men standing alone together in a cell. The old Grand Inquisitor studies the face of Jesus for a long time, and says to him, '"Is it you? You?" Receiving no answer, however, he quickly adds: "No, do not reply, keep silent. And in any case, what could you possibly say? I know only too well what you would say. And you have no right to add anything to what was said by you in former times. Why have you come to get in our way? For you have come to get in our way, and you yourself know it..."' The inquisitor speaks at length to his prisoner, threatening to burn him at the stake 'as the most wicked of heretics'. He is uneasy because 'the Prisoner has listened to him all this time with quiet emotion, gazing straight into his eyes and evidently not wishing to raise any objection. The old man would like the Other to say something, even if it is bitter, terrible. But He suddenly draws near to the old man without saying anything and quietly kisses him on his bloodless, ninety-year-old lips. That is His only response. The old man shudders. Something has stirred at the corners of his mouth; he goes to the door, opens it and says to Him: "Go and do not come back ... do not come back at all ... ever ... ever!"'

During this holy season of Advent, we await the coming of Our Saviour. When he comes, will he find us awake, ready to receive him with welcome hearts? Or out of fear that he may force us to confront our own inner darkness, will we command him to depart: 'Go and do not come back ... do not come back at all ... ever ... ever!'?

Reflections for the year of Mark

SECOND SUNDAY OF ADVENT

(YEAR B)

> *And so it was that John the Baptist appeared in the wilderness, proclaiming a baptism of repentance for the forgiveness of sins.* (Mark 1:4)

Two psychiatrists met at a convention and it wasn't long before they began talking about difficult cases they'd encountered. One asked the other: 'What is the most difficult case that you solved?'

The other answered: 'Once I had a patient who lived in a pure fantasy world. He believed that somewhere in South America he had an incredibly rich uncle who was going to leave him a fabulous fortune. Every day, all day long, day after day, he waited for a letter from some fictitious lawyer telling him that his uncle had died and the inheritance was his. He never went out or did anything. He just sat around, waiting, waiting, waiting.'

The other psychiatrist was intrigued by the case and asked: 'What became of the man? How did that case turn out?'

His confrere stood tall and with an air of authority, if not arrogance, said: 'It was an eight-year struggle, but with determined skill and penetrating insight, I finally cured him.'

'Absolutely amazing,' said the other psychiatrist. 'Yes, it was incredible. I had him cured. And then the lawyer's letter arrived!'[14]

Waiting is one of the key themes of this Sunday. We are a people who are waiting, and waiting is usually a time of tedium, uncertainty and anxiety. Samuel Beckett's play *Waiting for Godot* is, as the name suggests, about waiting. Two tramps, Vladimir and Estragon, are waiting for someone by the name of Godot. Seven times during their long wait they're tempted to leave, but one says to the other:

> Let's go.
> We can't.
> Why not?
> We're waiting for Godot.[15]

I've seen the play in performance twice, and I've watched a television production. On each occasion I was thoroughly bored. Nothing much happens in the play, and the audience is left wondering whether Godot even exists. Perhaps this play is Beckett's reflection on human life – a long, boring and tedious wait for someone who may not even exist. We become impatient with waiting. It 'saps our energies and stifles our enthusiasm'.[16] Many of us are like a man who jumped into a taxi and yelled impatiently at the driver, 'I'll make it worth your while to drive as fast as you can.' With screeching tyres, the taxi took off at great speed. After a few minutes had passed,

---

14 Adapted from William J. Bausch, *Telling Stories, Compelling Stories*, Twenty-Third Publications, Mystic, CT, 1992, p. 36.
15 Samuel Beckett, *Waiting for Godot*, Faber Paperbacks, London, 1977, pp. 14, 48, 68, 71, 78, 84, 92.
16 Dianne Bergant and Richard Fragomeni, *Preaching the New Lectionary, Year B*, The Liturgical Press, Collegeville, MN, 1999, p. 8.

the passenger thought to ask the driver, 'Do you know where we're going?' 'No sir, but I'm going as fast as I can!'

Fr Timothy Radcliffe points out that our society tries to eliminate waiting. As an illustration of what he means he offers the example of a plane crash in Canada in October 2004. The pilots were carrying fresh vegetables from Africa to Western markets and had been flying for almost twenty-four hours.

> Consumers expect to find mange-tout, asparagus and snap peas in the supermarkets all year round. They do not wish to wait until the due season. They want them now. In order to provide fruit and vegetables at competitive prices, the supermarkets buy them off companies that fly old planes which have not been properly serviced, registered in countries whose safety standards are not as high, as in this case in Ghana. The pilots fly for dangerously long hours. This is the fourth crash of a plane of this company since 1992. The founder of the company said that it is not the fault of the supermarkets. They are merely responding to market demands, which tolerate no waiting.[17]

Amidst the hurly-burly of parties and Christmas shopping, Advent invites us to stand aside from the constant busyness of our lives, to enter the wilderness, and to wait.

One woman has likened Advent to pregnancy. She says:

> Waiting is an impractical time to our way of thinking. It's good for nothing, but mysteriously necessary to all that is coming. As in pregnancy, nothing of value comes into being without a period of quiet incubation. Not a healthy baby, not

---

17 Timothy Radcliffe, *What is the Point of Being a Christian?*, Burns & Oates, London, 2005, pp. 75-6.

a loving relationship, not a reconciliation, not a work of art, and never a human transformation. Brewing, baking, simmering, fermenting, ripening, germinating, gestating, are all processes of becoming, and they all demand a period of waiting.[18]

One of the great spiritual writers of our time, Carlo Carretto, once spent several years living alone as a hermit in the Sahara desert. And what did the solitude and silence say to him? Carretto believes that 'God is telling us: learn to wait – wait – wait for your God, wait for love, be patient with everything. Everything that is worthwhile must be waited for!'[19]

In the sixth century before Christ the Jewish people languished in exile 'by the rivers of Babylon', hoping and waiting for their deliverance. Isaiah's words of consolation promise a new Exodus: 'Prepare in the wilderness a way for the Lord. Make a straight highway for our God across the desert.' The wilderness, it would seem, is a necessary prelude to the new creation. John the Baptist emerges from the wilderness proclaiming a baptism of repentance. His preaching is a prelude to one who is more powerful than he is.

In the wilderness of Advent we are called to prepare a way for the Lord in our own lives, to see with renewed or transformed minds, which is what repentance (*metanoia*) means. A large multinational company engaged the services of an efficiency expert, technically

---

18   William Bausch, *Storytelling the Word*, Mystic, Twenty-Third Publications, Mystic, CT, 1996, p. 245.
19   Quoted in Ronald Rolheiser, *Against an Infinite Horizon*, Hodder & Stoughton, London, 1995, p. 45.

known as a work-measurement engineer. The task of such a person is to direct time-and-motion studies that will promote efficient and economical utilisation of personnel and facilities. The expert gathered the employees together and invited them to watch an experiment. He took a large glass jar and began to fill it with rocks about the size of his fist. Within a short time the jar was filled, and he asked the question, 'Can I fit any more in the jar?' 'No', the employees answered. The expert then took several handfuls of pebbles and began dropping them into the jar. They easily slid between the larger rocks. A second time he asked, 'Can I fit any more in the jar?' Anticipating what was going to happen next the employees were astute enough to answer, 'Yes, you probably can.'

'You're right,' the expert replied as he took several scoops of fine sand and added it to the jar. The sand easily filtered between the larger rocks and the smaller pebbles. 'Is it full now?' he asked. 'I suppose you could add something else,' replied one employee.

'You're right,' the expert said as he poured a jug of water into the jar. 'Now what does all that demonstrate?' the expert asked. Certain that he was on the right wavelength, one employee volunteered, 'Well, it just goes to show that no matter how full your day seems to be, you can always find time for something else.'

The expert smiled. 'That may or may not be true, but what this experiment says to me is that if you don't put the rocks in first, there won't be any room for them afterwards.'

The rocks are, of course, those people and things that we claim are most important in our lives – our family and our faith, for example.

Releasing the Captive

The pebbles, sand and water are the thousand-and-one other things that demand our time and attention, that leave us emotionally and physically drained. During this season of waiting, let us take time to look again at our lives and how we spend our time. Looking back over his many years in prison, Nelson Mandela had this to say: 'There is no prospect about prison which pleases – with the possible exception of one. One has time to think. In the vortex of the struggle, when one is constantly reacting to changing circumstances, one rarely has the chance to consider carefully all the ramifications of one's decisions or policies. Prison provided the time ... to reflect on what one had done and not done.'[20]

---

20 Nelson Mandela, *Long Walk to Freedom*, Abacus, London, 1994, p. 509.

Reflections for the year of Mark

THIRD SUNDAY OF ADVENT

(YEAR B)

'Who are you? We must take back an answer to those who sent us. What have you to say about yourself?' (Jn 1:22)

When the Jews sent priests and Levites from Jerusalem to interrogate John, they confronted him with the most basic questions: 'Who are you? ... What have you to say about yourself?' After a lifetime spent in the wilderness, John responded unequivocally, telling them that he is not the Christ, nor is he Elijah, nor is he the prophet. 'Why, then,' they persist, 'are you baptising if you are not the Christ, and not Elijah, and not the prophet?'

Most of us spend a lifetime grappling with those fundamental questions that were put to John, 'Who are you?' and 'Why are you doing what you are doing?' The following letter was written in 1970 to the editor of *The Times* by Mrs Valerie Eliot on the occasion of the death of Bertrand Russell at the age of ninety-seven. Mrs Eliot's husband, the famous Anglo-American poet, had died some five years earlier in 1965.

> Sir, My husband, T.S. Eliot, loved to recount how late one evening he stopped a taxi. As he got in, the driver said: 'You're T.S. Eliot'. When asked how he knew, he replied: 'Ah,

Releasing the Captive

I've got an eye for a celebrity. Only the other evening I picked up Bertrand Russell, and I said to him: 'Well, Lord Russell, what's it all about', and, do you know, he couldn't tell me.'

Yours faithfully,
Valerie Eliot[21]

Do we find ourselves smiling at the predicament of one of the great philosophers and mathematicians of the twentieth century, seemingly perplexed and floundering when asked the most simple yet profound question a human being can pose? Or are we more amused at the casual impudence of a taxi driver who expected a brief and concise answer while dispensing the change? In as few words as possible, he seems to be saying, give me a capsule answer to the meaning of life!

Some time ago *The Sydney Morning Herald* reported the story of a seventy-year-old Ugandan woman whose flight plans went disastrously wrong at Bombay airport. The woman, who spoke only an obscure Ugandan dialect, had travelled by bus from Kampala and boarded her flight in Nairobi. She was to have changed planes at Bombay en route to visit family in Australia, but an administrative bungle left her stranded at the airport for two and a half days with only ten dollars and the clothes she wore. During her whole lifetime this woman had never ventured more than a few kilometres from her local village, so an international airport was a totally alien environment and she spoke a language nobody understood. It requires little

---

21   Kenneth Gregory (ed.), *The First Cuckoo*, Unwin Paperbacks, London, 1978, p. 309.

imagination to see in this woman's plight a metaphor of profound dislocation and alienation. It was only through her daughter's initiative and persistence that she was eventually rescued from a personal nightmare.[22]

'What's it all about?' is a question that refuses to go away. Before attempting to respond, we must rest with the question and resist the temptation to give glib and superficial answers. Laurence Freeman, repeating the wisdom of John Main, stresses the importance of the right question rather than the right answer:

> Get the question right before getting confused or intoxicated by the variety of answers. First of all, to hear the question demands that we pause, pay attention and repeat the question.[23]

John Main reflects upon the ancient myth of the Fisher King to illustrate the power of a question to change the world. In this myth 'the land has been blighted by a curse that has frozen all the waters and turned the earth to stone. No power in the land can lift the curse and the king sits silently fishing through a hole in the ice, despondent, waiting.'[24]

Laurence Freeman continues the story:

> Parsifal, a knight of the Round Table, meets Anfortas, the Fisher King, who has been wounded by a lance through both

---

22 Mike Secombe, 'The day Air India's magic carpet stranded granny', *The Sydney Morning Herald*, 18 February 1988.
23 Laurence Freeman, *Jesus: The Teacher Within*, Continuum, New York, 2000, p. 25.
24 John Main, *Word into Silence*, Darton, Longman and Todd, London, repr., 2003, p. 25.

thighs. The king is restricted to lying down and fishing from the bank of a river. Around him his kingdom languishes, a wasteland of freezing mists. On his first meeting with the Fisher King, during which he actually sees the Holy Grail, Parsifal does not ask any question of the king. This is a mistake, as he soon realises. His failure to ask a question threatens the very existence of the Round Table, the symbol of global order. Realizing his sin of omission, Parsifal swears never to spend more than two nights in the same place until he has found his way back to the King and discovered the meaning of the Grail.

After five gruelling years he finds Anfortas's castle again. Going straight up to the king, who is still lying prone with pain, Parsifal poses his question: "Who serves the Grail?" Immediately the Grail appears before them. Parsifal falls to his knees and prays that the king's suffering may be ended. Then he turns again to Anfortas and puts his second question, "What ails you?" Instantly Anfortas rises healed. With the king's newfound wholeness, the whole land is restored to life and fertility. Trees flower; streams flow; animals breed. Parsifal had simply asked his questions: one about the meaning of life, the other conveying compassion.'[25]

Freeman calls such questions redemptive, but stresses that they are not in themselves magic solutions. 'They initiate a process of redemption.'[26] A redemptive question is 'not like other mundane questions. It does not expect an ordinary, rational, correct answer. Instead, it opens up a deeper level for experiencing the truth.' Such questions often trigger 'definitive awakenings'.[27] Redemptive ques-

---

25 Laurence Freeman, p. 25.
26 Ibid., p. 26.
27 Ibid.

tions take us into the realm of mystery, and as Charlie Brown reminds us, 'In the Book of Life, the answers are not in the back.' We may be tempted, though, 'to cheat on the challenge of the mystery of life by reducing it to the status of a problem'.[28] Problems have answers that can be fatally attractive because they are clear and concise and readily amenable to verification. 'They make us feel we can bottle the truth in a slogan, a dogmatic definition or scientific formula.'[29] Here we need to heed the advice Linus offers Charlie Brown: 'There's a difference between a philosophy and a bumper sticker!'[30] G.K. Chesterton puts it this way: 'The poet only asks to get his head into the heavens. It is the logician who seeks to get the heavens into his head. And it is his head that splits.'[31] George Weigel points out that we 'think' with our brains, our senses, and our emotions. 'Thinking with only our brains gives us a headache; it also gives us an aching soul. The deepest longings within us – for communion with others, wisdom, joy, accomplishment, love – cannot be satisfied by reducing the world to syllogisms. Human beings were made for a wider infinity, for a more ample eternity.'[32]

Tuesdays with Morrie tells the story of Mitch Albom's weekly meetings with his old professor Morrie Schwartz. Morrie is dying of what we in Australia call motor neurone disease, but he faces his

---

28 Ibid., p. 27
29 Ibid.
30 Charles M. Schulz, *The Complete Peanuts*, 1975 to 1976, Fantagraphics Books, Seattle, WA, 2010, p. 92.
31 Quoted in George Weigel, *Letters to a Young Catholic*, Basic Books, New York, 2004, p. 89.
32 George Weigel, op. cit., p. 91.

imminent death with great peace. During one of their weekly meetings Morrie tells Mitch, 'Once you learn how to die, you learn how to live.'[33] He goes on to explain that 'most of us all walk around as if we're sleepwalking ... we're half-asleep.' Facing death changes all of that. 'When you realize you are going to die, you see everything differently.'[34]

Malcolm Muggeridge would agree. In *Jesus Rediscovered* he wrote,

> I am old, and in at most a decade or so will be dead ... Now the prospect of death overshadows all others. I am like a man on a sea voyage nearing his destination. When I embarked I worried about having a cabin with a porthole, whether I should be asked to sit at the captain's table, who were the more attractive and important passengers. All such considerations become pointless when I shall so soon be disembarking. As I do not believe that earthly life can bring any lasting satisfaction, the prospect of death holds no terrors. Those saints who pronounced themselves in love with death displayed, I consider, the best of sense.[35]

The ancient Greek historian Herodotus (c. 484 BC–c. 425 BC) writes that towards the end of Egyptian feasts, when partygoers were at their most exuberant, servants entered the banqueting hall and passed between the tables carrying skeletons on stretchers. Regrettably, he doesn't record what effect of this reminder of death had on the merrymakers. Did it make them keener to carry on with their merrymaking, or did it send them home in a more sombre mood?

---

33   Mitch Albom, *Tuesdays with Morrie*, Hodder, Sydney, repr. 1999, p. 82.
34   Ibid., p. 83.
35   Malcolm Muggeridge, *Jesus Rediscovered*, Fontana Books, London, 1969, pp. 57-8.

Alain de Botton observes that the effect of the thought of death 'is perhaps to usher us towards whatever happens to matter most to us ... (and) encourage us to pay less attention to the verdicts of others, who will not, after all, have to do the dying for us. The prospect of our own extinction may draw us towards the way of life we value in our hearts.'[36]

The right questions 'constantly refresh our awareness that life is not fundamentally a secular problem but a sacred mystery. Mysteries are not solved. They are entered upon and they embrace us.'[37] In his poem *The Rock*, T.S. Eliot writes:

> O my soul, be prepared for the coming of the Stranger,
> Be prepared for him who knows how to ask questions.[38]

In this holy season of Advent let us allow the questions put to John to resonate within our own lives: Who are you? What have you to say about yourself? Why are you doing what you are doing?

---

36 Alain de Botton, *Status Anxiety*, Hamish Hamilton, Camberwell, Vic., 2004, pp. 231-2.
37 Laurence Freeman, p. 27.
38 T.S. Eliot, *Selected Poems*, Faber and Faber, London, repr. 1980, p. 117.

Releasing the Captive

FOURTH SUNDAY OF ADVENT

(YEAR B)

Let it happen to me as you have said. (Lk 1:38)

David and Mary had one thing in common. By human reckoning they were both unlikely candidates for their roles in the Divine plan. When God told the prophet Samuel that he had chosen the future ruler of Israel from among the sons of Jesse, the prophet is impressed by Eliab, one of David's brothers. But the Lord says, 'Take no notice of his appearance or his height, for I have rejected him; God does not see as human beings see; they look at appearances but Yahweh looks at the heart.'

Jesse presents seven of his sons to Samuel, but the Lord rejects them all. Somewhat exasperated, Samuel then asks, 'Are these all the sons you have?' Almost as an afterthought Jesse replies that there is still one left, David the youngest, but he is looking after the sheep. David is summoned, and as soon as he appears the Lord tells Samuel, 'Get up and anoint him: he is the one!' (cf. 1 Sam 16:1-13).

Mary is betrothed to Joseph. Jewish matrimonial procedure consisted of two steps. Firstly, a formal exchange of consent before witnesses, and secondly the subsequent taking of the bride to the groom's family home. After the betrothal, something that usually happened when the girl was between twelve and thirteen, Mary was

Joseph's wife. After the betrothal the wife continued to live at her own family home for about a year. In first century Galilee, the wife had to be taken to her husband's home as a virgin, and Matthew and Luke both make it quite clear that Mary was indeed a virgin when the angel Gabriel appeared to her.[39] God chose a young twelve- or thirteen-year-old girl from Nazareth when everyone knows that nothing good can come from that place! (Jn 1:46).

Nazareth is never once mentioned in the Old Testament. Nothing of any importance ever happened there; no one of any significance had ever lived there. God's choice of David and Mary reflects a recurring pattern in Israel's history: 'Now again, He by-passed academics, clergy, politicians, judges, councillors, to rest His favour on simple unlettered folk: Farm-workers, fishermen, shepherds, donkey-drivers, peddlers, tanners, tax-collectors, beggars, harlots. All of them without influence, power, prestige.'[40]

Two teenagers became pivotal in God's plan, and for each of them that plan reaches fulfillment through God's supreme power. David desired to build a house (temple) for the Lord, but is promised instead that God will establish a house (dynasty) for him. That promise comes to its fulfillment in Mary's gracious acceptance, 'Let what you have said be done to me.'

I've often reflected on artistic representations of the annunciation, and I've noticed that very few paintings present Mary as a young teenager, puzzled and afraid. Invariably she is portrayed as a

---

[39] Raymond Brown, *The Birth of the Messiah, An Image Book*, New York, 1979, pp. 123-4.
[40] Ronan Kilgannon, 'Still to the Lowly Soul', Unpublished homily, 2005.

slightly older woman, serene and unperturbed, thoroughly unfazed by the angelic appearance. Mary's initial reaction was surely one of fear, not only because of the awesome nature of an encounter with God's messenger, but also because she is being asked to leap into the abyss of faith. Denise Levertov's poem 'Annunciation' captures the mood of this encounter:

> She did not cry, 'I cannot, I am not worthy.'
> nor, 'I have not the strength.'
> She did not submit with gritted teeth,
> raging, coerced.
> Bravest of all humans,
> consent illumined her.
> Consent,
> courage unparalleled,
> opened her utterly.[41]

In the movie *Indiana Jones and the Last Crusade*, Indy finds himself at the edge of a great abyss, and yet he must cross to the other side if he is to find the Holy Grail. A cryptic clue from his father's diary is his only guide: 'Only in the leap from the lion's head will he prove his worth.'

Looking around, Indy discovers the image of a lion's head etched into the rock above, but he can plainly see that the abyss is far too wide to leap. At that moment he realises that the cryptic clue is talking about a different kind of leap – 'It's ... a leap of faith. Oh God.' And we see him do it. He leaps off the edge of the abyss, but in doing so he lands on a bridge built by the first Crusaders but cleverly camouflaged.

---

41 Quoted in John Shea, *Eating with the Bridegroom: Year B*, Liturgical Press, Collegeville, MN, 2005, pp. 37-8.

The leap of faith is never easy because we have no guarantee where it will lead and what changes it might demand. As W.H. Auden writes:

> We would rather be ruined than changed.
> We would rather die in our dread than
> Climb the cross of the moment
> And see our illusions die.[42]

I cherish the freewheeling, autonomous me, 'in charge of my own destiny and captain of my soul.' The paradox is, though, that 'the more I learn to surrender my self, a more generous and available me comes into existence.'[43] Mary is not the only human being to receive an 'annunciation.'

Denise Levertov reflects on the annunciations in all of our lives:

> Aren't there annunciations
> of one sort or another
> in most lives?
> Some unwillingly
> undertake great destinies,
> enact them in sullen pride,
> uncomprehending.
> More often
> those moments
> when roads of light and story
> open from darkness in a man or woman
> are turned away from
> in dread, in a wave of weakness, in despair
> and with relief.

---

42 Quoted in Alan Jones, *Soulmaking: The Desert Way of Spirituality*, HarperCollins San Francisco, 1989, p. 122.
43 Alan Jones, *Passion for Pilgrimage*, Morehouse Publishing, Harrisburg, PA, 1989, p. 95.

Releasing the Captive

> Ordinary lives continue.
> God does not smite them.
> But the gates close, the pathway vanishes.[44]

Annunciations demand courage. When, like Mary, we courageously let go, God's plan is fulfilled in ways that we had not imagined possible.

There once lived an old man who loved his native island of Crete with a deep and beautiful intensity. When he knew that his time to die was close at hand, he had his sons bring him outside and lay him down on the beloved soil of Crete. As he drew his last breath, he clutched some earth in his hands and died a happy man.

He now appeared before heaven's gates, and St Peter greeted him warmly. 'You have been a kind and loving man during your life, come now and enter into the joys of heaven.' But as he was about to pass through the pearly gates, St Peter said, 'You must let go of that handful of soil.'

The old man was adamant, 'Never!' And so, St Peter had to leave him outside, for it was impossible to enter heaven while he still clutched the soil of Crete in his hand. Time passed by, and eventually one of his old drinking companions came out to talk with him, hoping to persuade him to let go of the soil and come inside. But still he refused. He was so stubborn that he remained outside for ages and ages.

Eventually his granddaughter came out to speak with him. 'Oh, grandpa, we all miss you. Please come inside with me.' She reached

---

44 Quoted in John Shea, *Eating with the Bridegroom*, p. 38.

out to take his hand in hers, and as he did so, he let go of the precious soil of Crete. And so, hand in hand, they entered through the pearly gates of heaven.

And the first thing that he saw as he entered heaven was his beloved island of Crete.[45]

---

[45] Adapted from William Bausch, *Storytelling: Imagination and Faith*, Twenty-Third Publications, Mystic, CT, 1984, pp. 127-8.

CHRISTMAS DAY

And the shepherds went back glorifying and praising God for all they had heard and seen. (Lk 2:20)

A mother and her young daughter knelt before the crib in their parish church. Pointing to the statue of the baby the mother explained, 'That's baby Jesus.' Then pointing to Our Lady she said, 'That's Mary, the mother of Jesus.' The little girl shook her head defiantly and said, 'No, Mummy, that's not Mary.' She then pointed to the statue of a shepherd nursing a young lamb and said, 'That's Mary.' Somewhat amazed, the mother replied, 'No, dear, that's not Mary. Mary is over here next to the baby Jesus.' But her daughter was insistent that the shepherd was Mary. 'Whoever told you that the shepherd was Mary?' the mother asked. 'Mummy, everyone knows: "Mary had a little lamb!"'

Today we celebrate the birth of the eternal word of God. Today we celebrate that truth at the heart of our Christian faith. In the person of Jesus Christ, God enters the human condition and becomes are we are. Not born in splendour, amidst the mighty and powerful, but born in a stable, amidst animals and hay. He came that that we might have life, life in abundance. He came in poverty that we might share in his riches. He is the true light that enlightens all people, and to those who accept him, he gives the power to become children of God.

Once upon a time there was an extremely wealthy landowner named Carl. He was a proud and pompous man who took great delight in riding his horse throughout his vast estate, congratulating himself on his enormous wealth.

One day, as he rode through his estate, he came across Hans, an elderly tenant farmer. Hans was loved by everyone. He was a kind, generous and compassionate man who had worked hard all his life. He owned very little, having given away most of his possessions to the poor and needy. He had just sat down to eat his lunch in the shade of a great oak tree, his head bowed in prayer. Startled by the sudden arrival of the landowner, he looked up and said, 'Oh, excuse me, sir. I didn't see you. I was giving thanks for my food.'

'Humph!' snorted the rich man, noticing the coarse dark bread and cheese that made up the old man's lunch. 'If that were all I had to eat,' he sneered, 'I don't think I'd feel like giving thanks.'

'Oh,' replied Hans, 'it's quite sufficient. But it's remarkable that you should ride past today because I feel that I have to tell you something. Last night I had a strange dream.'

'Oh, and what did you dream?' asked Carl with a cynical smile smeared all over his face.

'I heard a voice saying "The richest man in the valley will die tonight".'

Carl laughed out aloud. 'Nonsense!' And he turned and galloped away. 'Die tonight! How ridiculous. What a superstitious old fool.'

Releasing the Captive

But Carl couldn't push the old man's crazy dream out of his mind. So, just to make sure, he called in to see the doctor on his way home to the manor. Carl told the doctor of the old man's dream that the richest man in the valley would die this very night.

'Ah' said the doctor. 'It sounds like poppycock to me, but for your own peace of mind, let me examine you.' When the doctor had completed the examination he was full of smiles and assurances. 'Carl, you're as strong and healthy as that horse you ride. There's no way you're going to die tonight.'

Just at that moment a messenger arrived out of breath at the doctor's doorstep. 'Doctor, doctor,' he cried, 'come quick! It's old Hans. He just died in his sleep.'[46]

A Christmas Carol,[47] Charles Dickens's delightful story of transformation, is about Ebenezer Scrooge, a greedy and hard-hearted man whose obsession with money has isolated him from everyone. 'Bah! Humbug!' is his response to the festive season. 'If I had my way, every idiot who goes about with "Merry Christmas" on his lips should be boiled with his own pudding, and buried with a stake of holly through his heart.' When approached by some local businessmen seeking contributions for the poor and destitute, Scrooge is

---

46. Adapted from William J. Bausch, *Storytelling the Word*, Twenty-Third Publications, Mystic, CT, 1996, pp. 187-8.
47. A complete version of the story can be downloaded from http://www.online-literature.com/dickens/christmascarol/

totally bereft of compassion. 'I don't make myself merry at Christmas and I can't afford to make idle people merry.' With the greatest reluctance Scrooge begrudgingly gives his long-suffering clerk, Bob Cratchit, all of Christmas Day off work. 'It's not convenient, and it's not fair. Why should I pay a day's wage for no work?'

The beginning of Scrooge's conversion occurs when he is confronted by the ghost of his deceased business partner Jacob Marley. Marley's ghost, bound in chains, offers a solemn warning: 'I wear the chain I forged in life. I made it link by link, and by my own free will I wore it. Why did I walk through crowds of fellow-beings with my eyes turned down? I am here tonight to warn you, that you have yet a chance and hope of escaping my fate.' Scrooge is then told that three spirits will visit him.

The first spirit, the Ghost of Christmas Past, recalls a time of innocence, long before Scrooge had become obsessed with money. As he enters middle age Scrooge slowly succumbs to avarice, and his fiancé Belle decides to leave him, realising that she has been displaced in his affections by another idol: 'A golden one,' she tells him. 'Gain engrosses you.'

Then the Ghost of Christmas Present appears, and Scrooge is spirited away to the Cratchit household. Tiny Tim, Bob's young son, is gravely ill and will surely die if the shadows of the present remain unaltered. As the family shares a Christmas meal, Bob proposes a toast to his employer, much to the utter disgust of his wife. 'He is such an odious, stingy, hard, unfeeling man.'

Releasing the Captive

It is the third spirit, the Ghost of Christmas Yet to Come, that confronts Scrooge with his own inner darkness. Standing beside the ghost, Scrooge looks upon a bed where, beneath a ragged sheet, there lies something covered up. He does not have the strength to remove the sheet, for he knows it covers a body. The ghost then takes him to the Cratchit household, only to find a household in mourning. Tiny Tim has died also.

With great trepidation Scrooge asks, 'Spirit, tell me what man was that we saw lying dead.' By way of answer the spirit takes Scrooge to a churchyard. Seeing the words 'Ebenezer Scrooge' engraved upon a tombstone he undergoes a change of heart: 'Spirit, I am not the man I was. I will honour Christmas in my heart and try to keep it all the year.' And Scrooge is as good as his word. He becomes a man of compassion, making amends for his hard-heartedness. He joins his nephew's family for Christmas dinner, an invitation previously spurned, and the following day promises Bob Cratchit a pay rise with a promise to assist his struggling family. He becomes a second father to Tiny Tim.

And so the story ends with Scrooge becoming as good a friend, as good a master, and as good a man, as the good old city knew. Some people laughed to see the alteration in him, but he let them laugh, and little heeded them. His own heart laughed: and that was quite enough for him.

SOLEMNITY OF MARY, MOTHER OF GOD

But Mary treasured all these words and pondered them in her heart.
(Lk 2:19)

Today's gospel records three different reactions to the birth of Jesus. The first reaction is that of the shepherds. Once the angel had announced the news of great joy, the shepherds hurried away to Bethlehem and found Mary and Joseph and the baby lying in the manger, wrapped in swaddling clothes. They couldn't contain their joy and repeated to all whom they met what they had been told about the newborn child.

But we never hear of the shepherds again in any of the four gospels. Had they all died by the time that Jesus began his public ministry? Had they dismissed the events of that night as a fanciful dream and gone back to tending their sheep? We'll never know.

The second reaction to the birth of Jesus recorded in today's gospel is that of the people who heard the good news from the shepherds. We're told they were 'astonished' at what the shepherds said to them. But there is no indication that this astonishing news led to faith, to any kind of commitment or transformation. Their reaction doesn't go beyond: 'Wow', 'Amazing!' 'What an incredible story!' The very fact that these people didn't make any attempt to see for themselves the new born child is a clear indication that they didn't really take seriously this fanciful tale told by some shepherds. Or if they did, they didn't want to get involved.

The third reaction to all that had happened is that of Mary. We are told that 'she treasured all these things and pondered them in her heart.' Often throughout the Bible, women and men receive revelations from God that are beyond their immediate understanding. But the person of true faith, unable to understand the mystery of God's ways, treasures what has happened with trust in God, waiting to be led where God wills.

So it was with Mary. Though unable to understand fully what has happened to her, she has already said her 'yes', and from that moment onwards laid herself completely open to the plan of God.

Note that the text of the gospel says that Mary pondered all these things, not in her head, but in her heart. These events which so intimately involved her were not an intellectual puzzle to be unravelled, a cryptic crossword to be solved, but rather a truth to be absorbed and lived, a truth that contains the power to transform.

The English word 'creed' comes from the Latin credo, which in turn comes from the Latin words *cor*, meaning heart, and *dare*, which means 'to give.' When we recite the creed we are not reciting a list of propositions to which we give intellectual assent; rather we are proclaiming heartfelt truths.

Reflections for the year of Mark

There is a Sufi story about Nuri Bey, a respected Albanian who married a wife much younger than himself. When he returned home one evening a trusted servant came to him and said, 'Your wife, my mistress, is acting suspiciously.'

He went on to explain that the young wife was in her apartments with a huge chest, large enough to hold a man. The chest had belonged to the master's grandmother.

The servant explained, 'It should contain only a few ancient embroideries, but I believe that there may now be much more in it. But she will not allow me, your oldest retainer, to look inside.'

Nuri went to his wife's room and found her sitting disconsolately beside the massive wooden box. 'Will you show me what is inside the chest?', he asked.

'Are you asking me because of the suspicion of a servant, or because you do not trust me?'

Nuri replied: 'Would it not be easier just to open it, without thinking about the undertones?'

His wife did not think it was possible.

'Is it locked?' Nuri asked.

'Yes,' she replied.

'Where is the key?'

She held up the key and said, 'Dismiss the servant and I will give it to you.'

The servant was dismissed and the woman handed over the key and herself withdrew, obviously troubled in mind. Nuri Bey thought for a long time, then he called four gardeners from his estate. Together they carried the chest by night, unopened, to a distant part of the grounds, and buried it. The matter was never referred to again.[48]

Stories such as this are not like algebra, with a correct answer in the back of the book, but I suspect that we're meant to see Nuri's wife and her chest as a vessel of mystery. Nuri's first instinct is to open the vessel and have the mystery explained, but he thinks better of it.

The intellect works

> with reasons, logic, analysis, research, equations, and pros and cons. But the soul practises a different kind of math and logic. It presents images that are not immediately intelligible to the reasoning mind. It insinuates, offers fleeting impressions, persuades more with desire than with reasonableness.[49]

Peter O'Connor makes the observation that contemporary psychology seems to have become increasingly occupied with what is broadly termed the scientific model:

> As a direct consequence of this, a considerable amount of its focus has been on issues of proof and evidence for its assertions. In this sense psychology can be seen as reflecting the Western obsession with rationality and the denigration of the non-rational aspects of mind and being.[50]

Rainer Maria Rilke wrote, 'Do not seek answers; live the questions.'[51] This is not saying 'Don't question your faith!' or 'It's wrong to doubt.'

---

48 Adapted from Thomas Moore, *Care of the Soul*, HarperPerennial, New York, 1994, pp. 123-4.
49 Thomas Moore, p. 122.
50 Peter O'Connor, *Understanding Jung*, Mandarin, Port Melbourne, 1988, p. 1
51 Quoted in Phil Cousineau (ed.) *Soul: An Archaeology*, Harper, San Francisco, 1994, pp. xxviii.

Reflections for the year of Mark

If we are honest we must surely admit that faith is a cocktail of belief and doubt, with variable quantities of each ingredient. Thérèse of Lisieux, a saint

> who looks so naïve and unproblematical ... a person apparently cocooned in complete security, left behind her, from the last weeks of her passion, shattering admissions which her horrified sisters toned down in her literary remains and which have only now come to light in the new verbatim editions. She says, for example, 'I am assailed by the worst temptations of atheism'.[52]

We must learn to live with mystery, even though it is a source of uneasiness in a society where 'truth' is synonymous with 'fact', which can be demonstrated, confirmed and proved by scientific methods. Science has debunked many self-evident truths held passionately in past ages, not the least of which was the commonly held belief that the earth was at the centre of the universe.

The scientific and philosophical revolutions that gave birth to the modern world view confidently affirmed the autonomy and self-sufficiency of human reason. The legacy of the Enlightenment dismissed metaphysical speculation as 'idle intellectual fantasy' that was a 'disservice to humanity'.[53] Science, reason and empirical data were to be the Enlightenment's lethal weapons in the battle against dogmatic religion and popular superstition.[54]

---

52 Joseph Ratzinger, *Introduction to Christianity*, Search Press, London, 1968, pp. 17-18.
53 Richard Tarnas, *The Passion of the Western Mind*, Ballantine Books, New York, 1991, p. 310.
54 Ibid., p. 312.

Such weapons have scaled the battlements of 'problem', but 'mystery' remains an inviolable fortress unless we become like Mary who 'treasured all these things and pondered them in her heart.' As Blaise Pascal observed, 'The heart has its reasons which are unknown to reason,'[55] or in slightly different words: 'We come to know the truth not only by reason, but still more so through our hearts.'[56]

---

55 Martin Turnell (trans. and ed.), *Pascal's Pensées*, Harper & Row, New York, 1962, p. 95.
56 Quoted in Paul Johnson, *A History of Christianity*, Penguin Books, London, 1990, p. 349.

Reflections for the year of Mark

FEAST OF THE HOLY FAMILY

The parents of Jesus took him up to Jerusalem to present him to the Lord.
(Lk 2:22)

The gospel of Luke tells us of three ancient ceremonies that the holy family observed following the birth of Jesus. First, Jesus is circumcised and named. Circumcision was so sacred a ritual that the ceremony could be carried out even on the Sabbath, a day on which the Jewish law forbade almost every act that was not absolutely essential. When a boy was circumcised, he then bore in his flesh the sign that he was a member of God's chosen people.

Secondly, the child was brought to the Temple to be redeemed. According to the Torah (Ex 3:2), every firstborn male, both of humans and cattle, was sacred to God. But the child could be bought back from God for the sum of five shekels. Finally, the mother had to be purified after childbirth. A woman was deemed unclean for a period of forty days if she bore a boy, and eighty days if her child was a girl. The mother could go about her household duties and her daily business, but she could not enter the Temple or share in any religious ceremony. At the end of that time, she had to bring a lamb to the Temple as a burnt offering, and a young pigeon for a sin offering. That was a rather expensive offering, so the law laid down that if the mother could not afford the lamb she might bring another pigeon. The offering of the two pigeons instead of the lamb and the pigeon was technically called the offering of the poor. It was the offering of the poor that Mary brought to the Temple.

These ancient rituals seem strange to us. Circumcision has certainly fallen out of favour; the redemption of the firstborn male is blatantly sexist; and the notion that a woman is ritually unclean after childbirth would be offensive to most people today. But behind all of these rituals is the conviction that a child is a gift of God. The Greek Stoics used to say that a child was not given to a parent, but only lent by God.[57]

The main character in the 1968 movie *Rachel, Rachel* (directed by Paul Newman and starring Joanne Woodward) is Rachel, a 35-year-old unmarried school teacher who feels as though she's wasted her life. She lives at home with her mother and has devoted her life to teaching other people's children rather than having a family of her own. Rachel complains to another woman, who is a mother, how difficult it is for her to work intimately with her students in the classroom, to get to know them so well, only to have them move onwards at the end of the year, and inevitably grow away from her. Rachel envies women who have their own children, but a mother who has been listening to Rachel says in reply: 'It's not so different for a parent. You also get to have young children only for a short time. They move on and grow away from you. They have their own

---

57 Cf. William Barclay, *The Gospel of Luke*, The Saint Andrew Press, Edinburgh, 1953, pp. 18-20.

lives and don't belong to you. In the end, even for parents, your kids are never really your own!'⁵⁸

When I reflect upon my own family life there are three important lessons that I learnt. The first lesson was that of prayer. In the 1950s the American priest Fr Patrick Peyton visited Australia to promote the Rosary and family prayer. The title of his book was *The Family that Prays Together Stays Together*. Fr Peyton certainly influenced my parents, and every night we prayed the Rosary together as a family. I won't pretend that I always found it a deeply spiritual experience, and I was easily distracted. We'd say the Rosary in the lounge room, but my father didn't turn off the television set. Instead he turned down the volume and swiveled it around so that we couldn't see the screen. Well sometimes the television set wasn't turned completely around and I did my best to see what I was missing out on!

The second lesson I learned from my family was love. The American author Fr John Powell has written a number of books on relationships and spirituality in general. One of his books is entitled *The Secret of Staying in Love*. He tells of being in hospital by his dying father's bedside.

> It was the day my father died. It was a bleak, cold, and blustery day in January. In the small hospital room I was supporting him in my arms, when his eyes suddenly widened with a look of awe I had never seen before. I was certain that the angel of death had entered the room. Then my father slumped back, and I lowered his head gently onto the pillow. I closed his eyes, and told my mother who was seated by the

---

58   Cf. Ronald Rolheiser, *Against an Infinite Horizon*, Hodder & Stoughton, London, 1995, p. 73.

bedside praying: 'It's all over, Mom. Dad is dead.' She startled me. I will never know why these were her first words to me after his death. My mother said: 'Oh, he was so proud of you. He loved you so much.' Somehow I knew from my own reaction that these words were saying something very important to me. They were like a sudden shaft of light, like a startling thought I had never before absorbed. Yet there was a definite edge of pain, as though I were going to know my father better in death than I had ever known him in life. Later, while a doctor was verifying death, I was leaning against the wall in the far corner of the room, crying softly. A nurse came over to me and put a comforting arm around me. I couldn't talk through my tears. I wanted to tell her: 'I'm not crying because my father is dead. I'm crying because my father never told me that he was proud of me.' Of course I was expected to know these things. I was expected to know the great part I played in his life and the great part I occupied of his heart, but he never told me.[59]

The Australian Jesuit Fr Richard Leonard said that he read some of Fr Powell's books when he was 16 and felt challenged to tell the members of his family that he loved them. He wrote to his sister who was then working with Mother Teresa in Calcutta, and to his brother who was working interstate, telling them that he loved them. With his heart pumping and stomach churning he approached his mother after tea while she was watching the news. 'Mum, I have something important to tell you.' 'Oh, yes, what's that?' 'Mum,' he responded, 'I love you.' To which she replied, 'Well I certainly hope

---

59   John Powell, *The Secret of Staying in Love*, Argus Communications, Niles, IL, 1974, p. 68

so,' and promptly turned back to the television. His brother and sister wrote back to his mother asking what was wrong with Richard? The openness that Fr Powell advocates might sit uneasily with many Australians, but however we do it, family members need to hear that they are loved. It can so easily be taken for granted.

The third lesson my family taught me is the lesson of compassion. The story is told of a family that always dined very elegantly, but grandfather invariably soiled the tablecloth and frequently broke pieces of expensive china. Eventually the father decided to sit the grandfather at a table of his own where he could eat from a wooden bowl. Not long after grandfather's exile, the father noticed his young son busily making something on the bench in the garage. 'What are you making, son?' the father asked. 'It's for you, Dad, for when you get old like grandpa. It's a wooden bowl.'

Families are the school of holiness. We must experience prayer, love and compassion as lived rather than learnt realities; they are caught not taught. A photograph published in *The Sydney Morning Herald* some time ago showed a young girl being swung around by her father. The father had a camera strapped to his chest and the camera automatically took photographs as he swirled his daughter around. As you look closely at the photograph of the smiling daughter, you can see the image of her father reflected in her eyes. That, surely, is a parable of family life.

FEAST OF THE EPIPHANY

Then, opening their treasures, they offered him gifts of gold and frankincense and myrrh. (Mt 2:11)

The opening chapter of Barbara Tuchman's Pulitzer prize-winning history of World War I, *The Guns of August*, is entitled 'A Funeral'. The funeral is that of the British monarch Edward VII, who died in 1910, almost four years before the beginning of World War I. The chapter functions as an overture, sounding a note that will resonate throughout this history of the war. The obsequies for Edward were attended by nine kings, five heirs apparent, 40 more imperial or royal highnesses, seven queens and a scattering of special ambassadors from uncrowned countries. 'Together they represented seventy nations in the greatest assemblage of royalty and rank ever gathered in one place and, of its kind, the last.'[60] This funeral functioned symbolically as the death knell of the old Europe. Lord Esher wrote in his diary after the funeral, 'All the old buoys which have marked the channel of our lives seem to have been swept away.'[61] The infancy narratives in the gospels of Matthew and Luke also function as an overture, sounding notes that will resonate throughout the gospel. In both gospels, the news of the birth of the Messiah is

---

60   Barbara W. Tuchman, *The Guns of August*, Ballantine Books, New York, p. 1.
61   Ibid., p. 14.

announced to outsiders – to shepherds in Luke (2:8), and to wise men from the East (and therefore Gentiles) in Matthew. The infancy narratives must also be read within their Roman context. The Roman emperor Caesar Augustus was said by his biographers to have been conceived by the god Apollo in the womb of his mother, Atia. His titles, 'Son of God', 'Lord', 'Saviour of the World' and 'Bringer of Peace on Earth' were inscribed on coins, temples and public monuments. The gospels are subversive. It is Jesus, not Caesar, who is Son of God, Lord, Saviour and Bringer of Peace on Earth.

But let us turn to today's feast of the Epiphany. 'We three kings of Orient are ...' So goes the popular carol celebrating the journey of the wise men from the East, who came bearing gifts of gold, frankincense and myrrh. However, a closer reading of the text reveals that Matthew's gospel – and they're mentioned only in Matthew's gospel – doesn't refer to them as kings, but as magi (magus in the singular, from which we get our English word 'magician'). Nor does Matthew tell us how many wise men there were, only that they brought three gifts. The popular notions that there were three, and that they were kings is a tradition that begins with Origen (c. 185–254 AD), quite possibly influenced by Psalm 72, which is today's responsorial psalm. This psalm, originally written as a coronation hymn for one of Israel's kings, speaks of the kings of Tarshish and the sea coasts paying tribute, and the kings of Sheba and Seba bringing gifts for the newly-crowned king. It didn't take the Christian imagination long to interpret this psalm in the light of Matthew's gospel, and the wise men are transformed into kings bearing gifts.

Releasing the Captive

And, of course, it wasn't all that long before these wise men were given names. Their names, Gaspar, Melchior and Balthasar are first mentioned in the sixth century, and by the Middle Ages they were venerated as saints. Their relics are now enshrined in Cologne Cathedral.[62] A much later tradition adds a fourth wise man, Artaban. There are several versions of this story, and although none of it is biblical, it does capture a beautiful truth. It is appropriate, therefore, that we should listen to it on the feast of Epiphany.

Like Gaspar, Melchior and Balthasar, Artaban was also a Persian and a man of great wealth and learning. Like many Persians they were familiar with the Jewish scriptures, for centuries earlier the Persian king Cyrus had liberated the Jewish people from exile in Babylon. The wise men that we know as the Magi were convinced that the rising star they had seen would lead them to the long-awaited Messiah of Israel. Artaban converted his considerable wealth into precious jewels, a gift for the newborn king of the Jews. With faith and hope he embarked upon this great journey, intending to accompany Gaspar, Melchior and Balthasar as they followed the rising star. A few hours into the journey he came across a traveller who had been brutally attacked by robbers and left for dead by the roadside. Being a compassionate person, he did all that he could to revive the traveller and heal his wounds. In a scenario reminiscent of the parable of the Good Samaritan, Artaban took the wounded traveller to an inn, and paid the innkeeper with one of his precious stones to

---

62 'Magi' in F.L Cross and E.A. Livingstone, *The Oxford Dictionary of the Christian Church*, Oxford University Press, Oxford, repr. 1997, p. 1020.

take care of the man. But this unexpected delay had made Artaban anxious, for he knew that his companions would not be able to wait for him. The wounded traveller, anxious to repay a debt of kindness, confided in Artaban. 'I am Jewish, and I can assure you that the One whom you seek will be born in Bethlehem. That is surely where your companions have headed.'

When Artaban arrived at the small town of Bethlehem he went anxiously from house to house, asking if anyone had seen his companions. Sensitive to his distress, one family invited him to join them for a meal, but their news was not good. The husband and wife, nursing their young son, assured him that three Persian visitors had left several days earlier.

As they began the meal they were disturbed by a loud commotion in the town. Amidst much shrieking and screaming Herod's soldiers were mercilessly slaughtering all young male children of a certain age. The parents were terrified when a soldier burst into their house and rushed at the young mother as she clutched her baby in her arms.

At that moment, Artaban stepped forward, 'Captain, would you be interested in some precious jewels? They are yours if you leave this house now and do not ask any questions.'

Grabbing the jewels, the captain gleefully shouted at his soldiers, 'There is no baby in here.'

When the soldiers had gone, the young mother spoke to Artaban, 'Thank you. You have saved my baby's life.'

As he was about to leave, she took him aside. 'I was told that your friends went to see a couple who were visitors from Nazareth – Mary and Joseph and their young son. Joseph had a premonition that something bad was about to happen and set out quickly with his family for Egypt.'

Artaban set out for Egypt, but he became hopelessly lost and more confused as he made enquiries at one village after another. As he travelled, he was deeply touched by the poverty that he encountered, and so he gave generously to the poor – here a ruby, there a sapphire, to another a diamond. But he would not give up the search. For ten years, for 20 years, for over 30 years he searched.

Hearing rumours of a prophet in Israel who was healing the sick, casting out devils, and welcoming sinners, Artaban set out for Jerusalem, hoping that this man might be the one whom he sought. He was now an old man, sick and close to death. But with only one jewel left to offer as a gift he set out for Jerusalem.

When at length he reached the ancient walled city he shuffled through the narrow and crowded streets, praying for a sign from God. It was then that he saw some soldiers leading a screaming young woman to the slave market. She was crying out in Persian, his own language, so he stopped the soldiers to ask who she was. They explained that she had accompanied her father to Jerusalem, but he had died suddenly leaving substantial debts. The girl was to be sold to satisfy her father's debtors. With his last jewel Artaban bought the girl's freedom.

At that moment he was distracted by a commotion close by. Crowds of people were making their way to a rocky outcrop called

Golgotha, just outside the city walls. A prisoner was being led to his execution.

The young Persian girl explained that this man, Jesus from Nazareth, was to be crucified. The authorities had mockingly referred to him as the 'King of the Jews'. In a moment of insight, Artaban realised that this man was the one whom he had sought all these years, but now he had arrived too late. Both he and the young man from Nazareth were soon to die.

As the condemned man passed by, carrying his cross, Artaban was startled. As he looked into the eyes of Jesus, he saw in an instant the faces of all those people whom he had helped during his long journey. Artaban then died, knowing that many times during the past 30 years he had indeed met the king of the Jews and paid him homage.

Releasing the Captive

ASH WEDNESDAY

'Remember that you are dust, and unto dust you shall return.'
(Liturgy for Ash Wednesday)

In Karel Capek's play *The Makropulos Case*, Elina Makropulos has lived for 342 years, thanks to an elixir of eternal life concocted by her alchemist father. She was 42 years of age when she first took the formula, and after 300 years life has become boring. What more can she do that she hasn't already done? Life has become predictable and joyless. She decides not to take the elixir again, having come to the realisation that human life should not last too long. The brevity of human life gives it its value.[63]

During today's liturgy we are reminded of our mortality: 'Remember that you are dust, and unto dust you shalll return.' Ironically, preparation for death is preparation for life. Confronted by the undeniable truth that we have a limited span of time upon this earth, let us pause to ask some fundamental questions: In my life, who and what are important and life-giving? Is my time and emotional energy truly invested in those relationships and commitments that I claim are at the heart of my life? Or am I too busy?

---

63 Edward L. Beck, *Soul Provider*, Image Books Doubleday, New York, 2007, p. 56.

Reflections for the year of Mark

Henri Nouwen writes that 'one of the most obvious characteristics of our daily lives is that we are busy. We experience our days as filled with things to do, people to meet, projects to finish, letters to write, calls to make, and appointments to keep. Our lives often seem like over-packed suitcases bursting at the seams.'[64]

Alan Jones, Dean of San Francisco's Grace Cathedral, says that a friend of his 'asks his students what truth they want to become by the end of their lives.' Many of us, Jones writes, 'have been telling a story to ourselves and to the world about what we think is true and real for us so long that we have come to believe it absolutely.'[65] Lent summons us into the desert to be probed. 'About what? About yourself and the story you've been telling yourself about yourself. How far is it a lie?'[66]

Repentance is on-going because we are forgetful. The Hindu tradition tells us that a child in the womb sings, 'Do not let me forget who I am.' But once the child has been born, the song becomes, 'Oh, I have forgotten already.'[67] Marcus Borg shares a story he heard about a three-year-old girl who was excited when she found out that her mother was expecting a baby. When the mother returned home from hospital with the newly born child (a boy) his little sister made a rather unusual request. She wanted to be alone with her new brother in his room with the door shut. The parents were a little

---
64 Henri Nouwen, *Making All Things New: An Introduction to the Spiritual Life*, Doubleday, New York, 1981, p. 23.
65 Alan Jones, *Living the Truth*, Cowley Publications, 2000, p. 117.
66 Ibid., p. 118.
67 Jack Kornfield, *After the Ecstasy, the Laundry*, Bantam Books, New York, 2000, pp. 3-4.

uneasy about her being alone with the baby and the door closed, but they had installed an intercom system in the baby's bedroom, so they could be in the room in an instant if they suspected that something strange was happening. So they let the little girl spend some time with her brother in private. Through the intercom the parents heard their daughter move across the room, and they imagined her leaning over the baby's crib. But then they heard her speaking to her three-day-old brother, 'Tell me about God – I've almost forgotten.'

As Borg observes, the story is both haunting and evocative,

> for it suggests that we come from God, and that when we are very young, we still remember this, still know this. But the process of growing up, of learning about this world, is a process of increasingly forgetting the one from whom we came in whom we live.[68]

Repentance is on-going because we forget: we become tired and listless, immobilised and overcome by what the spiritual tradition calls *acedia*, or spiritual apathy. Scott Peck, author of the best seller *The Road Less Travelled*, speaks of the force of entropy. The force of entropy is an inbuilt resistance, an inclination to keep things the way they are, 'to cling to the old maps and old ways of doing things, to take the easy path.'[69] Entropy causes us 'to stay at the comfortable, easy rung where we now are or even to descend to less and less demanding forms of existence.'[70] Entropy is a form of laziness, and laziness is the 'only one impediment' to spiritual growth. It is a form

---

68 Marcus J. Borg, *The Heart of Christianity*, HarperSanFrancisco, 2003, pp. 113-4.
69 M. Scott Peck, *The Road Less Travelled*, Arrow Books, London, repr., 1999, p. 285.
70 Ibid., p. 322.

of non-love because it is 'the unwillingness to extend one's self.'[71] Repentance bids us to journey beyond forgetfulness and spiritual lethargy; it beckons us to begin yet again.

Consider this contemporary parable about the continual need for repentance. On a dangerous seacoast where shipwrecks often occur there was once a crude little lifesaving station. The building was just a hut, and there was only one boat, but the few devoted members kept a constant watch over the sea, and with no thought for themselves went out day or night tirelessly searching for the lost. Many lives were saved by this wonderful little station, so that it became famous.

Some of those who were saved, and various others in the surrounding areas, wanted to become associated with the station and give of their time and money and effort for the support of its work. New boats were bought and new crews were trained. The little lifesaving station grew.

Some of the new members of the lifesaving station were unhappy that the building was so crude and so poorly equipped. They felt that a more comfortable place should be provided as the first refuge of those saved from the sea. So they replaced the emergency cots with beds and put better furniture in an enlarged building. Now the lifesaving station became a popular gathering place for its members, and they redecorated it beautifully and furnished it exquisitely, because they used it as a sort of club.

---

71 Ibid., p. 290.

Releasing the Captive

Fewer members were now interested in going to sea on lifesaving missions, so they hired life boat crews to do this work. The lifesaving motif still prevailed in this club's decoration, and there was a liturgical lifeboat in the room where the club initiations were held.

About this time a large ship was wrecked off the coast, and the hired crews brought in boat loads of cold, wet and half-drowned people. The beautiful new club was in chaos. So the property committee immediately had a shower house built outside the club where future victims of shipwreck could be cleaned up before coming inside.

At the next meeting, there was a split in the club membership. Most of the members wanted to stop the club's lifesaving activities as being unpleasant and a hindrance to the normal social life of the club. Some members insisted that lifesaving was their primary purpose and pointed out that they were still called a lifesaving station. But they were finally voted down and told that if they wanted to save the lives of people who were shipwrecked in those waters, they could begin their own lifesaving station down the coast.

And so they did. As the years went by, the new station experienced the same changes that had occurred in the old. It evolved into a club, and yet another lifesaving station was founded. History continued to repeat itself, and if you visit the seacoast today you will find a number of exclusive clubs along that shore. Shipwrecks are frequent in those waters, but most of the people drown![72]

---

72 This parable originally appeared in an article by Theodore O. Wedel, 'Evangelism – the mission of the church to those outside her life', *The Ecumenical Review*, (October 1953), p. 24. This paraphrase by Richard Wheatcroft appeared in *Letter to Laymen* (May–June 1962), 1, and is reproduced in Howard Clinebell, *Basic Types of Pastoral Care and Counselling*, Abingdon Press, Nashville, rev. edn, 1984, pp. 13-14.

Reflections for the year of Mark

A monk was once asked, 'What do you do there in the monastery?' He replied: 'We fall and get up, fall and get up, fall and get up again.' Standing at the edge of the Lenten desert, let us get up again from our torpor and begin yet again.

Releasing the Captive

FIRST SUNDAY OF LENT

(YEAR B)

*The Spirit drove Jesus out into the wilderness
and he remained there for forty days. (Mk 1:12)*

In the 1940s a collection of essays by eminent British and American contributors was published under the title *This I Believe*. In about 600 words each of the contributors attempted to express his or her beliefs about life. The introduction to the 1949 edition explained the rationale behind such a book. It said that

> among people generally material values are gaining and spiritual values declining. The reasons are obvious: the uncertainty of the economic future, the shadow of war, the atom bomb, army service for one's self or loved ones, the frustration of young people facing the future. Seldom has there been a time when an inventory of one's personal beliefs and sense of values seems to be more needed.

John Marsden, perhaps best known as a children's author, came across a copy of *This I Believe* while he was browsing in a second-hand bookshop sometime during 1965. It made such an impression upon him that he approached a publisher and suggested that a book similar to *This I Believe* would be timely for Australia. The publishers agreed, and Marsden began compiling a list of eminent Australians who might contribute to a local version of the book.[73] The only criteria were that they had to be interesting people who represented a range of views and experiences. In the case of adult contributors, they also had to have achieved distinction in their field. Marsden writes in the introduction that the most important function of the book is to help all of us – both contributors and readers alike – to stop and confront something that we don't think about often enough. He asks, 'What kind of society have we become that we don't even think about our beliefs anymore? There are few things more important that we as humans can do, yet we hardly ever do it.'

Marsden wrote to about 800 people. He found their responses fascinating. Many simply didn't answer his letter. Many wrote courteous, often regretful refusals. A couple refused quite aggressively, as though they were angry to have been asked. In general, architects, theatre people, religious leaders, sports players and writers were the keenest to contribute. Artists, journalists and politicians tended to accept the invitation but were often not heard from again, despite many attempts to contact them. By far the most difficult people to contact, according to Marsden, were business leaders. And why? Well, they invariably declined on the grounds of 'busyness'. An interesting response, is it not? Business leaders were so busy that they didn't have time to stand back from their lives to articulate their basic beliefs. There is no shortage of people in our society who work harder and harder to climb the ladder of success, without

---

73 John Marsden (ed.), *This I Believe*, Random House, Sydney, 1996.

ever stopping to ask whether the ladder is even leaning against the right wall. Many guests on Caroline Jones's highly successful ABC radio programme, *The Search for Meaning*, told her that although the broadcast interview made them vulnerable, 'they were glad of the push it gave them to review their values and direction. It was like a personal stocktaking which revealed unacknowledged assets and also a few places where the cupboard was bare.'[74]

In May 2002, Eugene O'Kelly was elected chairman and chief executive of KPMG, one of America's Big Four accounting firms, and by 2006, if all went well, he expected to become chairman of the global organisation. In May 2005, O'Kelly went to the doctor to check out a drooping cheek that he attributed to stress. He received a devastating diagnosis: he was told that he had late-stage brain cancer and only three months to live.

Strange as it might seem, he welcomed that diagnosis as a blessing.

> I was blessed. I was told I had three months to live. You think that to put those two sentences back to back, I must be joking. Or crazy. Perhaps that I lived a miserable, unfulfilled life, and the sooner it was done, the better.

That was far from the truth:

> I loved life. Adored my family. Enjoyed my friends, the career I had, the big-hearted organizations I was part of, the golf I played. And I'm quite sane.[75]

---

74 Caroline Jones, *An Authentic Life*, ABC Books, Sydney, 1998, p. 10.
75 Eugene O'Kelly, *Chasing Daylight*, McGraw-Hill, New York, 2008, p. 1.

Reflections for the year of Mark

What becomes clear in *Chasing Daylight*, O'Kelly's account of how his impending death transformed his life, is that he was incredibly driven. His job as CEO was tough, relentless and full of pressure.

> My calendar was perpetually extended out over the next 18 months. I was always moving at a hundred miles an hour. I worked all the time. I worked weekends. I worked late into many nights. I missed virtually every school function for my younger daughter. My annual travel schedule averaged, conservatively, 150,000 miles. For the first ten years of my marriage, when I was climbing the ladder at KPMG, Corinne and I rarely went on vacation. After that, vacations were mostly rolled into the corporate outings I was required to attend.[76]

Eugene O'Kelly was forced to think seriously about his own death, to think more deeply about his life than he'd ever done. Not long before he died he wrote about the importance of the inner journey:

> I had long believed that a successful businessperson could, if so inclined, live a spiritual life, and that to do so it wasn't necessary to quit the boardroom, chuck it all, and live on an ashram, as if only a physical departure that dramatic would confirm a depth of feeling about larger issues, including one's soul. After my diagnosis, I still believed that. But I also discovered depths to which a businessperson rarely goes, and learned how worthwhile it was to visit there, and sooner rather than later, because it may bring one greater success as a businessperson and as a human being. You can call what I went through a spiritual journey, a journey of the soul. A journey that allowed me to experience what was there all along but had been hidden, thanks to the distractions of the world.[77]

---

76 Ibid., p. 23.
77 Eugene O'Kelly, pp. 12-13.

How true! A handful of people are called to a life of solitude, but most of us are called into the desert amidst the frantic busyness of life. And the desert alerts us to what was there all along, but hidden beneath the distractions of the world. In Scetis, south of Alexandria in Egypt, a brother went to Abba Moses to ask for advice. He said to him, 'Go and sit in your cell, and your cell will teach you everything.'[78]

The Australian social commentator Hugh Mackay has noticed that we Australians are famous for greeting each other by asking a question, and then almost immediately supplying the answer. 'How y'goin? Orright?' But lately Mackay has observed a subtle variation to that greeting. Instead of: 'How y'going? Orright?' We're now greeting each other by saying: 'How y'goin? Busy?' The preferred answer is, of course, 'Flat out!' It wouldn't do to mumble something like: 'Busy? No. Not really. I'm actually taking it a bit easier so I can spend a little more time fiddling around with my poetry.' Mackay argues that we have become obsessed by the need to appear busy. 'Busy-busy' has become a kind of mantra in our lives.[79] And keeping busy is one sure way to avoid listening. Frantic busyness can be a wonderful hiding place. If you stay busy for long enough, you might never have time to listen, you might never have time 'to take a closer look at the things and people one would rather not see, to face situations one would rather avoid, to answer questions one would rather forget'.[80] If

---

78 Benedicta Ward, *The Desert Fathers: Sayings of the Early Christian Monks*, Penguin Books, London, 2003, p. 10.
79 Hugh Mackay, 'Flat out, but are we really doing anything?'
80 Alessandro Pronzato, quoted in John Moses, *The Desert: An Anthology for Lent*, p. 57.

you'd rather not answer those questions or face those situations, C.S. Lewis tells you how:

> Avoid silence, avoid solitude, avoid any train of thought that leads off the beaten track. Concentrate on money, sex, status, health and (above all) on your own grievances. Keep the radio on. Live in a crowd. Use plenty of sedation. If you must read books, select them very carefully. But you'd be safer to stick to the papers. You'll find the advertisements helpful; especially those with a sexy or snobbish appeal.[81]

This holy season of Lent begins in the desert. We are called into the wilderness. In *The Tibetan Book of Living and Dying* there is an interesting discussion about laziness. The author contrasts Eastern and Western types of laziness, and argues that Western laziness is quite different. 'It consists of cramming our lives with compulsive activity, so that there is no time at all to confront the real issues.'[82]

The desert invites us to journey within, to stop and confront the real issues, the questions we don't think about often enough. Thomas Moore believes that the great malady of the 20th century is 'loss of soul.' 'Soul' is impossible to define precisely, but it has to do with 'genuineness and depth, as when we say certain music has soul or a remarkable person is soulful.'[83]

Loss of soul is reflected in emptiness, meaninglessness, vague depression, disillusionment about marriage, family, and relationship,

---

81 C.S. Lewis, *Christian Reflections*, Eerdmans, Grand Rapids, MI, 1967, pp. 168-9.
82 Sogyal Rinpoche, *The Tibetan Book of Living and Dying*, Rider, London, 1992, p. 19.
83 Thomas Moore, *Care of the Soul*, p. xi.

a loss of values, yearning for personal fulfillment, and a hunger for spirituality.[84] The desert summons us to undertake a personal stock-take. In his *Letters to a Young Poet*, Rainer Maria Rilke offers this advice: 'Go into yourself and see how deep the place is from which your life flows'.[85] John Marsden concludes his introduction in words that are extremely appropriate for Lent. He writes, 'Perhaps after browsing through *This I Believe* you might challenge yourself to do what these one hundred people have done. Believe me, it's not easy! But believe me, it's worth it!'

---

84 Ibid., xvi.
85 Quoted in Thomas Moore, *Care of the Soul*, p. 299.

SECOND SUNDAY OF LENT

(YEAR B)

Let us make three tents, one for you, one for Moses and one for Elijah.
(Mk 9:5)

When Jesus was transfigured in the presence of Peter, James and John, the experience was so overwhelming that Peter did not want it to end. 'Let us make three tents, one for you, one for Moses and one for Elijah.' But the moment passes, and 'they saw no one with them any more but only Jesus.'

Such numinous moments are blessings on our journey of faith, but the spiritual masters counsel us to be wary of placing too much importance upon such experiences. When a nun told St Teresa of Avila that she had just seen a vision of the Blessed Virgin Mary, the saint replied, 'Never mind, dear, it will go away!' And St Philip Neri told one of his followers who reported having a similar vision, 'Next time she appears, spit in her eye!' When he did so, it is said, the devil appeared.[86]

Peter, James and John encountered the divine presence on Mt Tabor (the traditional site of the transfiguration), and God put

---

86   Alan Jones, *Passion for Pilgrimage*, p. 131.

Releasing the Captive

Abraham to the test on Mt Moriah, but for those with eyes to see, nowhere is bereft of God's presence. Fr Ronald Rolheiser makes the observation that

> what we need to have in order to possess a sense of God's presence in everyday life, are not the kind of miracles that so drastically change ordinary reality so as to prove beyond the shadow of a doubt that there is a world of the supernatural beyond our natural world (miracle in the common sense understanding). No. What we need to have so as to move us beyond our practical atheism is a deeper sense of how God is already present and acting in the seemingly ordinary events of our lives. We need to read the signs of the times, to be able to see in the conspiracy of accidents within ordinary life, the finger of God.[87]

Fr Rolheiser tells a story shared by a woman who attended a class he was teaching. She had been raised in a religious home and had been a pious and regular churchgoer. During her years as a university student her interest and practice in religion progressively slipped so that by the time that she graduated she no longer attended church or prayed. Several years later she spent some time with a married sister to do some skiing. She arrived on a Saturday evening and her sister invited her to go to Mass with her the following morning. She politely refused and went skiing instead. On her first run down the ski-slope she hit a tree and broke her leg. She was released from hospital the following Saturday and the next morning her sister again invited her to come to Mass. This time she accepted the invitation.

---

87 Ronald Rolheiser, *The Shattered Lantern*, Hodder & Stoughton, London, 1994, p. 156.

Reflections for the year of Mark

It happened to be Good Shepherd Sunday and the celebrant was a visiting priest from Israel. During the homily he told of a custom among shepherds in Israel that existed at the time of Jesus and is still practised today. Sometimes very early on in the life of a lamb a shepherd senses that it is going to be a congenital stray, one forever drifting away from the flock. What the shepherd does then is to take the lamb and deliberately break its leg so that he has to carry it until its leg is healed. As a result the lamb becomes so attached to the shepherd that it never strays again.

Coming out of church that morning, supported by crutches and sporting a huge cast, she reflected, 'I may be dense, but given my broken leg and this chance coincidence, hearing this woke up something inside me. Fifteen years have passed since then and I have prayed and gone to church regularly ever since!'[88]

The Jewish biblical scholar Geza Vermes entitled his autobiography *Providential Accidents* because, he writes, 'here I am, recently turned seventy, seeking to piece together and make sense of my life story, which I can best sum up, mixing religious and secular imagery, as an amazing series of providential accidents'.[89]

James Mackey, quoting George Santayana, suggests that divine providence is a conspiracy of accidents.[90] Such providential accidents are guides from beyond for those 'who see every event of their lives against a divine horizon, who see in the conspiracy of accidents that make up their daily lives the finger and providence of God'.[91]

---

88 Ibid., p. 155.
89 Geza Vermes, *Providential Accidents*, Rowman & Litterfield, Lanham, MD, 1999, p. xi.
90 Ronald Rolheiser, *The Shattered Lantern*, p. 155.
91 Ibid., p. 157.

Releasing the Captive

When Jack Kornfield became a Buddhist monk in Thailand over thirty years ago he had to learn how to bow, a practice he found awkward at first. Each time a Buddhist monk enters the meditation hall he falls to his knees and bows – a practice of reverence and mindfulness. The monk also bows each time he takes his seat with the master. After a week or two in the monastery one of the senior monks took Kornfield aside and told him that he must bow not only when entering the meditation hall and when receiving instruction from the master, but also when he meets his elders. Being the only Westerner in the monastery he was not sure who his elders were. 'It is traditional,' he was told, 'that all who are older in ordination time, who've been monks longer than you, are your elders'. That meant everybody was his elder!

And so Kornfield began to bow to all of the other monks. He had no difficulty in bowing before those monks whom he judged to be wise and worthy elders of the community, but he felt ridiculous bowing before some 21-year-old monk who had been ordained only a week before him, a lad full of hubris who had joined the monastery only to please his parents or to eat better food than he could at home. It was even difficult bowing to a sloppy old rice farmer who had come to the monastery the season before on the farmers' retirement plan, a man who constantly chewed betel nut and had never meditated a day in his life.

As a way of dealing with the inner conflict that this constant bowing caused, Kornfield began to look for some worthy aspect of each person that he could acknowledge with his bow. 'I bowed to the wrinkles around the retired farmer's eyes, for all the difficulties he had seen and suffered through and triumphed over. I bowed to the vitality and playfulness in the young monks, the incredible possibilities each of their lives held yet ahead of them.'

And so he began to enjoy bowing because he saw it as a way of greeting with a respectful and kindly heart all that life presents to us.

Bowing to the providential accidents that life presents to us is often difficult, 'but it is one of the most useful and honourable practices'.[92] The Persian poet Rumi expresses this truth in these words:

> This being human is a guest house.
> Every morning a new arrival.
> A joy, a depression, a meanness,
> some momentary awareness comes
> as an unexpected visitor.
> Welcome and entertain them all
> Even if they're a crowd of sorrows,
> who violently sweep your house
> empty of its furniture.
> Still treat each guest honourably,
> He may be clearing you out
> for some new delight.
> the dark thought, the shame, the malice,
> meet them at the door laughing,
> and invite them in.
> Be grateful for whoever comes,
> because each has been sent
> as a guide from beyond.[93]

---

92 Jack Kornfield, After the Ecstasy, the Laundry, p. ix-xi.
93 Quoted in Kornfield, After the Ecstasy, the Laundry, p. xi.

THIRD SUNDAY OF LENT

(YEAR B)

Jesus answered them, 'Destroy this temple and in three days I will raise it up.' (Jn 2:19)

The desert was our symbol for the first Sunday of Lent. Last week we accompanied Jesus up a mountain, and today we focus on the Temple. The desert, the mountain, and the Temple are three powerful symbols for our Lenten journey. What was the significance of the Temple for the Jewish people?

About 1000 BC King David conquered the ancient city of Jerusalem and made it his capital. David wanted to build a temple in Jerusalem, but the prophet Nathan dissuaded him, telling the king that it was a task to be undertaken by his son Solomon. Solomon completed the task in about 960 BC, and by all accounts the Temple was a majestic building. When it was completed the Ark of the Covenant was solemnly placed in the inner sanctum of the Temple, the Holy of Holies or *devir* in Hebrew. The Temple was not originally intended to be a house of prayer, but a house or tabernacle for the Ark. Hence it was called the house of the Lord, in much the same way that the palace was the house of the king.[94] The basic term for temple in the

---

94 *Encyclopedia Judaica*, CD Rom, under 'Temple'.

Hebrew Bible is *bêt Yahweh* or *bêt 'elōhîm*, 'house of Yahweh' or 'house of God'.[95] The Temple didn't fulfil the same function as a Christian church. Our churches are built to accommodate a large congregation gathered for worship. The Temple building itself 'was not a place of public gathering and prayer, although its courtyards were the scene of such activity. Rather, the Temple in conception was a dwelling place on earth for the deity of ancient Israel'.[96] The Jewish Temple also served as a place for offering sacrifices.[97] It was the religious centre of Israel and the seat of the divine presence. The Temple was also the sign of election. 'God himself chose to live among his own, and he chose to live in this city and in this Temple.'[98]

The Babylonians conquered Jerusalem and destroyed the Temple in 586 BC. Many of the Jews were taken into exile, and they languished by the rivers of Babylon for almost eighty years. Babylon in its turn was conquered by the Persian king, Cyrus, and the Jews were allowed to return home. A huge task lay ahead of them. Jerusalem had been destroyed and the Temple lay in ruins. They set about rebuilding the Temple, but they did not have the resources to adorn it with the same splendour as the former building. It was said that many of the old men who had seen the First Temple in all its glory wept when they saw the modest proportions of the new building.

---

95 Carol Meyers, 'Temple, Jerusalem', in David Noel Freedman (ed.), *The Anchor Bible Dictionary*, Volume 6, Si – Z, Doubleday, New York, 1992, p. 352.
96 Ibid., p. 351.
97 Paula Fredriksen, *Jesus of Nazareth, King of the Jews*, Macmillan, London, 1999, p. 208.
98 Roland de Vaux, *Ancient Israel: Its Life and Institutions*, Darton, Longman & Todd, London, 2nd edn, 1965, p. 327.

Releasing the Captive

In 20 AD King Herod (37–4 BC) began rebuilding the Temple, and by all accounts it was a magnificent building. Herod's grandiose project so frightened the Jews that he had to promise that he would have all the materials ready before touching a stone of the old edifice.[99] It was Herod's temple that we read of in the gospels, although it was not finally completed until 63 AD, just seven years before its destruction.[100] Some 40 years after the death of Jesus, the Roman emperor Titus and the Tenth Legion Fretensis 'turned the magnificent holy compound into smoldering uninhabitable ruins in the year 70 AD.'[101] If any of Herod's building had survived the destruction wrought by Titus it would have been swept away by Hadrian in 135 AD when he rebuilt Jerusalem, renaming it *Colonia Aelia Capitolina*. The sole remnant of the Temple is the so-called Wailing or Western Wall.

Why was the Temple so important for the Jews? The Temple was the most sacred place on earth, the navel of the universe, the axis mundi. It played a central role in the religious and cultic life of Israel. The Holy of Holies (the *davir*) was its innermost sanctum, accessible only to the high priest, and only on the Day of Atonement. From about 20 AD onwards the high priest was compelled to sleep in his official room in the Temple. This occurred when the high priest Simeon was touched by an Arab's spittle on the eve of the day, thereby

---

99 Jerome Murphy-O'Connor, *The Holy Land: An Archaeological Guide from Earliest Times to 1700*, Oxford University Press, 3rd edn, 1992, p. 85.
100 Raymond E. Brown, *The Gospel According to John I-XII*, Doubleday & Company, New York, 1966, p. 116.
101 Carol Meyers, 'Temple, Jerusalem', in David Noel Freedman (ed.), *The Anchor Bible Dictionary*, p. 365.

rendering him unable to officiate.[102] Orthodox Jews will not walk onto the Temple mount lest they inadvertently walk into the space where the davir or Holy of Holies once stood.

Now that the State of Israel exists, why don't the Jews rebuild the Temple? Many Jews would love to rebuild the Temple, but there is a problem. The site of the Temple is now an Islamic shrine that marks the spot from which the prophet Muhammad was said to have ascended to heaven. The Dome of the Rock (Qubbet es-Sakhra), completed in 691 AD, was the first major sanctuary built by Islam, and despite its antiquity, it has survived essentially intact.[103] Were the Dome of the Rock to be destroyed in order to rebuild a Jewish temple it would surely lead to World War III!

In today's gospel, Jesus says he will destroy the Temple, and in three days raise it up. He was not speaking of the magnificent temple that towered over him. He was speaking, rather, of the temple that was his body. John's gospel places this incident at the beginning of Jesus' public ministry, so what does it mean? Let us respond to that question by asking why Jesus was so irate? He drove merchants and money changes from the Temple, accusing them of 'turning my Father's house into a market.' But these were in fact legitimate transactions, essential for the smooth running of the Temple cult. Jewish visitors from around the world visiting the Temple to celebrate major feasts would hardly have brought with them animals for sacrifice. These would have to be purchased in the Temple precincts, but not

---

[102] Joachim Jeremias, *Jerusalem in the Time of Jesus*, SCM Press, London, 1969, pp. 153-4.
[103] Jerome Murphy-O'Connor, *The Holy Land*, p. 90.

in the Temple proper. Moreover, Roman coins, bearing an image of Caesar's head or sometimes an image of pagan gods, were unfit for Temple use, so many changers provided an essential service.[104]

While the merchants and money changes may have been guilty of petty profiteering, Jesus' anger is directed at something more radical. His action is a parable in action, and the interpretative key is the allusion to the prophet Zechariah (14:21) – 'and there will be no more traders in the Temple of Yahweh Sabaoth, when that Day comes' – and the text from Psalm 68 that the disciples remember: 'Zeal for your house will devour me.'

At the very outset of his ministry (as John tells the story) Jesus is laying all his cards out on the table. He is making a double claim. 'First, by driving the merchants out of the Temple precincts, he announces that the time of fulfillment has come. Second, identifying God as his Father affirms his right to make such a claim and to act in accord with it.'[105]

In other words, the old order of worship will be replaced by a new one, an order focused on the body of Christ, and not the temple.[106] The divine presence no longer dwells in a temple, a building made by human hands; it now dwells in the humanity of Jesus.[107]

The Jewish Temple was about exclusion. Non-Jews could go no further than the Court of the Gentiles; women no further than the

---

[104] Dianne Bergant and Richard Fragomeni, *Preaching the New Lectionary, Year B*, p. 109.
[105] Ibid., p. 109.
[106] Reginald H. Fuller, *Preaching the New Lectionary: The Word of God for the Church Today*, The Liturgical Press, Collegeville MN, 1979, p. 341.
[107] Verna Holyhead, *Ashes to Breaking Waters*, John Garratt Publishing, Mulgrave, Vic., 1996, p. 28.

Court of Women; non-priests no further than the Court of the Israelites; and priests no further than the Court of the Priests. Only one man, the Jewish high priest, had access to the *devir*, the Holy of Holies, and then only on one day of the year, the Day of Atonement. In Jesus, we all have access to the Holy of Holies.

There is a further point worth considering. Temple sacrifice was essentially about exchange.

> Worshipers give God something; God gives worshipers something. The worshiper gives God a sacrificial animal and, in return, God gives the worshiper forgiveness for sins and help in various endeavours ... In this way the mentality of the marketplace so permeates Temple worship that it degenerates into deal making.

But the Father of Jesus is not a deal maker.

> He does not exchange favours for sacrifices. The Father is a free flow of spiritual life and love that cannot be bought, bartered, bargained, or bribed.[108]

The 2003 movie *House of Sand and Fog* stars Ben Kingsley as Massoud Amir Behrani, an Iranian refugee to the United States. Towards the end of the movie Behrani is wracked with grief when his son is tragically shot dead. 'If you let my son live,' he instinctively prays, 'I will lie in the park, put bird seed on my eyes, and let the birds eat my eyes out.' Such deal-making is hardwired into the human condition and comes out of hiding during times of stress and tragedy.[109]

---

108 John Shea, *Eating with the Bridegroom: Year B*, Liturgical Press, Collegeville, MN, 2005, pp. 90-1.
109 Ibid., p. 94.

The Temple, the place of our encounter with God, is not a marketplace where a deal can be struck for the right price. When Jesus identified himself as the new temple, he was claiming to be 'the presence of God in the midst of the community.'

He is the true temple, 'the place where the glory of God has chosen to make his dwelling.'[110] And so, when we accept him in faith, 'We are agreeing that he is the centre of our universe, the medium of our communication with God, the presence of God in our midst.'[111] Where once only the high priest could enter, we now have gracious access through our crucified and risen Lord.

---

110 Tom Wright, *John for Everyone, Part 1*, SPCK, London, 2002, p. 26
111 Dianne Bergant and Richard Fragomeni, *Preaching the New Lectionary, Year B*, p. 110.

FOURTH SUNDAY OF LENT

(YEAR B)

For God sent his Son into the world not to condemn the world, but so that through him the world might be saved. (Jn 3:16)

The gospel reading alludes to an episode that occurred during the Exodus, the chosen people's great journey of homecoming. When the Israelites lost patience and complained that Moses had brought them out of Egypt to die in the desert, God sent fiery serpents among the people, and their bite brought death to many. The people repented and begged Moses to intercede with the Lord. God then instructed Moses to make a serpent out of bronze and raise it up as a standard. Those bitten by a serpent were saved by looking upon the bronze serpent (Num 21:4-9).

Just as the bronze serpent was a life-giving antidote to the deadly venom, Jesus tells Nicodemus that 'the Son of Man must be lifted up as Moses lifted up the serpent in the desert, so that everyone who believes may have eternal life in him.' The gospel assures us that God sent his Son into the world, not to condemn the world, but so that through him the world might be saved.

Releasing the Captive

From what, I ask myself, do I need to be saved? First, I need to be rescued from exile. Just recently I celebrated the funeral of a parishioner who had migrated from Italy with her husband at the age of 29. She was 80 years old when she died, and despite living in this country for 51 years she never felt truly at home in Australia. In fact, she had made up her mind to return to Italy, her husband having died three years earlier, but that was not to be.

Today's readings present us with an image of exile. For 70 or 80 years the Jewish people languished 'by the rivers of Babylon' longing to return home. The scriptures begin with a story of exile. God created the man and the woman (we know them as Adam and Eve), settled them in the Garden of Eden, and told them they were free to eat from any of the trees of the garden except one. They are tempted by the serpent, the most cunning of all the animals, and they eat the forbidden fruit. As a result, they are banished from the garden, and the entrance was guarded by an angel with a fiery sword.

They are banished from paradise forever, but why? Surely not because they ate a piece of fruit? The act responsible for their expulsion from Eden was disobedience. God gave them a command and they disobeyed it. God could just as easily have said, 'Please don't eat the daisies.' The emphasis is on the disobedience itself, not on what the act of disobedience was.[112]

We have a 'fractured, broken, and sinful heart,'[113] we are exiled by the rivers of Babylon, rebellious in the wilderness of Sinai. Our

---

[112] Marcus J. Borg, *Reading the Bible Again for the First Time*, HarperSanFrancisco, 2002, p. 78.
[113] Alan Jones, *Soul Making: The Desert Way of Spirituality*, HarperCollins, San Francisco, 1989, p. 111.

Reflections for the year of Mark

lives, like those of the Israelites in the desert, have been 'twisted and bent out of shape by wrong turns, infidelities, and betrayals'.[114] I'm not whom I should be. I am an exile. The word 'alienation' is another way of describing the same experience, the Latin word *alius* meaning 'another person'. I am alienated because I am not my true self.

I also need to be saved from the tyranny of the ego. Salvation is placing God at the centre of everything, but, like the mythical Narcissus, we are beguiled and obsessed by our own image. Narcissus, a youth of exceeding beauty and vanity, was the son of the river god Cephissus. Echo, a mountain nymph, fell madly in love with Narcissus, but her love was totally unrequited and she pined away to become a mere voice.

Angered by this, the god Nemesis determined to punish Narcissus for his vanity. When Narcissus went to drink from a certain pool he saw his own reflection in the water and was overcome by the sight of his own beauty. He falls in love with himself, and 'thus, turned inward and paralysed by his obsession with himself, he eventually withered away and became a flower which still bears his name.'

Fr Ronald Rolheiser writes that 'few images are as apt to describe the contemporary mindset as is that of narcissism.'[115] Salvation is displacing ourselves at the centre of the universe and becoming eccentric, off-centre. Alan Jones writes,

> I have wasted a great deal of my time trying to run the universe – and if not the universe, then my own little part of

---

[114] Alan Jones, *The Soul's Journey*, Cowley Publications, Cambridge, MA, 2001, p. 115.
[115] Ronald Rolheiser, *The Shattered Lantern*, pp. 24-5.

it. I have tried to make others conform to my view of things, often for their own good. I have bullied friends, coerced children, and been hard on myself for the sake of wanting to be in control.[116]

I also need to be saved from the 'gap'. In the London Underground prominently displayed signs warn travellers to 'Mind the gap'. It's a warning that alerts commuters to the gap between the subway platform and the train carriage, but perhaps we can see it as a metaphor for another kind of gap. 'We all live in the 'gap' between the person we are today and the person we ought to be.'[117]

Fr Edward Beck tells of a deacon who commenced his homily wearing a rubber Halloween horror mask. The congregation laughed and applauded, but as the church quieted, he slowly removed the mask and began to speak about the masks we wear in our lives, and about God's desire to help us peel them off so that our true selves may be revealed.[118]

I also need to be saved from the illusion of invincibility. I call it the 'Superman syndrome'. Like the fictional Clark Kent, I can change into the 'man of steel' whenever I want. I can overcome any obstacles if I put my mind to it. I am invincible!

This is not salvation. Salvation is about letting go of the controls. The plethora of self-help books caters to the fantasy that if I set my mind to it, I can become the kind of person I want to be. Rick Warren makes the observation that

> Self-help books, even Christian ones, usually offer the same predictable steps to finding your life's purpose: Consider your

---

116 Alan Jones, *The Soul's Journey*, p. 174.
117 George Weigel, *Letters to a Young Catholic*, p. 113.
118 Edward L. Beck, *God Underneath*, Image Books, New York, 2002, p. 64.

dreams. Clarify your values. Set some goals. Figure out what you are good at. Aim high. Go for it! Be disciplined. Believe you can achieve your goals. Involve others. Never give up.[119]

The emphasis here is on what I can achieve, and human wholeness is not ultimately about me. The 'I-can-save-myself' approach to salvation has a long pedigree. Pelagius, a fourth-century British theologian and biblical scholar, argued that human beings always have the power to choose what is good. In a nutshell, I can achieve perfection through my own unaided effort. Human beings are responsible for their own actions, he taught, and, if only they have the courage to will it, there is no height of sanctity that they may not attain. According to Pelagius, God gave each of us existence, and it is our responsibility to sanctify ourselves.

He was vigorously opposed by St Augustine and condemned by two local church councils in North Africa and by the Council of Ephesus.[120] Warren tells of a time when he was lost in the mountains. When he stopped to ask for directions to the campsite, he was told, 'You can't get there from here. You must start from the other side of the mountain!' In the same way, he writes, 'You cannot arrive at your life's purpose by starting with a focus on yourself. You must begin with God, your Creator.'[121]

M. Scott Peck uses the myth of Icarus to illustrate our illusion of invincibility. Icarus and his father attempted to escape from prison

---

[119] Rick Warren, *The Purpose Driven Life*, Zondervan, Grand Rapids, MI, 2002, p. 19.
[120] Gerald O'Collins and Mario Farrugia, *Catholicism: The Story of Catholic Christianity*, Oxford University Press, Oxford, 2003, pp. 35-6.
[121] Rick Warren, *The Purpose Driven Life*, p. 18.

by imitating the birds. They constructed wings of feathers and wax and began their flight to freedom. Icarus became enthralled by the experience and soared towards the sun. But of course, as he flew closer to the sun the wax on his wings began to melt, and he plummeted to his death. We are not omnipotent, and Peck writes that a major learning on the journey is 'the art of surrender'.[122] The first step in the Alcoholics Anonymous programme reads:

> We admitted we were powerless over alcohol – that our lives had become unmanageable. Secondly, we came to believe that a Power greater than ourselves could restore us to sanity. And thirdly, we made a decision to turn our will and our lives over to the care of God as we understood Him.[123]

Scott Peck tells of an alcoholic executive who came to see him because AA wasn't working for him. In fact, he'd been going to meetings on alternate nights. On the nights he didn't attend meetings he got blind drunk. This executive could recite the first step, but ultimately he was unable to admit that he was powerless over alcohol. He shifted the blame to a 'kind of biochemical defect' in his brain that caused alcohol to take over after the first drink. In other words, he could not surrender and admit that he was powerless over alcohol both before and after that first drink.[124]

---

122 M. Scott Peck, *Further along the Road Less Travelled*, Simon & Schuster, New York, 1993, p. 107.
123 *Twenty-Four Hours a Day*, Collins Dove, Melbourne, 1972. Pages not numbered.
124 M. Scott Peck, *Further along the Road Less Travelled*, pp. 140-1.

To use the imagery of today's gospel, he preferred darkness to light. We must first acknowledge our brokenness before the healing can begin. In the words of Leonard Cohen's song *Anthem*'

> Forget your perfect offering
> There is a crack, a crack in everything
> That's how the light gets in.[125]

Paul's letter to the Ephesians reminds us that we have been saved by grace. In other words, we were not saved by anything that we have done. Salvation is a gift, totally unmerited. It comes free of charge to people who have not merited it and do not deserve it. Salvation is not egocentric; it is centred in Christ; it is not gazing at our own image; it is looking upon the Son of Man 'who has been raised up in both ignominy and exaltation'.[126]

---

[125] http://www.azlyrics.com/lyrics/leonardcohen/anthem.html
[126] Dianne Bergant and Richard Fragomeni, *Preaching the New Lectionary, Year B*, p. 114.

FIFTH SUNDAY OF LENT

(YEAR B)

Anyone who loves his life loses it; anyone who hates his life in this world will keep it for the eternal life. (Jn 12:25)

Passover is approaching, and many Jews have made the pilgrimage to Jerusalem to celebrate the great festival that commemorates the liberating power of God in the Exodus. Among the pilgrims were two Greeks. Such people were called 'Godfearers' – Gentiles who admired and lived Judaism as best they could. We're told that they want to see Jesus. This entails more than a casual meeting or simple curiosity. To see Jesus means to enter into his revelation, to accept his role as the revealer. This is the sight that these Greeks desire.[127] Just as the grain of wheat must die if it is to yield a rich and abundant harvest, it is also true that the ego's distorted view of the world must die if we are to 'see' Jesus.

And what is the vision of Jesus? He expresses it succinctly to Andrew and Philip: 'Anyone who loves his life loses it; anyone who hates his life in this world will keep it for the eternal life.' In trying

---

[127] John Shea, *Eating with the Bridegroom*, p. 100; Francis J. Moloney, *Signs and Shadows: Reading John 5-12*, Wipf & Stock, Eugene, OR, 2004, pp. 186-7.

to come to terms with these words of Jesus, let us remember that Semitic thought often expresses truths forcefully, using black and white imagery.

The idea of loving or hating life is a perfect example of what I mean. This black-and-white imagery is to be treated cautiously. Elsewhere in the gospels Jesus tells us that no one can come to him unless they hate their mother and their father. Well, how does that square off with the commandment to honour one's father and mother? Is Jesus exhorting us to hate our mother and father? Or, rather, is he using a forceful Semitic idiom to remind us that our commitment to God's kingdom must come before everything else in our lives; that it must be our top priority; that it must even come before family commitments? Jesus also exhorts us to love our neighbour as we love ourselves (Mt 22:36-39). That therefore presupposes that we love, not hate, ourselves.

The author M. Scott Peck worked as a psychiatrist in the United States army. In *Further along the Road Less Travelled*, he tells of the army's interest in knowing what makes successful people click. A dozen successful soldiers were gathered together for this study, men and women from different branches of the services who had all been markedly successful. They had been promoted ahead of their contemporaries, but they were also popular. Those who were married seemed to have successful family lives and their children were well adjusted and doing well in school. Why were they so successful?

As part of the study, they were asked to write down – independently of each other – the three most important things in their life, in order of priority. Peck noted that they all took the task seriously. The first to return the answer sheet took forty minutes completing the task, and the others took more than an hour. What, however, was remarkable was that while the second and third items on their list varied enormously, all twelve came up with exactly the same answer for number one: 'Myself'. Scott Peck concludes,

> And that, I suggest, was an expression of mature self-love. Self-love implies the care, respect, and responsibility for and the knowledge of the self. Without loving one's self one cannot love others. But do not confuse self-love with self-centredness.[128]

Self-love involves dying to self. The American writer Joseph Campbell has studied myths from many different cultures and from different periods of human history, and he observed how the same fundamental themes emerge time and again. One of his most popular works is entitled *The Hero with a Thousand Faces*.[129] Campbell outlines a number of key stages in the journey of the hero. It begins with the call to adventure, the hero's summons to leave behind familiar shores and launch out into the unknown.

This involves crossing a threshold, and here we encounter what Campbell calls the guardian of the threshold. The guardian symbolises all of those intimidating forces, both from within and without, that attempt to prevent us from embarking upon the adventure: the fear of failure, the loss of safety and security, the fear of leaping into

---

128 M. Scott Peck, *Further along the Road Less Travelled*, p. 88.
129 Joseph Campbell, *The Hero with a Thousand Faces*, Fontana Press, London, 1993.

the unknown. After crossing the threshold, the hero then enters the belly of the whale. The term 'belly of the whale' comes from the story of Jonah. You may recall that Jonah received a call from God: 'Jonah, go to Nineveh and preach repentance!' Jonah couldn't stand the Ninevites, and he hoped that God would wipe them off the face of the earth. But if he preached, the Ninevites might repent and be spared. So instead of heading eastwards towards Nineveh, Jonah ran off in the opposite direction and boarded a ship bound for Tarshish, which is in Spain.

A great storm arose and the sailors cast lots to find out who was to blame. Everything pointed to Jonah, who then came clean and admitted what he'd done. The sailors threw him overboard, and Jonah was swallowed by a great fish. He remained in the belly of the whale for three days and three nights. The whale obviously suffered from acute indigestion, and spat Jonah out onto dry land. The Lord then told Jonah a second time: 'Off to Nineveh!' And Jonah went on to greatness. The belly of the whale symbolises the death of Jonah's wilfullness and obduracy.

So, the life that we hate is the self-centred self, the tyranny of the ego typified by Narcissus. False love uses and manipulates others as a crutch for our own frail egos. Remember the movie *Rainman*, starring Tom Cruise, who plays a selfish, hustling salesman named Charlie Babbitt, and Dustin Hoffman who plays his older autistic brother Raymond?

Charlie Babbitt, kicked out of home as a teenager, didn't even know he had an older brother, yet alone an autistic one. To make matters worse, Charlie has been left a 1949 Buick convertible, but Raymond has been left three million dollars. Since Charlie has run into financial difficulties and is about to lose his exotic car dealership, he needs that money. Charlie is the perfect example of self-centred love, spending most of his time trying to cheat Raymond out of his inheritance.

But during the course of the movie, almost against his will, Charlie begins to care for Raymond. Before he knows it, for the first time in his life, he is thinking more of another person than himself. Slowly he begins to die to self and to live for Raymond. And slowly he becomes a different person. The scheming and conniving self that sought only to manipulate Raymond for his own selfish end falls away, and a deeper self emerges. The seed falls on the ground and dies to yield a rich harvest.[130]

Just as the seed must die, so must we. Alan Jones, Dean of San Francisco's Grace Cathedral, believes that 'All of us look outside ourselves for causes of our distress. We cling to the role of victim because finding a cause inside ourselves would be unbearable.'[131]

I would be happier if only I could change this or that, him or her, yet it is I who must change. The Sufi Bayazid once said that he was a revolutionary when he was young and his prayer to God was: 'Lord give me the energy to change the world.'

As he approached middle age and realised that half his life was gone and he hadn't changed a single soul, the changed his prayer to:

---

130 I am indebted to William J. Bausch, *More Telling Stories, Compelling Stories*, Twenty-Third Publications, Mystic, CT, 1994, p. 97, for the reference to Rainman.
131 Alan Jones, *The Soul's Journey*, p. 35.

Reflections for the year of Mark

'Lord, give me the grace to change all those who come in contact with me. Just my family and friends, and I shall be content.' As an old man, aware that his days were numbered, his one prayer was: 'Lord, give me the grace to change myself. If I had prayed for this right from the start I should not have wasted my life.'[132]

Dying to self means emptying the self. On the day that Thomas Merton began his solitary life as a hermit he asked for the prayers of the Gethsemane community in these words:

'And when you pray for me, all I ask that you pray for is that above all I should completely forget my own will and completely surrender to the will of God, because ... this is all I want to do.'[133]

A distinguished man once came to visit a Zen master, seeking the meaning of life. The visitor began to tell the master about his achievements and successes in life; he spoke at length of the degrees and diplomas he had been awarded. As the visitor continued his never-ending success story, the master placed a beautiful china cup before him and began filling it with tea. After the cup was filled, the master kept pouring tea into it. The visitor quickly moved away from the overflowing cup, saying 'Stop pouring, the cup is full! No more tea will fit in the cup.'

The master replied, 'Like this cup, you are overflowing with your own opinions and achievements. How can I teach you anything unless you first empty your cup?'

---
[132] Anthony de Mello, *The Song of the Bird*, Gujarat Sahitya Prakash, Anand, India, 1985, pp. 174-5.
[133] John Howard Griffin, *Follow the Ecstasy: The Hermitage Years of Thomas Merton*, Orbis Books, New York, 1993, p. 32.

Releasing the Captive

Charlie Babbit likewise emptied himself, died to himself, and a transformation began. In the words of the German poet Goethe:

> And so long as you haven't experienced
> This: to die and so to grow,
> You are only a troubled guest
> On the dark earth.[134]

---

134 Robert Bly (ed.), *The Soul Is Here for Its Own Joy: Poems from Many Cultures*, Ecco Press, Hopewell NJ, 1995, quoted in John Shea, *Eating with the Bridegroom*, p. 103.

Reflections for the year of Mark

PASSION SUNDAY (PALM SUNDAY)

My God, my God, why have you forsaken me? (Mk 15:34)

Karl Rahner, one of the greatest Catholic theologians of the 20th century, tells a story about Romano Guardini on his deathbed. Guardini was Rahner's predecessor in the chair of theology at the university of Munich. Guardini had told a friend that at the Last Judgment that he would willingly be interrogated by the Recording Angel, but he would also like to ask one question himself. He firmly hoped, the account goes on, that the angel would not deny him the true answer to the question which no book, not even the Bible, no dogma and no teaching authority, not even his own theology, had ever been able to answer for him. Guardini's unanswered question was: 'Why, God, these fearful detours on the way to salvation, the suffering of the innocent, why sin?'[135]

Bishop Geoffrey Robinson writes that 'There are certain fundamental questions about life that all people are constantly asking themselves: Who am I? Where do I come from? Where am I going? What is the purpose and meaning of my existence?'[136] We instinc-

---

135 Quoted in E. Biser, 'Interpretation und Veranderung', in *Karl Rahner, Theological Investigations*, vol. 19, Darton, Longman & Todd, London, 1983, p. 208.
136 Geoffrey Robinson, *Confronting Power and Sex in the Catholic Church*, John Garratt Publishing, Mulgrave, Vic, 2007, p. 299.

tively seek to discover a meaning in what happens to us. Francis Collins, one of America's leading geneticists and head of the Human Genome Project, notes that 'science is powerless to answer questions such as "Why did the universe come into being?" "What is the meaning of human existence?" "What happens after we die?", and yet one of the strongest motivations of humankind is to seek answers to such profound questions.[137] We could also add, 'Why do people suffer?'

Rabbi Harold Kushner tells of a Jewish legend about Moses. As he climbed down from Mount Sinai with the two stone tablets on which God had written the Ten Commandments, he had no trouble carrying them even though they were large and heavy slabs of stone and the path was steep. As he approached the Israelite camp he saw the people dancing around the golden calf. According to the legend the words took flight and disappeared from the stone tablets. Now that they were blank stones again, Moses found the weight unbearable and he could no longer carry them.

The point of the legend is clear. We can endure any burden if we believe there is some meaning or purpose to it.[138] Human suffering is not a problem that has black and white answers. It is a mystery, and the way in which human beings have come to terms with mystery is through story. Stories offer us a way of seeing into the mystery. So consider these two stories.

---

137 Francis S. Collins, *The Language of God*, Free Press, New York, 2006, p. 6
138 Harold S. Kushner, *When Bad Things Happen to Good People*, Pan Books, London, 1981, p. 142.

Reflections for the year of Mark

The early Australian novel *For the Term of His Natural Life*, written by Marcus Clarke, tells the story of an Englishman, Rufus Dawes, wrongfully arrested for murder and transported as a convict to Australia. In the penal colony of Van Dieman's land, he experienced excruciating suffering and brutality.

The only person able to reach out to Dawes, and then only briefly, is the Anglican chaplain, the Reverend Mr North. Mr North's brief moment of triumph was certainly not due to the fact that he was a minister of religion. It was due to the fact that he had suffered. He had not suffered in the same way as Rufus Dawes, who had been flogged almost to death. Mr North suffered because he was an alcoholic, tormented by anguish and guilt, and overcome by a profound sense of unworthiness. In this man, the hardened convict perceived a companion in suffering, and the author makes this observation about the brief meeting between the two men: 'He who would touch the hearts of men must have had his own heart seared.'[139]

The Jewish author Elie Wiesel describes in his book *Night* the horrifying scene of the hanging of a thirteen-year-old boy in a Nazi concentration camp. When the power failed at a central electric plant the Gestapo concluded that it was sabotage and the young boy was implicated. He was condemned to death, along with two other inmates who had been found to possess arms. Wiesel writes:

> The SS seemed more preoccupied, more worried, than usual. To hang a child in front of thousands of onlookers was not

---

[139] 'Marcus Clarke, For the Term of His Natural Life', in Michael Wilding (ed.) *Portable Australian Authors: Marcus Clarke*, University of Queensland Press, Brisbane, 1976, p. 289.

a small matter. The head of the camp read the verdict. All eyes were on the child. He was pale, almost calm, but he was biting his lips as he stood in the shadow of the gallows ...The condemned prisoners together stepped onto the chairs. In unison, the nooses were placed around their necks. 'Long live liberty!' shouted the two men. But the boy was silent. 'Where is merciful God, where is He?', someone behind me was asking. At the signal, the three chairs were tipped over. Total silence in the camp. On the horizon, the sun was setting. 'Caps off!' screamed the Lageralteste. His voice quivered. As for the rest of us, we were weeping ... Then came the march past the victims. The two men were no longer alive. Their tongues were hanging out, swollen and bluish. But the third rope was still moving: the child, too light was still breathing ... And so he remained for more than half an hour, lingering between life and death, writhing before our eyes. And we were forced to look at him at close range. He was still alive when I passed him. His tongue was still red, his eyes not yet extinguished. Behind me, I heard the same man asking: 'For God's sake, where is God?' And from within me, I heard a voice answer: 'Where He is? This is where – hanging here from this gallows' ... [140]

Today's story of the passion is not an attempt to answer the question 'Why do people suffer?' It does, though, proclaim a fundamental truth: Jesus did not come to abolish suffering, but rather to fill it with his presence. He who would heal us has had his own heart seared on Calvary.

---

[140] Elie Wiesel, (trans. Marion Wiesel), *Night*, Hill and Wang, New York, 2006, pp. 64-5.

Reflections for the year of Mark

MASS OF THE LORD'S SUPPER (HOLY THURSDAY)

This is my body, which is for you; do this as a memorial of me.
(1 Cor 11:24)

A few years ago I had the opportunity of making a week's retreat on the Scottish island of Iona. The great missionary St Columba had founded a monastic community on Iona as early as the sixth century. The Benedictines came to the island and set about building an abbey at the beginning of the 13th century, but sadly, in the wake of the 16th-century Reformation the abbey was abandoned and gradually fell into a state of ruin. In the 1930s a Church of Scotland minister, George MacLeod, undertook an ambitious project to rebuild the ruined abbey. He involved unemployed men from Glasgow in his grand plan, together with young men training for the ministry in the Church of Scotland. The Iona Community grew out of that experience.

During my week's retreat at the abbey, I attended a holy communion service conducted by a Church of Scotland minister. It was the first time I had attended a eucharist presided over by a woman. The minister used an ordinary loaf of bread for the eucharist, but only a fraction of it was consumed at communion time. Later that evening, I was in the kitchen, rostered for washing up after the evening meal.

Releasing the Captive

The minister who had presided at the eucharist earlier that day came into the kitchen with the remainder of the loaf that had been used at the communion service. She simply placed the loaf in the breadbasket to be sliced and toasted for breakfast the following morning. The minister intended no disrespect. She was simply following the belief and practice of the Church of Scotland. But what she did certainly jarred Catholic sensitivities. For John Calvin, the guiding spirit of Scottish Presbyterianism, the bread and wine were no more than a sign of Christ's body and blood. He taught that believers received Christ spiritually in the act of taking communion. The bread and wine, for Calvin, remained but bread and wine.

Let us now go to the other extreme. The winner of the 1997 Pulitzer Prize, *Angela's Ashes*, is Frank McCourt's memoir of a Catholic upbringing in New York in the 1930s and in Ireland in the 1940s. The American-born McCourt is at school in Ireland, preparing for his first communion. The teacher tells the boys to be careful to stick out their tongues far enough, so that the communion wafer won't fall to the floor. And why? Well, apparently that's the worst thing that can happen to a priest.

> If the wafer slides off your tongue that poor priest has to get down on his two knees, pick it up with his own tongue and lick the floor around it in case it bounced from one spot to another. The priest could get a splinter that would make his tongue swell to the size of a turnip and that's enough to choke you and kill you entirely.

When the moment of holy communion arrived, the young McCourt experienced a moment of crisis. When the priest placed the host on his tongue it stuck; he had 'God glued to the roof of (his) mouth.' At this point he remembered a warning his teacher had given: 'Don't let that host touch your teeth for if you bite God in two you'll roast in hell for eternity.' As he tried to dislodge the host from the roof of his mouth with his tongue the priest hissed at him: 'Stop that clucking and get back to your seat.' But the problem eventually resolved itself: 'God was good. He melted and I swallowed Him and now, at last, I was a member of the True Church, an official sinner.'[141]

But the story of McCourt's first communion doesn't end there. The first communion breakfast at his grandmother's house was, literally, more than he could stomach. He'd obviously eaten too much. 'The food churned in my stomach. I gagged. I ran to her backyard and threw it all up.' His grandmother came storming outside and was horrified, accusing him of throwing up the body and blood of Jesus in her back yard. 'What am I goin' to do? I'll take him to the Jesuits for they know the sins of the Pope himself.'

So the young McCourt was dragged through the streets of Limerick and thrust into the confessional box. He begins his confession: 'Bless me Father, for I have sinned. It's a day since my last confession.' The priest asks what sins he could have possibly have committed in a day. 'I threw up my First Communion breakfast. Now Grandma says she has God in her backyard and what should she do?' Obviously doing his best to stifle a laugh, the Jesuit confessor offers this advice: 'Ah ... ah ... tell your grandmother to wash God away with a little

---

[141] Frank McCourt, *Angela's Ashes*, HarperCollins, London, 1996, p. 128.

water, and for your penance say one Hail Mary and One Our Father. Say a prayer for me, and God bless you, my child.'[142]

What do we have here? At one extreme, bread left over from the communion service toasted for breakfast. Bread – no more than a sign pointing to a reality beyond it. At the other extreme a consecrated wafer spoken of as 'God bitten in two,' 'God in the backyard' – a crude physicalist understanding of eucharist.

In our Catholic tradition, we refer to the consecrated bread and wine as a sacrament. In fact, we often use the term the blessed sacrament. A sacrament is more than a sign. A sign, to be effective, has to have one clear, unambiguous meaning. Traffic signs are a good example. A stop sign, for example, means that we must bring our vehicle to a complete stop, and proceed when it is safe to do so. Accidents would occur if the meaning of a sign was not clear or unambiguous.

A sacrament is more than a sign, for a sign merely points to a reality beyond itself. A sacrament is also more than a symbol. Water, for example, can be a symbol. But symbols, unlike signs, are ambiguous. Water can sometimes be a symbol of life; at other times a symbol of destruction. Drought, the absence of life-giving water; flood, the destructive force of water in abundance.

In the long-running cartoon in *The Sydney Morning Herald*, Hagar the Horrible is comfortably ensconced in a chair with a beer in his hand. His long-suffering wife remarks, 'You remind me of a mighty river!' Somewhat flattered, he replies, 'You mean I'm powerful and

---

142 Ibid., p. 129.

fast-moving?' 'No,' says his wife. 'I mean you're big and wide and rarely go dry.'[143]

But symbols are important to us. A couple whose marriage I celebrated recently came to see me not long after they'd returned from their honeymoon. They asked me to bless another wedding ring because the groom had lost his ring while surfing during their honeymoon. The ring was insured, and a jeweller was able to make an identical copy of the original. But from another point of view, the original ring was irreplaceable. It was a symbol given by the bride to her husband at the very moment when they made a lifelong commitment to each other. That was a unique and unrepeatable moment. The ring symbolised their love. Through the marriage ritual that ring had become immersed in the story of their love. But ultimately, the ring – a band of metal – didn't embody that love. The newlyweds didn't suddenly fall out of love when the ring was lost.

Sacrament takes us beyond symbol. A sacrament participates in the reality it symbolises. It mediates the reality it symbolises. When we receive communion, we encounter Christ's real presence through eating and drinking the transformed elements of bread and wine. Consider for a moment the story of the two disciples walking to Emmaus after the death of Jesus. The mysterious stranger who joins them is the risen Lord, but they fail to recognise him. Nor do they recognise him when he explains how all that has just happened in Jerusalem is the unfolding of God's plan. It is only when they sat

---

[143] Dirk Browne, 'Hagar the Horrible', in *The Sydney Morning Herald*, 20 April, 2000.

down for a meal that the disciples suddenly recognised Jesus, and they recognised him in the breaking of the bread (Lk 24:13-35).

On this sacred night we remind ourselves again that each time we gather around the table of the Lord, we encounter him in the breaking of the bread, as did the disciples on the road to Emmaus. He is truly present among us in this most blessed sacrament, and we bend the knee in adoration. In the words of the 13th century hymn composed by St Thomas Aquinas, and translated so eloquently by Gerard Manly Hopkins:

> Godhead here in hiding, whom I do adore
> Masked by these bare shadows, shape and nothing more,
> see, Lord, at thy service low lies here a heart
> lost, all lost in wonder at the God thou art.

GOOD FRIDAY

It is fulfilled. (Jn 19:30)

In AD 30, Jesus of Nazareth was in Jerusalem for the approaching feast of Passover. On Thursday evening, 6 April, Jesus celebrated a solemn farewell meal with his inner circle of disciples, and later that night he was arrested in the Garden of Gethsemane. He was first interrogated by some Jewish officials and then handed over to Pilate early on the morning of Friday, 7 April, Pilate quickly condemned him to death by crucifixion. By all accounts crucifixion was an excruciatingly painful way to die. The Jewish historian Josephus, who witnessed men dying by crucifixion during Titus' siege of Jerusalem in 70 AD, calls it 'the most wretched of deaths.'[144] After being scourged, Jesus was crucified at Golgotha or 'Place of a skull' outside the walled city of Jerusalem. He was dead by the evening of Friday, 7 April 30 AD. He was about 36 years old, and his public ministry had lasted a little over two years.[145]

From this nucleus of history fact, some of which is conjecture, how does a Christian understand the crucifixion? In Dry Salvages, T.S. Eliot writes, 'We had the experience but missed the meaning.' What does Jesus' death mean? Why did his life end in this way? St Anselm of Canterbury (c. 1033–1109) wrote a book on theology

---

[144] Josephus, The Jewish War, 7, 203, quoted in Gerald G. O'Collins, 'Crucifixion', David Freedman (ed.), *The Anchor Bible Dictionary*, Volume 1, Doubleday, New York, 1992, p. 1207.
[145] John P. Meier, *A Marginal Jew: The Roots of the Problem and the Person*, Volume I, Doubleday, New York, 1991, p. 407.

that he first entitled *Fides quarens intellectum* (later known as *Proslogion*) – 'faith seeking understanding'. In the introduction he explains, 'I have written this little work from the viewpoint of persons trying to raise their mind to contemplate God and seeking to understand what they believe.'[146] How, then, can we understand Jesus' death? Why did he die?

Any response to that question involves interpretation. The New Testament itself uses a variety of metaphors, symbols and images to explore the meaning of the death of Jesus. St Paul depicts the death of Jesus as effecting a new or renewed access to God (Rom 5:2; Eph 2:18). The image here is that of 'the opening of a road after an avalanche, or the discovery of the Northwest Passage.' Paul also uses images from the law courts, particularly 'the decree of acquittal read to one unfortunate enough to have been arraigned on some charge before them (Rom 5:9 passim).'

Elsewhere the imagery is drawn from the marketplace, particularly that of the slave-market. 'Now the death of Jesus is our redemption or our ransom, the act of buying us back or the price paid (Rom 3:24; Mk 10:45).' Another image is that of 'being reconciled with a friend after a period of estrangement' (2 Cor 5:17-21). Then there are images from the medical profession, where the death of Jesus becomes our healing or 'salvation' (Rom 5:9, 2:16). In some New Testament texts the imagery is drawn from the ritual experience of Judaism – the sprinkling of blood that sealed a covenant (Mk 14:24);

---

146 Charles Hill, *Making Sense of Faith: An Introduction to Theology*, E.J. Dwyer, Sydney, 1995, p. 6.

or the priestly sacrifice on the Day of Atonement (Heb 9:11-14); or that of the Passover lamb. Finally, the sense of liberation 'experienced on all kinds of occasions, from getting out of tight trousers to getting out of death row in a state penitentiary, is evoked in an attempt to let us know what the death of Jesus means to us (Gal 1:4).'[147]

Reflecting on these images, James Mackey suggests that 'the worst mistake that could be made here would be to take any of these, or all of them, literally. To do so would be to mistake the nature of symbolism in a very elementary way, and to mistake, consequently, the true significance of the death of Jesus which these writers are trying by means of these rich images to bring to our notice and appreciation.'[148]

In one way or another, all of these images are expressions 'of the radical nature of the love which gives itself completely, of the process in which one is what one does, and does what one is; it is the expression of a life that is completely being for others.'[149]

The cross is Jesus' final act of love. 'It draws to a climax all those actions throughout his ministry – his touching of a leper, his tenderness toward the chronically sick or bereaved, his tears at Lazarus' grave – in which we see the deeply human, and ... characteristically God-filled Jesus truly at work. When John declares that Jesus, having loved his own who were in the world, now loved them to the uttermost (Jn 13:1), this is not a later theological spin being overlaid

---

[147] James P. Mackey, *Jesus the Man and the Myth*, Paulist Press, New York, 1979, pp. 74-5.
[148] Ibid., p. 75.
[149] Joseph Ratzinger, *Introduction to Christianity*, p. 214.

Releasing the Captive

on top of events that were originally not like that at all. This is simply telling it like it was.'[150]

An ancient legend about Judas tells how he went out and hanged himself, having betrayed Jesus for thirty pieces of silver. In death, Judas found himself languishing at the bottom of a dark and dank pit, and there he lay in distress for countless millions of years. There came a time when, through the darkness, he thought he saw a glimmer of light, high above him at the mouth of the pit. He was instinctively drawn to the light, and with great difficulty he began to climb towards the light. For years he climbed, often slipping back to the bottom, but he persisted. After what seemed like an eternity he came close to the mouth of the pit, and the light grew stronger. Eventually, after many aeons, he pulled himself over the edge and, much to his astonishment, found himself in an Upper Room where a young rabbi was having a meal with his friends. The young rabbi came over to him, helped him to his feet and said, 'Judas! Welcome! We've been waiting for you. We couldn't continue the supper without you.'[151]

The cross, surely, is the place of healing. 'God, in Jesus, is the one who waits and waits with infinite patience. He is still waiting. Please come home!'[152]

---

150 N.T. Wright, *The Challenge of Jesus*, InterVarsity Press, Downers Grove, IL, 1999, p. 94.
151 Adapted from Alan Jones, *Passion for Pilgrimage*, p. 92.
152 Ibid.

Reflections for the year of Mark

EASTER SUNDAY

They killed him by hanging him on a tree, yet three days afterwards God raised him to life.
(Acts 10:39-40)

If I were asked to summarise the entire Bible as concisely as possible, I would do it in three words: Exile and return. The Bible begins with a story of exile. God created the man and the woman and settled them in the Garden of Eden to cultivate and take care of it. They were free to eat the fruit of all of the trees in the garden with one exception. You know the story. The man and the woman were tempted, and they ate. Their sin was not eating a piece of fruit. God could just as easily have said 'Don't pick the roses.'

Their sin was an act of defiance and rebellion. And so they were banished from the garden, and a great winged creature with a fiery flashing sword stood guard at the entrance. The man and the woman were exiled, a theme that continues throughout the scriptures. God's people live in exile in Egypt, and much of the Pentateuch tells the story of the long trek to the Promised Land. Exile is a theme that resonates throughout the writings of the prophets. Isaiah tells of the destruction of the northern kingdom in the eighth century BC, and then of the exile to Babylon in the sixth century. Ezekiel is the prophet of exile, offering hope to a people languishing by the rivers of Babylon.

Releasing the Captive

The concluding paragraph of John's account of the Passion, read on Good Friday, offers us a seemingly unimportant detail. We're told that 'At the place where he had been crucified there was a garden, and in this garden a new tomb in which no one had yet been buried.' (Jn 19:41) The synoptic gospels don't mention a garden, but it's obviously significant for John because he mentions it twice within one sentence. Later, when the risen Lord appears to Mary Magdalene, she fails to recognise him and mistakes him for the gardener. This mention of the garden is John's way of telling us that the death and resurrection of Jesus is the beginning of the return. The man and the woman (we know them as Adam and Eve) were banished from the garden. Jesus, the new Adam, has come to bring us home.

The garden is the central symbol of Frances Hodgson Burnett's children's classic *The Secret Garden*, first published in 1911 and subsequently made into a film and Broadway musical. It is the story of Mary Lennox whose parents died as the result of a cholera epidemic in the Indian village where she was born. Mary, a very plain young girl, is sent home to England to live with her uncle, Archibald Craven, and entrusted to the care of Mrs Medlock, the housekeeper at Misselthwaite Manor, a large 600-year-old house on the edge of the Yorkshire moors.

Mr Archibald is overwhelmed by grief following the tragic death of his wife some ten years earlier. He refuses to see people, and spends most of his time away. When he is at home he lives as a virtual recluse, shutting himself up in the west wing of the manor. None of this makes Mary feel cheerful: 'A house with a hundred rooms, nearly all shut up and with their doors locked – a house on the edge of a moor – whatsoever a moor was – sounded dreary. A man with a crooked back who shut himself up also!'[153]

In a variation of the Genesis theme in which the man and women are free to eat the fruit of all the trees in the garden but one, Mary is restricted to two rooms and told to keep to them. She is free, however, to roam about the extensive grounds which include several walled gardens, one of which is locked. The gardener, Mr Pitcher, explains that Mr Craven gave orders to lock the garden following the death of his wife. 'It was her garden. He locked th' door an' dug a hole and buried th' key.'[154] Mary's curiosity is aroused and she finds out more about the garden from Martha, one of the servants. It was Mrs Craven's garden, and she just loved it. She tended to it, and none of the gardeners was ever allowed to go in. Mr Craven and his wife spent hours together in the garden, reading and talking. But there was one tree with a branch bent like a seat on it, and Mrs Craven would sit there. One day a falling branch from that tree struck and killed her, and no one has gone into the garden since.

But the secret garden is not the only strange thing about Misselthwaite Manor. Mary is certain that she can hear a childish whine from somewhere inside the house. Again, her curiosity is aroused, and defying Mrs Medlock's strict instructions, Mary sets out to find the source of this strange crying. And that's how she meets Colin, the bedridden son whom Mr Craven had emotionally abandoned

---

[153] Frances Hodgson Burnett, *The Secret Garden*, Michael Joseph, London, 1986, p. 18.
[154] Ibid., p. 30.

after the death of his wife. Colin stays in his room and doesn't want to be moved out of it because it tires him too much. 'I am like this always, ill and having to lie down,' he tells Mary. And when asked if his father comes to see him, he replies 'Generally when I am asleep. He doesn't want to see me.' Colin had become 'a hysterical, half-crazy little hypochondriac who knew nothing of the sunshine.'[155]

A friendship develops between the two children, each of whom has been spoiled, although in different ways. Colin is convinced that he shall become a hunchback and soon die, but Mary cannot stand his self-pity: 'There's nothing the matter with your horrid back – nothing but hysterics!'.[156] Mary soon finds the door to the secret garden, covered by a wall of ivy, and a friendly robin redbreast shows her where the key is hidden. Plans are soon afoot to introduce Colin to the garden, a difficult undertaking given his frail health and the fact that he is confined to a wheelchair.

The garden is a magical experience, and Colin is soon transformed, physically and emotionally. His doctor is amazed: 'The boy is extraordinarily better. His advance seems almost abnormal.'[157] Soon he is able to walk and run as other children, liberated from the wheelchair and no longer confined to his room.

But Colin's is not the only healing. Returning home from abroad, Colin's father makes his way to the garden to be met by his son: 'Father, I'm Colin. You can't believe it. I scarcely can myself, I'm Colin.' And Mr Craven's soul 'shook with unbelieving joy'. As father

---
155 Ibid., p. 209.
156 Ibid., p. 135.
157 Ibid., p. 190.

and son return to the manor the servants can't believe what they are seeing: 'Across the lawn came the Master of Misselthwaite, and he looked as many of them had never seen him. And by his side, with his head up in the air and his eyes full of laughter, walked as strongly and steadily as any boy in Yorkshire – Master Colin!'[158]

This is the story of Easter, a story of rebirth and the transformation of lives broken by tragedy, loss and grief. It is a journey from exile, of coming home. On this Easter day, Jesus has come to lead us back into the garden, to bring us home from exile. The victory has been won. Alleluia!

---

158 Ibid., p. 224.

Releasing the Captive

SECOND SUNDAY OF EASTER

(YEAR B)

Thomas, called the Twin, who was one of the Twelve, was not with them when Jesus came. (Jn 20:24)

In Book V of his *Confessions*, St Augustine writes of the years prior to his conversion. At this time a Manichean teacher named Faustus had recently arrived at Carthage, a man who was 'very well versed in all the higher forms of learning and particularly in the liberal sciences.'[159] Manichaeism was a form of Gnosticism, and Augustine had been involved with the Manicheans for some nine years and eagerly awaited the arrival of Faustus. Other members of the sect had been unable to answer all of Augustine's questions, but they assured him that once Faustus arrived he had only to discuss his doubts with him 'and he would have no difficulty in giving me a clear explanation of my queries and any other more difficult problems which I might put forward.'[160]

Alas, Augustine waited in vain. Although Faustus was 'a man of agreeable personality, with a pleasant manner of speech,' he did

---
159 St Augustine, *Confessions*, trans. by R.S. Pine Coffin, Penguin Classics, Harmondsworth, 1961, Book V, 6. 96.
160 Ibid., p. 97.

little more than patter off 'the usual Manichean arguments with a great deal more than the usual charm.' But Augustine's thirst was not satisfied, 'however precious the cup and however exquisite the man who served it.' Those who had assured Augustine that all his doubts would be allayed once Faustus had arrived were 'poor judges' who 'thought him wise and thoughtful simply because they were charmed by his manner of speech.'[161] Augustine had been suffering from what Gerald O'Collins calls 'the waiting-for-Faustus' syndrome. He was expecting someone really special to satisfy his hungry heart.[162]

Today's gospel focuses on Thomas. Thomas, like us, is called to believe on the testimony of others. 'The faith required of him is, in a way, more demanding than that required of those who actually encountered the risen Lord. Viewed in this way, his doubt is understandable.'[163]

As much as we might hope for a Faustus who will dispel all doubt, belief and unbelief are inextricably woven into the fabric of every believer's soul. Sometimes our faith seems unassailable; at other times we are riddled with doubt. A story from the Jewish tradition illustrates the point well. A rumour had spread quickly among the Jewish community in a small medieval village. Abraham the cobbler had become an atheist. The rumour was insidious and stretched credulity to the limits, for Abraham was the most devout person in the village. And yet, when the Sabbath came around all eyes in the

---

161 Ibid.
162 Gerald O'Collins, *Experiencing Jesus*, E.J. Dwyer, Sydney, 1994, p. 22.
163 Dianne Bergant and Richard Fragomeni, *Preaching the New Lectionary*, Year B, p. 176.

synagogue were fixed on the place where Abraham had sat from time immemorial. It was empty! Perhaps he was ill, perhaps he lay dying at home. How else could his absence be explained? Perhaps, worse still, the rumour was true after all!

No one could concentrate during the service, and once it was over the entire congregation rushed to the house of Abraham, fearing he may be dead. But no. There he was, working in his garden, the very picture of good health. The villagers immediately delegated Yussel the tailor to pose the obvious question. And so, tentatively, Yussel approached Abraham and spoke. 'Abraham, the village has delegated me to ask this question: Are you or are you not an atheist?'

Abraham stood before him in silence, and without saying a word turned his back and continued working in the garden. Everyone was amazed, and it was certain that no work would be done in the village until the question of Abraham's mysterious behaviour was resolved.

So again, a few days later, Yussel was delegated a second time to approach Abraham with the same question. Yussel confronted Abraham and said: 'Abraham, everyone wants to know, are you or are you not an atheist?' Abraham looked at his old friend and said simply and straightforwardly, 'Yes, it is true. I am an atheist.'

Yussel was flabbergasted, but soon regained his composure. 'Then why didn't you answer me the first time I asked you?' Abraham seemed genuinely surprised and shocked by the question: 'You wanted me to tell you I was an atheist … on the Sabbath?'[164]

---

[164] Adapted from William Bausch, *Storytelling: Imagination and Faith*, Twenty-Third Publications, Mystic, CT, 1986, p. 52.

Reflections for the year of Mark

When the risen Lord first appeared to his disciples Thomas was not with them, according to John's gospel. He refused to believe their testimony unless he could see and touch the wounds for himself. As so often happens in John's gospel, we are invited to identify with the people who meet and experience Jesus. There is something in all of us that demands proof, but a great deal of life is not, in the words of Karen Armstrong, 'amenable to the logic of grammar and neat sentences that put things into an order that makes sense.'[165] We are people who 'tend to look at life with a literalist squint and believe not only in the myth of objectivity but also in the easy accessibility of meaning. We want to move straight past Go, collect our 200 dollars, and move on. We want unequivocal answers to our deepest questions.'[166]

The religious quest is ultimately an attempt to express the inexpressible. What T.S. Eliot said of poetry is true of the religious quest: it is a 'raid on the inarticulate'.[167] We must therefore agree with the Greek Orthodox claim

> that any statement about God had to have two characteristics. It must be paradoxical, to remind us that God cannot be contained in a neat, coherent system of thought; and it must be apophatic, that is, it should lead us to a moment of silent awe or wonder, because when we are speaking of the reality of God we are at the end of what words or thoughts can usefully do.[168]

---

165 Karen Armstrong, *The Spiral Staircase: A Memoir*, HarperCollins, London, 2004, p. 75.
166 Alan Jones, *The Soul's Journey*, p. 7.
167 Karen Armstrong, *The Spiral Staircase*, p. 323.
168 Ibid., p. 327.

St Augustine put it this way, 'If you have understood, then what you have understood is not God!'[169]

John's gospel is saying that

> pure faith is trust in God, not because of the evidence for such trust but precisely in spite of the absence of such evidence! Our culture is captivated 'with a pseudoscientific mind-set'. Christianity, as John understood it, stands at the opposite side of the issue: 'Blessed are those who have not seen and yet have come to believe.'[170]

'I am an atheist, but I certainly can't tell you that on the Sabbath!' 'I want Faustus to give me some straight answers.' 'I want to feel and touch, to test and verify.'

Lord, I have faith. Help my lack of faith.

---

[169] Alan Jones, *Passion for Pilgrimage*, p. 131.
[170] Robert Kysar, *Preaching John*, Fortress Press, Minneapolis, 2002, p. 162.

Reflections for the year of Mark

THIRD SUNDAY OF EASTER

(YEAR B)

Touch and see for yourselves; a ghost has no flesh and bones as you can see I have. (Lk 24:39)

In a book on Jesus entitled *Joshua, The Man They Called Jesus*, the author Ian Jones tells of a time when, at the age of twenty-four, he was close to death in St Mary Abbot's Hospital, London. He reveals that one of the nurses who watched over him during his stay in hospital had been killed in an air raid eleven years before. Such an encounter would surely leave most of us wondering: Was I dreaming? Was I hallucinating? Was it a drug-induced fantasy? If I were certain that I had been watched over by a nurse who had long since died, I've wondered what effect it would have upon my life, and especially upon my faith. Jones says only that his encounter with this nurse was 'brief but unforgettable', and he doesn't return to the subject again even when he writes about the resurrection of Jesus in the final chapter of his book.[171]

In *The Waters of Siloe*, Thomas Merton tells the story of a similar encounter, but with a markedly different outcome. A cosmopolitan

---

171 Ian Jones, *Joshua, The Man They Called Jesus*, Lothian Books, Port Melbourne, 1999, p. iii.

Releasing the Captive

Frenchman, 'a businessman, and an important one', books into one of the big Paris hotels. He walks through the lobby 'like a man who is used to stopping at the best hotels.' He suddenly becomes aware that someone is looking at him, and when he turns around he sees a woman, 'and to his astonishment she is dressed in the habit of a nun.'

Had he known anything about the habits worn by different religious orders of nuns, he would have recognised the white cloak and brown robe as belonging to the Discalced Carmelites. But he was 'far too important and too busy to worry his head about nuns and religious orders – or about churches for that matter,' although he occasionally went to Mass as a matter of form. 'The most surprising thing of all is that the nun is smiling, and she is smiling at him. She is a young sister, with a bright, intelligent French face, full of the candour of a child, full of good sense: and her smile is a smile of frank, undisguised friendship.'

As the businessman signs the hotel register he enquires of the clerk, 'Who was that nun that just passed by?' The clerk is nonplussed. 'You are mistaken, monsieur. A nun, in a hotel, at this time of night! Nuns don't go wandering around town, smiling at men!' The businessman protests that he has seen a nun smiling at him, right there in the hotel lobby. The clerk shrugs. 'Monsieur, you are the only person that has come in or gone out in the last half hour.' A few days later, while visiting some friends, he saw a picture of the very same nun. His friends told him that her name was St Thérèse of the Child Jesus. This mysterious encounter with a nun, long since dead, in a hotel lobby, changed the man's life. Now 'he was no longer an important French industrialist', but a monk wearing a brown habit with a brown scapular over it, with a thick leather belt buckled around the waist. His head was shaved and he had grown a beard. 'He had become a Trappist in a southern French abbey.'[172]

In today's gospel the disciples encounter Jesus. At first, we're told, they thought they were seeing a ghost. But Jesus invites them to see and touch for themselves; 'a ghost has no flesh and bones as you can see I have.' Jesus still had his human body, but it was changed, it was somehow different. They could touch Jesus, so he was flesh and blood, but he could also go through locked doors. He could eat and drink, but he could also appear and disappear.

Stuart Jackman's novel *The Davidson Affair* invites us to imagine how modern media might have covered the death of Jesus (Davidson – that is, Son of David). Suspend your disbelief and listen as Cass Tennel, a reporter with the Rome-based Imperial Television Corporation, appears on local television with an update of events following the crucifixion of Jesus. Tennel tells his television audience that Jesus was arrested at a secret rendezvous outside the city limits, betrayed to the Sanhedrin by one of his closest friends. The atmosphere in Jerusalem was electric. At Passover time the city struggled to contain ten times its normal population. The Sanhedrin sat through the night and on Friday morning presented their verdict to Pontius Pilate, the Roman governor. His Excellency signed the necessary order and Davidson was executed just before noon that same day. The revolu-

---

[172] Thomas Merton, *The Waters of Siloe*, Sheldon Press, London, 1949, pp. xiii-xv.

tion – if revolution it was – was over. Throughout Saturday's festival Sabbath celebrations every precaution was taken to ensure that there would be no further incidents triggered off by supporters of the dead leader. At the end of the day the police were able to report that all was quiet. But something happened at Davidson's tomb. There was a disturbance of some kind, and the Jewish army guard was rattled. As a result of this disturbance there had been a widespread and persistent rumour that Davidson was somehow alive again.

Tennel seeks permission to interview Pilate, and the Roman governor is only too happy to put his own spin on the absurd allegations that an executed criminal has risen from the dead. Tennel asks Pilate if he would care to make a comment on the current crisis. Pilate insists that there is no crisis, that everything is under control, and there's absolutely no cause for alarm. The governor assures him that Davidson is dead and buried, and he can see no point in discussing the point further. But Tennel raises the questions of persistent rumours that he is alive again. Pilate assures him: 'Mr Tennel, he was executed by soldiers of the Tenth Legion. They're not amateurs, you know. They're some of the toughest troops in the Roman Army. When they kill a man, he's dead and he stays dead.' Tennel agrees, but argues that the rumours are very persistent. Pilate replies: 'But of course, this is Jerusalem, my dear chap. The Middle-East. We thrive on rumour here. It's meat and drink to these people. We're in the middle of a great religious festival. The Jews are an emotional people. Work it out for yourself, Mr Tennel. Of course there are rumours – and very splendid some of them are too. But when you've lived here as long as I have you'll not worry your head about bazaar gossip …' Pilate has no time for wild rumours. 'Rumours are not important, Mr Tennel. Only facts. And the fact is that Davidson is dead.' So when Tennel asks 'Do you think we've heard the last of Davidson?' Pilate is able to answer unequivocally: 'I do.'[173]

Pilate's complacency was justified. In first century Palestine there was no shortage of messianic pretenders who managed to attract a band of followers. The Romans viewed them with suspicion, and once the leader had been executed they disbanded, never to be heard of again. What was so different about the people who followed Jesus? On the face of it they were not leadership material. One of them betrayed Jesus for 30 pieces of silver; another, Simon Peter, the rock on which the new movement was to be built, denied three times even knowing Jesus. And when Jesus was arrested the gospel of Mark tells us that 'they all deserted him and ran away' (14:50).

What happened to change these terrified and fearful disciples? Reginald Fuller observes,

> Even the most skeptical historian has to postulate an "X", as M. Dibelius put it, to account for the complete change in the behaviour of the disciples, who at Jesus' arrest had fled and scattered to their own homes, but who in a few weeks were found boldly preaching their message to the very people who had sought to crush the movement launched by Jesus by disposing of its leader.[174]

---

173 Stuart Jackman, *The Davidson Affair*, Faber and Faber, London, 1966. An edited and adapted account from pages 25-31.
174 R.H. Fuller, *The Formation of the Resurrection Narratives*, SPCK, London, 1972, p. 2.

The 'X' factor is, of course, the resurrection of Jesus. The disciples were as puzzled by it as we would be. 'But they were all quite clear that it happened. It wasn't a corporate hallucination. It wasn't a grief-induced fantasy. It was for real.'[175]

Cass Tennel's television programme included an interview with Cleopas, one of two travellers who allegedly saw the risen Jesus. Cleopas explained that as he and his companion were telling the disciples about their experience of meeting Jesus on the road to Emmaus, Jesus appeared again. Tennel asks Cleopas if he's a little afraid of telling this story, given that the authorities are taking a very serious view of the situation.

Cleopas replies:

> Well, yes, in a way I suppose I am. I mean, I've never been one for sticking my neck out before. Kept in the background, sort of thing. Only now, well, it doesn't matter any more. You see, the worst they can do is to kill me. And death isn't important now. He's made that clear enough. Death isn't the end, it's only the beginning. Up to yesterday morning we only had half a life. People like you and me – half alive, that's all we were. But now – now it's different. He's alive again. And because he's alive, we're alive too. Really alive, for the very first time. You know something, Mr Tennel? It's like being born again. That's what it is, being born again.[176]

---

175 Ibid.
176 Stuart Jackman, *The Davidson Affair*, pp. 171-2.

Reflections for the year of Mark

FOURTH SUNDAY OF EASTER

(YEAR B)

The good shepherd is one who lays down his life for his sheep. (Jn 10:11)

In 1994, Kevin Carter, a South African photographer, won the Pulitzer Prize for feature photography after capturing the image of a vulture stalking a starving young girl in famine-ravaged Sudan. The award-winning photograph of a child barely alive and a vulture eager for carrion epitomised the horror and suffering of Sudan's famine. It was published first in *The New York Times* and also *The Mail & Guardian*, a Johannesburg weekly.

In 1993 Carter flew to southern Sudan to photograph the mass starvation caused by a devastating civil war. Once his plane had landed in the village of Ayod he began snapping photos of famine victims. Wandering into the open bush he heard a soft, high-pitched whimpering and saw a tiny girl trying to make her way to the feeding centre. As he crouched to photograph her, a vulture landed in view. Careful not to disturb the bird, he positioned himself for the best possible image. He would later say he waited about twenty minutes, hoping the vulture would spread its wings. It did not, and after he took his photographs, he chased the bird away and watched as the little girl resumed her struggle.[177] The good shepherd of today's gospel is willing to sacrifice his life for his sheep.

Kevin Carter's award-winning photograph portrayed the harrowing scene of a starving girl. But it also captured the image of the photographer as an aloof, impassive and detached spectator of the human condition. He is only a hired man and has no concern for the sheep. And who is the hired hand of today's gospel; who does Jesus have in mind? Quite obviously, the religious leaders of his own day. Jesus 'seems to be saying that the religious leadership of his day care very little for the people. They are not likely to defend the people against danger. Most certainly they will not sacrifice their lives for the people.'[178]

But before we start pointing the finger at the Jewish leadership in first century Palestine, let us listen to what this image of the Good Shepherd is saying to us today. Leaders in today's world, and especially in the church, can become so immersed in administration that they lose touch with the very people they are called to serve.

An old Talmudic riddle asks, 'Why did the Tower of Babel crumble?' And the answer is, 'Because the leaders of the project were more interested in the work than they were in the workers.' The rabbis explained that while the tower was under construction, if a person dropped dead, no one cared. On the other hand, if a single brick fell and broke they would all cry out saying, 'When will there be another

---

[177] I have consulted a number of internet sites, but especially Scott MacLeod, http://www.thisisyesterday.com/ints/KCarter.html
[178] Robert Kysar, *Preaching John*, p. 27.

like it?' God destroyed the tower, not because they were trying to reach heaven, but because they were more interested in bricks than bricklayers.[179]

In the second *Yes Minister* television series, an episode entitled 'The Compassionate Society' is about St Edward's, a newly-constructed hospital in northern London that is staffed with 350 administrators and 150 ancillary staff, but no doctors, nurses or patients, and it will be at least another 18 months before patients are admitted. Jim Hacker, the Minister for the Department of Administrative Affairs, sets up an enquiry into this sad state of affairs, a decision that isn't at all agreeable to his permanent secretary, Sir Humphrey Appleby.

Sir Ian Whitechurch, head of the Department of Health and Social Services (DHSS) discusses some issues that would have to be dealt with prior to the opening of the hospital: 'So, why is your minister interested in St Edward's Hospital?' Sir Humphrey: 'Well apparently he's greatly concerned that it has no patients.' Sir Ian: 'It takes all sorts ... How could there be patients when it has no nursing staff? ... We've found at the DHSS that it takes time to get things going. First of all, you have to sort out the smooth running of the hospital. Having patients around would be no help at all.' Sir Humphrey agrees, 'They'd just be in the way.'[180] How many hospital administrators, school principals or parish priests have thought that their hospital, school or parish would be far less bothersome without the persistent demands of patients, pupils or parishioners?

---

179 Cf. William J. Bausch, *More Telling Stories, Compelling Stories*, pp. 153-4.
180 http://www.yes-minister.com/ymseas2a.htm#YM%202.1

Releasing the Captive

> The good shepherd doesn't just love the sheep. The good shepherd is prepared to leave the 99 sheep that are safe, to seek out and find the one that is lost (Lk 15:1-7).

A man walking along a deserted beach at sunset noticed a young child in the distance. He watched as the child picked up small objects from the sand and threw them out into the sea. As he drew near to the child he asked what he was doing. 'I'm throwing these starfish back into the ocean. It's low tide now and they've been washed up into the shore. If I don't throw them back into the water they'll die.' Somewhat amused the man pointed out that there were countless thousands of starfish stranded on the beach. 'You can't possibly get to all of them. There are too many of them, and this is probably happening on hundreds of beaches along the coast. It's part of the cycle of nature. What you're doing won't make the slightest difference.' The young boy smiled as he bent down and picked up yet another starfish, and as he threw it back into the sea, he replied, 'Well, I made a difference to that one!'[181]

Anita Roddick, founder of The Body Shop and campaigner for any number of causes, was fond of quoting a saying of Betty Reese: 'If you think you are too small to be effective, you have never been in bed with a mosquito.'

Father Joe is Tony Hendra's touching story about his relationship with a Benedictine monk of Quarr Abbey, Fr Joseph Warrilow, 'the man who saved my soul'. This is an uplifting story of a good shepherd

---

[181] Adapted from Jack Canfield and Mark Victor Hansen, *Chicken Soup for the Soul*, Health Communications, Inc., Deerfield Beach, FL, 1993, pp. 22-23.

Reflections for the year of Mark

who cared intensely and individually for each of the sheep that came his way. For more than 40 years Fr Joe had been for Tony Hendra

> my still centre, the rock of my soul, as steady and firm as the huge oak on the curve of the hill where the monastery stands ... All my conscious life he was my strongest ally, the cherished gatekeeper of my lost Eden, a lighthouse of faith blinking away through the oceanic fogs of success and money and celebrity and possessions, my intrepid guide in the tangled rain forest of human love, my silken lifeline to the divine.[182]

But Fr Joe had also touched the lives of countless others. The Archbishop of Canterbury, Rowan Williams, spoke of Fr Joe as 'a listener of genius – someone who would be well on the way to meet you before you got there. He immediately flung open the doors.'[183] After Fr Joe's death Tony Hendra was surprised to read these words in an obituary: 'He touched the lives of so many people, in England and abroad, in his own Church and not (in his own church) ... it is hard to give full weight to the extent of his pastoral influence.'[184]

Hendra was surprised because Fr Joe had treated him as if he were the only one in his life. When he expressed his surprise to one of Fr Joe's fellow monks that he was 'Not The Only One' he was told, 'Ah yes – everyone thought they were Joe's best friend.'[185] Such is the good shepherd who knows his sheep.

---

182 Tony Hendra, *Father Joe*, Hamish Hamilton, Camberwell, Vic., 2004, pp. 4-5.
183 Ibid., p. 270.
184 Ibid., p. 268.
185 Ibid., p. 269.

FIFTH SUNDAY OF EASTER

(YEAR B)

Every branch in me that bears no fruit he cuts away, and every branch that does bear fruit he prunes to make it bear even more. (Jn 15:2)

In 600 AD St John Climacus, at 75 years of age, was persuaded by the monks of St Catherine's monastery at Mt Sinai to become their abbot. As abbot he wrote a guide to the spiritual life that has become a classic, *The Ladder of Divine Ascent*, a work that led to his being known as John of the Ladder.[186] John likens the Christian life to ascending a ladder with thirty rungs – one rung for each of the thirty years of Jesus' hidden life. Each of the thirty rungs represents a virtue to be acquired (fourteen of them), or a vice to be avoided (sixteen of them). If you Google *The Ladder of Divine Ascent* you'll see an icon, inspired by St John's book, that shows monks ascending (and falling from) the ladder to heaven. Winged demons armed with bows and arrows make the ascent difficult, but Jesus, with outstretched arms, welcomes those who reach the top of the ladder. The metaphor of the ladder is probably inspired by the story of Jacob's

---

186 The inspiration for this homily comes from Edward L. Beck, *Soul Provider*.

ladder in the Book of Genesis (28:10-13), and it offers a helpful insight into the steps that lead us from the false self to the true and authentic self.

John of the Ladder warns us that we cannot climb the ladder in a single stride, so let us content ourselves today with the first two rungs. Renunciation is the bottom rung. All the major religious traditions emphasise renunciation as a necessary path to spiritual maturity. Jesus urges us to deny our very selves, to take up our cross, and follow in his footsteps. Renunciation may involve voluntarily giving up legitimate pleasures or pastimes, but we must renounce whatever deadens our spiritual life.

In today's gospel Jesus likens his disciples to branches that draw life from him, the true vine. His father, the vinedresser, cuts away every branch that no longer bears fruit. That, in a nutshell, is what renunciation is all about – removing the dead wood from our lives. But the process of pruning may be painful. One of the recurring themes in the *Peanuts* cartoon strip is that of Linus and his blanket. 'My blanket! I can't live without my blanket' is an oft-repeated refrain.

On one occasion Linus has survived without his blanket for two weeks. His sister, Lucy, suggests that now is an ideal time to burn the blanket. 'You've gone without your blanket for two weeks now. That proves you no longer really need it.' With Linus in tow Lucy heads off to the backyard incinerator. 'We will now hold a "blanket burning" which will symbolize your new psychological freedom.' Linus is ambivalent: 'Couldn't we maybe use a symbolic blanket?' Lucy is undeterred: 'As I toss your blanket into the trash burner, your insecurities are symbolically destroyed forever!' Turning to her distraught brother, she assures him: 'There! You are now free from the terrible hold it once had on you. You are a new person!' Linus responds with a soul-searing cry of anguish: 'AAUGHH!!'[187]

Linus hates Mondays because it's washday. 'How can I relax with my blanket in the wash? Why does she have to wash it anyway? It wasn't very dirty! I GOTTA HAVE THAT BLANKET! I can't breathe! The walls are closing in on me! I'm getting weak! Gasp – Gasp – Help me, somebody! Help me!! AAAUGHH!'[188] In another variation on the same theme, Lucy smugly informs her brother that she has buried his blanket. 'You can't do that! I'll die without that blanket! I'll be like a fish out of water! I'll die! I'll die! Tell me where you buried it! Tell me! ... Tell me! Tell me! Tell me! Tell me! Oh, tell me!'[189]

We're talking here about much more than a blanket. Charles Schulz, creator of the Peanuts cartoon strip, has said that 'If you do not say anything in a cartoon, you might as well not draw it at all. Humour which does not say anything is worthless humour. So I contend that a cartoonist must be given a chance to do his own preaching.'[190] What, then, is my security blanket? It may be some-

---

187 Charles M. Schulz, *The Complete Peanuts*, 1967 to 1968, Fantagraphics Books, Seattle, WA, 2008, p. 110.
188 Charles M. Schulz, *The Complete Peanuts*, 1959 to 1960, Fantagraphics Books, Seattle, WA, 2006, p. 140.
189 Charles M. Schulz, *The Complete Peanuts*, 1961 to 1962, Fantagraphics Books, Seattle, WA, 2006, p. 2.
190 Quoted in Robert L. Short, *The Gospel According to Peanuts*, Fontana Books, London, 1969, p. 7.

Reflections for the year of Mark

thing, or someone, that I tell myself I can't live without. It might be wealth or the esteem of others, power or prestige – a thousand and one things that I grasp in my insecurity and neediness. But ultimately, the dead wood must be pruned if I am to experience life in its fullness.

The second rung is detachment. While the vinedresser cuts away the dead wood, he also prunes the branches that bear fruit. We may be reluctant to prune perfectly healthy branches, but unless that is done the vine will not yield an abundant harvest. Detachment isn't the same as renunciation. There are some things in life that we cannot give up entirely. Detachment is a way of ensuring that we are not dominated by what we cannot renounce.

During the past week I celebrated the funeral of Hilda, an elderly parishioner whose life was a perfect example of a non-grasping stance towards life, which is the essence of detachment. During the eulogy we heard a story about a time when Hilda's family and friends gave her a business class airline ticket to visit a dear friend overseas.

When she returned home everyone was curious to find out how she had enjoyed the comfort of business class. Rather sheepishly Hilda explained that in the departure lounge she got talking to a rather obese lady who was travelling on the same flight, but in economy class. 'A woman of her size would have been so uncomfortable squashed up in an economy class seat, so I suggested that we exchange our boarding passes. She travelled in business class, and I was happy enough to sit in economy. After all, there's not much of me, and I was quite comfortable.' Looking around the congregation as this story was told, I noticed a number of nodding heads. 'Yes,' they seemed to say. 'She was that kind of person.' The story made me feel uncomfortable. You'd need more than a pair of secateurs to prize a business class ticket from my grasp!

Renunciation and detachment are lessons to be learnt from a story about a monk who reached the outskirts of a village and settled under a tree for the night. As the monk slept one of the villagers had a vivid dream in which he saw a monk pass through the village carrying a pearl of great price. A voice told him that the pearl was his for the asking if he could find the monk. As soon as he awoke he rushed outside, and when he caught sight of a monk asleep beneath a nearby tree he rushed up to him and screamed, 'The pearl! The pearl! I must have the pearl.' The monk looked a little nonplussed and asked, 'What pearl?' 'The pearl in your bag,' replied the villager. 'Oh, I'd forgotten about it,' and rummaging through his bag he produced the pearl. 'Here it is. Take it if you want it.' The villager immediately grasped the pearl and hid it under his cloak. He rushed home, locked the door and pulled down the blinds, fearful that someone might steal his treasure. But as he gazed upon the pearl he became restless, and finally he could stand it no longer. He rushed to find the monk and gave him back the pearl. 'Take it back. I don't want it.' The monk then asked, 'Well, what do you want?'

The villager said, 'Give me the wealth that makes it possible for you to give the pearl away.'[191]

---

191 Adapted from Anthony de Mello, *The Song of the Bird,* p. 161.

SIXTH SUNDAY OF EASTER

(YEAR B)

This is my commandment: love one another, as I have loved you.
(Jn 15:12)

How do we decide what is right and what is wrong? In other words, what is the basis for morality? How do we distinguish between good and evil? Some people argue that society, and society alone, determines right and wrong. The extreme form of that view is called social determinism. In other words, we are born as a tabula rasa, a blank page. All judgements about right and wrong are determined solely by society.

That is a view put forward by one of the characters in David Williamson's play *Dead White Males*. Dr Grant Swain, a lecturer in literary theory, lays out the agenda for his students in his first class. Dr Swain tells them, 'This course will show you that there are no absolute truths, that there is no fixed "human nature" and what we think of as "reality" is always and only a manufactured reality.'[192]

---

[192] Quoted in David Williamson, 'Men, Women and Human Nature', in Peter Coleman (ed.) *Double Take: Six Incorrect Essays*, Mandarin, Port Melbourne, 1996, p. 9.

Releasing the Captive

If we were rigid social determinists we would have to conclude that nothing is absolutely right or wrong. We would also have to concede that certain kinds of behaviour considered evil by one society could be judged good and commendable by another society. Social determinism ultimately reduces morality to the same status as etiquette. In some cultures, for example, it is quite acceptable on formal occasions to eat food with our fingers. In other cultures, it is considered bad manners.

Are right and wrong decided in the same manner? Are the terms 'good' and 'evil' as arbitrary as good and bad manners? Or are some actions intrinsically evil under any circumstances? Would not the sadistic rape and murder of a young child be judged evil by all right-thinking people, no matter where they lived?

At the opposite end of the spectrum to social determinism is the belief that human beings have been programmed, just like a computer. If that is true, we would have to conclude that free will is only an illusion. No one could therefore be held morally responsible for their behaviour. You could hardly blame a robot for doing what it was programmed to do.

Free will verses fate or determinism is the theme of the *The Adjustment Bureau*, a 2011 American movie based loosely on Philip Dick's short story *Adjustment Team*. David Norris, played by Matt Damon, is an up-and-coming American politician who has just lost a senate campaign. He meets an attractive young English dancer, Elise (played by Emily Blunt), and falls in love with her. As the story progresses David arrives at work and witnesses something very bizarre taking place. Everyone is frozen in place, except for a number of mysterious men wearing felt hats who appear to be making some 'adjustments' to one of the frozen figures in the scene. These are the men from the adjustment bureau, and we soon discover that they're not human beings at all. They're more like angels whose job is to enforce the 'plan'.

The plan is devised by a person they call 'the chairman', who is clearly a God-like figure. When things go wrong with the plan for one reason or another, the adjustors are sent in to put things back on track. David is told that, according to the plan, he cannot fall in love with Elise, and they will block any attempt he makes to establish a romantic relationship. If he tells anyone about them they will immediately erase his memory and identity.

This is a story of fate (in the sense of divinely imposed order) verses freedom, and given the fact that this is an American movie set in the twenty-first century you won't win a prize for guessing the winner.

As you might expect, David's relationship with Elise progresses, despite all the efforts of the felt-hatted adjustors. At this point a more senior adjustor named Thompson appears on the scene. His job is put a definitive end to a situation that has not gone according to the plan.

He explains to David why this particular case is so important. David is destined to become the president, and Elise a great dancer, but neither destiny will be fulfilled if they have a romantic relationship. I won't reveal any more of the plot, just in case you haven't seen the movie. But the scene is set for a clash: a divinely conceived and imposed plan versus human freedom.

This movie presents us with two things that human beings seek: we want to be free, but at the same time we all want the plan, that is, we want some idea that the world makes sense, that we are not the victims of random chance, that things don't happen without rhyme or reason.

We want freedom, and we want the plan. The premise of this movie is that freedom and the plan are mutually exclusive; you can't have both at the same time. And that's why this movie's fundamental premise is based on bad theology, precisely because it sets up the problem in this way.

Do I, as a Christian, accept that I lose my freedom if I submit to the Divine plan? The Divine plan is set out for us in today's gospel: 'Remain in my love.' Does that rob us of our freedom?

St Augustine of Hippo, who lived during the fourth and fifth centuries, once wrote, 'Love, and do what you will.'[193] At first hearing, Augustine's dictum sounds like a licence to do whatever gives you pleasure, an endorsement of hedonism. But the words 'do what you will' are firmly anchored to that first word – 'Love'.

Before returning to the premise that drives *The Adjustment Bureau*, let us consider that word 'love'. In his first encyclical, *Deus Caritas Est*, Pope Benedict observes that 'Today, the term 'love' has become one of the most frequently used and misused of words, a word to

---

193 *Tractatus in Ep.* Joannis, vii.

which we attach quite different meanings.' Reflecting upon the vast semantic range of the word, he writes that

> we speak of love of country, love of one's profession, love between friends, love of work, love between parents and children, love between family members, love of neighbour and love of God.[194]

The Greek word used for love in today's gospel and in the first letter of St John is *agape*. The pope's encyclical describes *agape* as a love 'grounded in and shaped by faith.'[195] This love involves 'a real discovery of the other', that moves beyond selfishness. It is not self-seeking, but manifests itself in a 'concern and care for the other.' It 'seeks the good of the beloved: it becomes renunciation and it is ready, and even willing, for sacrifice.'[196]

So, is there a clash between God's plan for us, the law of love, and human freedom? Consider the example of playing a musical instrument. George Weigel, citing an example given by Servais Pinckaers, puts it this way:

> Anyone can bang away on a piano, but that's to make noise, not music ... At first, learning to play the piano is a matter of some drudgery, as we master exercises that seem like a constraint, a burden. But as our mastery grows, we discover a new, richer kind of freedom: we can play the music we like, we can create new music on our own. Freedom, in other words, is a matter of gradually acquiring the capacity to choose the good and to do what we choose with perfection, with excellence.[197]

---

194 Benedict XVI, *Deus Caritas Est*, n. 2.
195 Ibid., n. 7.
196 Ibid., n. 6.
197 George Weigel, *The Cube and the Cathedral*, Basic Books, New York, 2005, pp. 80-1.

Releasing the Captive

Thus God's law (the plan) is not the opposite of human freedom. God's plan educates us in freedom. The piano teacher is not limiting the student's freedom but rather awakening it. Having followed the 'plan' imposed by the teacher, the student as an accomplished pianist will be able to play whatever he or she wishes. God's plan does not crush human freedom, but awakens it. The command to love awakens us to our true destiny as human beings.

SEVENTH SUNDAY OF EASTER

(YEAR B)

I passed your word on to them.(Jn 17:14)

After the death of Judas the disciples gathered to choose someone to take his place among the Twelve. It was important that the person they chose had been with them the whole time, someone who was a witness to all that Jesus had said and done, someone who could act with them as a witness to his resurrection. Two candidates were proposed and they drew lots. The lot fell to Matthias, and he was listed among the Twelve.

In today's gospel Jesus prays for his disciples. He has entrusted the Father's word to them, and now he sends them into the world to be witnesses to the truth. But what if they should fail? Did Jesus have a plan B?

An ancient legend tells of Jesus' arrival in heaven, where a vast host of angels greeted him. Out of curiosity they asked him what arrangements he had made on earth to complete the work he had begun. Jesus replied, 'I have sent my twelve disciples into the world.' The heavenly host seemed puzzled. 'But what if this tiny group should fail?' Jesus replied, 'I don't have any other plan.'[198]

---

[198] Adapted from William J. Bausch, *A World of Stories*, Twenty-Third Publications, Mystic, CT, 1998, p. 336-7.

Releasing the Captive

This small band of disciples began to preach the word that had been entrusted to them, and that became the genesis of the gospels we read today. How did the gospels come to be written? Details about the life and teaching of Jesus were first handed on by word of mouth. This oral tradition was eventually committed to paper, and scripture scholars speculate that there was at least one major collection of the sayings and deeds of Jesus before any of the gospels were written.

The first gospel to be written was Mark, sometime during the mid-60s, and hence about 30 years after the death of Jesus. Some 15 or 20 years after the gospel of Mark, the gospels of Matthew and Luke were written. The gospel of John came another ten or 15 years after that, sometime towards the end of the first century. If one gospel was already in circulation, why were the other three gospels written? The authors of the gospels of Matthew, Luke and John obviously felt the need to present the life and teachings of Jesus in a different perspective for their own communities.

In their introduction to *The Penguin Book of Australian Jokes* Phillip Adams and Patrice Newell argue that there are, sadly, very few genuinely Australian jokes. The same core joke is recycled from somewhere overseas with variations on names, places and punchline. Classic Irish jokes are frequently retold as indigenous *Dad 'n Dave* jokes. And many of the most common political jokes these days are aimed at the prime minister of the day. Some of the most caustic jokes told about former prime minister Paul Keating, according to Adams and Newell, turn out to be recycled anti-Hitler jokes told in

Reflections for the year of Mark

Munich clubs in the 1930s, specifically by two courageous comedians who ended up in Dachau. Writers of novels, plays and feature films tell us that there are only about a dozen basic plots that are endlessly recycled. Adams and Newell conclude: 'If that is true of drama it seems trebly, painfully true of jokes.' The point is that the same basic joke is reworked to fit a different situation.[199]

The gospel writers were engaged in a similar enterprise. Let us consider Luke's gospel. Luke was written round about 80 AD, and hence some 50 years after the death of Jesus. We can say with certainty that Luke wasn't among the first disciples of Jesus. His audience was quite different to the congregation or church Matthew wrote for. In fact, Luke's gospel was written in two parts: the Acts of the Apostles is Part Two. It is addressed to someone by the name of Theophilus.

That's a Greek name, and Luke wrote his gospel in Greek. His Greek is elegant and educated, unlike, for example, the Greek of Mark. When Luke borrows sections of Mark, and incorporates some 60 per cent of Mark's gospel, he often has to tidy up Mark's poor grammar. Luke is addressing an audience which is primarily Gentile, in other words, they were not from a Jewish background. Luke's task, therefore, is to translate the gospel from one culture to another. His audience doesn't have the same background as Matthew's predominantly Jewish-Christian audience. And so, for example, Luke isn't interested in showing that Jesus is the fulfilment of Old Testament

---

[199] Phillip Adams and Patrice Newell, *The Penguin Book of Australian Jokes*, Penguin Books, Ringwood, 1994, p. 23.

prophecy. His audience wouldn't have been as familiar with the Old Testament as Matthew's community.

What is all of this saying to us? Even within the fifty years or so that the New Testament was written, there was an evident need to make the life and teachings of Jesus intelligible to people who lived in other cultures and spoke other languages. Jesus lived in Palestine and spoke Aramaic. Luke's gospel is addressed to a Greek-speaking community.

At the end of the scripture readings at Mass the lector says: 'The Word of the Lord', and we respond: 'Thanks be to God.' But we must keep in mind that this timeless Word of God is expressed in human words, in first-century words and images. Like all words, they are limited by the age which produced them. Each subsequent generation of believers, and each culture, must journey beyond those first-century words and images and allow the eternal Word of God to become incarnate in their own language and culture. After all, this is what Jesus himself did.

Consider an incident that Luke's gospel places towards the beginning of Jesus' public ministry. Returning to his home town of Nazareth, Jesus entered the synagogue and was handed the scroll of the prophet Isaiah. He deliberately searched for a particular passage from Isaiah, a prophecy that had been written over five centuries before Jesus himself was born. The passage he read aloud to the congregation was set during the Babylonian exile. It is known as one of the songs of the suffering servant and describes the work and suffering of someone who achieved God's work in that situation of exile in a totally unexpected way (Is 61:1-2). This text had a specific meaning in its original context. But when Jesus began to speak in the synagogue at Nazareth, he was not about to give a history lesson on the Babylonian exile. Rather, he made the astounding claim that the words of Isaiah were being fulfilled in his own day, in his own life and ministry, among his own people.

In the same way, we do not read the scriptures as a history lesson. We read this word because it is Truth. We are attentive to the Word of God telling us what happened over two thousand years ago because it enables us to understand God's presence among us here and now. Luke comes back to this theme at the end of his gospel when he tells the story of two disciples on the road to Emmaus (Lk 24:13-35). They are despondent as they discuss the events that had just taken place in Jerusalem. A mysterious stranger joins them – it is of course Jesus himself – and he begins to explain how Moses and the prophets are the key to understanding what has just happened. That is the challenge for every generation of believers, to receive freshly the Word of God and to find in it the interpretative key for the present moment. In the words of Claudius of Turin, 'Blessed are the eyes that see the Divine Spirit through the letter's veil.'[200]

---

[200] Quoted in Esther de Waal, *Seeking God*, Fount Paperbacks, London, 1984.

THE ASCENSION OF THE LORD

(YEAR B)

And so the Lord Jesus, after he had spoken to them, was taken up into heaven. (Mk 16:19)

Some experience just can't be put into words. T.S. Eliot reminds us that

> Words strain,
> Crack and sometimes break, under the burden,
> Under the tension, slip, slide, perish,
> Decay with imprecision, will not stay in place,
> Will not stay still.[201]

The movie *Good Will Hunting* starring Matt Damon and Robin Williams is the story of twenty-year-old Will Hunting who is highly intelligent but chooses to work as a construction labourer. He's arrested after attacking a police officer and faces the prospect of imprisonment. If he is to avoid jail he must see a therapist, and so he does. He treats the first few therapists with disdain and they refuse to work with him. Things are different with Sean Maguire

---

[201] T.S. Eliot, *Burnt Norton* (no. 1 of Four Quartets). http://famouspoetsandpoems.com/poets/t__s__eliot/poems/15132

(Robin Williams) because he is able to breach Hunting's defence mechanisms. In one memorable scene Maguire tells Hunting that what he knows comes out of books, not lived experience:

> So if I asked you about art you could give me the skinny on every art book ever written ... Michelangelo? You know a lot about him I bet. Life's work, criticisms, political aspirations. But you couldn't tell me what it smells like in the Sistine Chapel. You've never stood there and looked up at that beautiful ceiling ... If I asked you about war you could refer me to a bevy of fictional and non-fictional material, but you've never been in one. You've never held your best friend's head in your lap and watched him draw his last breath, looking to you for help. And if I asked you about love I'd get a sonnet, but you've never looked at a woman and been truly vulnerable. Known that someone could kill you with a look. That someone could rescue you from grief. That God had put an angel on Earth just for you. And you wouldn't know how it felt to be her angel. To have the love be there for her forever. Through anything, through cancer. You wouldn't know about sleeping sitting up in a hospital room for two months holding her hand and not leaving because the doctors could see in your eyes that the term 'visiting hours' didn't apply to you. And you wouldn't know about real loss, because that only occurs when you lose something you love more than yourself, and you've never dared to love anything that much.

Will Hunting had the words, but not the experience. The evangelists had the opposite problem. They've had the experience, but they struggle to put it into words. They are attempting to express the mystery of Christ's transition – a transition between that period during which Jesus of Nazareth was physically present, and the time that followed when he was no longer physically with them. The celebration of the ascension is a way of talking about Jesus' physical separation from the human story. It is a farewell scene, but unlike most partings it leaves the disciples rejoicing. Liberated now from all restrictions of time and space, the Lord is present forever in the lives of his disciples.

But where and how is the Lord present with us? What is the truth of the ascension for us today? The old green catechism, well-known to baby boomers, posed a fundamental question, 'Where is God?' And the answer, 'God is everywhere ...'[202] The catechism thus stated a truth at the heart of most of the world's great religions.

From the Islamic tradition comes a story about a holy man who set out on a pilgrimage to Mecca. At the outskirts of the holy city he lay down to rest, exhausted by the long journey. He had barely fallen asleep when he was brusquely awakened by an irate pilgrim. 'This is the time of day when all devout Muslims bow their heads towards Mecca in prayer. Not only are you asleep at the time of prayer, but it is your feet and not your head that you have pointed towards the holy city. What sort of Muslim are you?' The holy man opened his eyes and looked up at the irate pilgrim. 'Brother, would you do me a favour? Please place my feet in a direction where they won't be pointing towards God.'[203] The Jewish tradition expresses this insight beautifully in Psalm 139:

> O where can I go from your spirit,
> or where can I flee from your face?

---

202 *Catechism of Christian Doctrine*, Sydney, 1939, p. 11.
203 Adapted from Anthony de Mello, *The Prayer of the Frog*, p. 6..

> If I climb the heavens, you are there.
> If I take the wings of the dawn
> and dwell at the sea's furthest end,
> even there your hand would lead me,
> your right hand would hold me fast.
> If I say: 'let the darkness hide me
> and the light around me be night,
> even darkness is not dark for you
> and the night is clear as the day.[204]

God is with us everywhere. If you're familiar with the life of Moses, you'll recall the time he was tending a flock of sheep when God spoke to him from a burning bush (Ex 3). A story from the Jewish tradition tells of a pagan who approached Rabbi Joshua and asked, 'Why, of all things, did God choose the humble thornbush as the place from which to speak to Moses?' The rabbi replied: 'If God had chosen a carob tree or a mulberry bush, you would have asked the same question. Yet I will not let you go away without an answer to your question. God chose the humble thornbush to teach us that there is no place on earth bereft of the Divine Presence, not even a thornbush.'[205]

Therefore we need to be attentive to the present moment. Daisetsu Teitaro Suzuki, an exponent of Zen Buddhism in the West, was sitting at table with a number of distinguished scholars. The man seated beside him kept asking him questions, but Suzuki ate his dinner patiently and said nothing. The man, who obviously knew

---

204 *The Grail Psalms*, Collins Liturgical Publications, London, 1986, p. 202.
205 Jakob J. Petuchowski, *Our Masters Taught*, Free Press, New York, 1982, p. 103.

little or nothing about Zen, asked: 'How would you sum up Zen for a Westerner like me?' Suzuki looked the man in the eye and said: 'Eat!'[206] In other words, be aware of this moment and enjoy the meal that is before you. Be where you are.

In the words of the catechism, God is everywhere. But Christian tradition has always emphasised the presence of God within. At a funeral we incense the body of the deceased as a reminder that the body is a temple of God's Holy Spirit. St Paul tells the Galatians, 'God has sent into our hearts the Spirit of his Son (Gal 4:6). Christian mystics have had their own names for the place where God dwells within us: 'the inner chamber', 'the secret room', 'the hidden tabernacle', or 'the bridal chamber'.

Some young children went to spend some time with their grandparents. One morning their grandmother found them leaning over the wall of the well in the backyard, peering down into the water. When she asked what they were doing they replied: 'Grandfather said that if we looked hard enough we would see where God lives on earth.' With a smile on her face their grandmother asked, 'And have you seen it?' The children answered, 'No. All that we see is our own faces reflected in the water.' 'Well then,' said grandmother, 'you grandfather was right, for you have seen at least one place where God dwells here on earth – in yourselves, deep within you.'

In Matthew's gospel the ascension isn't mentioned explicitly. If we had only Matthew's gospel we'd be celebrating the feast of the disappearance of the Lord rather than the ascension of the Lord.

---

206 Thomas Moore, *Care of the Soul*, p. 219.

Reflections for the year of Mark

The gospel ends with Jesus commissioning his disciples, but assuring them of his presence with them always. Giacomo Puccini was dying of cancer when he wrote his final opera, *Turandot*.

His friends encouraged him to take it easy and rest, but he would always respond, 'I'm going to do as much as I can on my great masterwork and it's up to you, my friends, to finish it if I don't.' Puccini died before the opera was completed. His friends were faced with a choice. They could mourn their departed friend and wonder how great the completed opera might have been. Or they could complete the work he had started – which they decided to do. And so it happened that, in 1926, at the famous Opera House of Milan, La Scala, Puccini's completed opera was performed for the first time; conducted by Arturo Toscanini. When they reached that part of the opera where Puccini had stopped writing because he died, Toscanini stopped everything, turned around with eyes welling up with tears, and said to the large audience, 'This is where the master ends.' And he wept. But then, after a few moments, he lifted up his head, smiled broadly, and said, 'And this is where his friends began.'[207]

So it is with the ascension. The Master had finished his work on earth and he commissioned his disciples to continue, assuring them of his continued presence with them.

---

207 Adapted from William J. Bausch, *A World of Stories*, Twenty-Third Publications, Mystic, CT, 1998, p. 300.

PENTECOST SUNDAY

(YEAR B)

*You send forth your spirit, they are created;
and you renew the face of the earth. (Psalm 103:30)*

The Book of Genesis, the first book in the Bible, the book of beginnings, poetically describes God's creation of the world. We read: 'Now the earth was a formless void, there was darkness over the deep, with a divine wind sweeping over the waters.' Creation began with the divine wind sweeping over the waters. Today's first reading from the Acts of the Apostles tells of another beginning – the beginning of the church, and again we read of a wind: 'When Pentecost day came round, they had all met together, when suddenly there came from heaven a sound as of a violent wind which filled the entire house in which they were sitting.' Luke, the author of the Acts of the Apostles, invites his readers to see Pentecost as a new creation, or to be more precise, a renewal of creation. As we pray in today's responsorial psalm: 'You send forth your Spirit ... and you renew the face of the earth.'

Pentecost is a story of renewal and of profound change. Before the Spirit came upon the disciples they were timid and fearful. There are two faces of the human emotion of fear. On the one hand, fear alerts us to danger. In Herman Melville's epic saga on whaling, *Moby Dick*, Starbuck says that the only men he wants in his boat are men who are afraid of whales. Those who are afraid truly know the power and awesome strength of their adversary, and are not likely to be foolhardy. But fear can also be debilitating. We hear of people being paralysed with fear. The disciples were overcome by fear and overwhelmed by a terrible sense of failure and inadequacy.

Which reminds me of a mother who lived with her son in a house right next door to the local Catholic church. One Sunday morning, the mother roused her son, telling him that it was time to get up for Mass. The son replied, 'I don't want to go to Mass.'

'But darling, you must go to Mass.'

'I don't want to go to Mass, and for two reasons. Firstly, Mass is always so incredibly boring. And secondly, the people who go to Mass don't like me.'

'Now Son, there are two good reasons why you should go to Mass. Firstly, you're not a child any more. You're 50 years of age. And secondly, and more importantly, you've got to go to Mass because it's Sunday, and you're the parish priest!'

We will never know exactly what happened in that upper room on the first Pentecost day, but the effects were startling and dramatic. Disciples who had been overcome by fear went out and boldly proclaimed the Good News for all to hear. Today we listen again to this marvellous story of transformation, not because we are students of ancient history, curious and intrigued about the distant past. We listen again to this story because it assures us that the same Spirit who transformed the disciples is present and active among us.

In 1964, Jean Vanier moved into a house in Trosly-Breuil, a small village in France, with two intellectually disabled men, Raphael and Phillippe. He called the home L'Arche (the Ark, a symbol of life, hope, and covenant with God and humanity). In setting up this home, Jean chose to look at handicapped people in a radical way, one inspired by the life of Jesus and the Beatitudes. In a society that values production and competition, those with a mental handicap teach us the value of sharing, acceptance, and joy. At the heart of L'Arche is the idea of 'living with' and not just 'doing for' those with mental handicaps. Since 1964 L'Arche is now an international organisation with 126 communities in 31 countries, including Australia.

After visiting homes for the intellectually disabled Vanier gradually became aware of how deeply wounded people with learning disabilities are.

> Even if they are well cared for, they do not understand why they have been excluded, why they are not living in the same way as their brothers and sisters. They are also sometimes oppressed: throughout the world I have seen children chained up; I have seen 200 men and women piled into a room and living in filth ... My experience has shown me that their violence, their strange behaviour, their depression are pleas for true relationship: Am I worth taking care of? The only response to this question is another heart saying 'Yes, you're worth it. I am willing to commit myself to a relationship with you, because I want you to live'.[208]

---

208 Information obtained from the website of L'Arche Internationale, http://www.larche.org/front/home.php

Reflections for the year of Mark

Vanier is also co-founder of the Faith and Light movement. Faith and Light offers people with an intellectual disability, together with their family and friends, a supportive place of prayer and friendship. There are now over nine hundred Faith and Light groups throughout the world today. Jean Vanier is a person who knows a great deal about transformation, about helping wounded people to change. He believes that when intellectually handicapped people are locked away in institutions they wither. Their hearts and spirits are wounded. And so, they harden just to survive, then seethe with anger and bitterness.

Vivian was a young girl of ten when she came to live in one of Vanier's communities. She had spent almost all of her life in an institution. She had never experienced a permanent relationship. In one institution after another she managed to survive, but with a great deal of pain. When she first joined a L'Arche community she experienced pain yet again, because she found herself once more among strangers. She screamed continuously, and tested the helpers by her wild and crazy behaviour, her tantrums and fits. But slowly, over several months she made a momentous discovery. It is in fact one of the most delightful experiences in life – to realise, suddenly, that you are loved by someone else. Vivian began to feel secure. She will always remain fragile; she will always find relationships hard, but there is now peace in her heart. A new spirit had come upon her.

On Easter Sunday a few years ago, 12,000 members of Faith and Light made a pilgrimage to Lourdes. About a third of these people were intellectually handicapped, the others were friends, helpers and family. They processed to the main square in front of the basilica – some in wheelchairs, some walking with difficulty – all of them with their various wounds and handicaps. They came smiling with joy and cheering with excitement.

Vanier recalled a television journalist asking him the following morning: 'How do you explain this? I like my job. I'm well paid, I enjoy perfect health, but they have something I don't have. They have joy.' Vanier replied,

> 'The stone which the builders rejected has become the corner stone.' Those who have been sidelined by society have become the building blocks of a new community – a community of faith and light, of love and joy. They change when someone takes an interest in them. They come out of their shells and begin to grow. New energies are released in them, energies which had been hidden and locked up inside them.[209]

The miracle of human change. Pentecost is not about something that happened back then. Pentecost is about God's Spirit changing people now.

---

[209] The story of Vivian and the pilgrimage to Lourdes comes from Flor McCarthy, *Sunday and Holy Day Liturgies, Year A*, Dominican Publications, Dublin, repr. 1992, pp. 93-4.

Reflections for the year of Mark

TRINITY SUNDAY

(YEAR B)

And know that I am with you always; yes, to the end of time. (Mt 28:20)

The early centuries of the Christian era were marked by church councils and theological debates – all about the nature of God, and especially about the mystery that we now call the Trinity. Bishops and theologians of the time grappled with the question: How can we express – with accurate precision – the relationship between God the Father, God the Son and God the Holy Spirit? Gregory of Nyssa testifies to the endless debates at the time of the Second Ecumenical Council in Constantinople (381 AD):

> The whole city is full of it, the squares, the marketplaces, the cross-roads, the alley-ways; old-clothesmen, money-changers, food-sellers – they are all busy arguing. If you ask someone to give you change, they philosophise about the Begotten; if you enquire about the price of bread, you are told by way of reply that the Father is greater and the Son inferior; if you ask whether your bath is ready, the attendant answers that the Son was made out of nothing.[210]

---

[210] On the Deity of the Son and the Spirit (PG 46:557B), quoted in John Chryssavgis, *Light Through Darkness*, Darton, Longman and Todd, London, 2004, pp. 59-60.

Releasing the Captive

Any attempt to capture the reality of God in human language will always be in tension with the sublime mystery of God that utterly transcends the grasp of words and definitions. There will always be a tension between living in the mystery of God, and the very natural and understandable wish to articulate our religious experiences in words. Our words are not the Truth itself, but merely an attempt to express it in human terms. St Augustine once observed, 'If you have understood, then what you have understood is not God!'[211] But who is closer to the reality: those who live within the mystery of God and are thereby transformed by the power of that mystery, or those who know the correct formulas, who can describe the divinity with dogmatic precision? Leo Tolstoy's story of the three hermits, written in 1886, offers an interesting reflection on this question.[212]

A bishop was sailing home after completing business abroad. The voyage was a smooth one, the wind favourable and the weather fair. As the bishop strolled on deck he noticed a group of passengers gathered around an old fisherman, who was pointing to the sea and telling them something. He drew nearer to listen, and asked what the fisherman had been saying. One of the passengers replied, 'The fisherman was telling us about the hermits.'

'What hermits?' asked the bishop. 'Tell me about them.' The fisherman pointed to a little island, just now visible on the horizon. 'That is the island where the hermits live. They're holy men.

---

[211] Alan Jones, *Passion for Pilgrimage*, p. 131.
[212] Adapted from Leo Tolstoy, 'The Three Hermits', in Louise and Aylmer Maude (trans.), *Twenty-Three Tales*, Oxford University Press, Reprinted 1975, pp. 93-201.

Reflections for the year of Mark

I've heard people talk of them since I was a boy, but never chanced to see them myself till the year before last.' The fisherman went on to explain how once, when he was out fishing, he'd been stranded at night upon the island, not knowing where he was. In the morning, he wandered about the island and came across a hut, and met an old man standing near it. Very soon two others joined him. They fed him, dried his things and helped him repair his boat. 'And what were they like?' asked the bishop. 'One is a small man and his back is bent. He wears a priest's cassock and is very old; he must be more than a hundred years old. But he is always smiling, and his face is as bright as an angel's. The second is taller, but he also is very old. He wears a tattered peasant's coat. He's a strong man, and he, too, is kindly and cheerful. The third is tall, and has a beard as white as snow reaching to his knees. He is stern, with overhanging eyebrows; and he wears nothing but a piece of matting tied around his waist. The bishop then asked: 'Did they speak to you?'

'For the most part they did everything in silence, and spoke very little, even to one another. One of them would just give a glance, and the others would understand him.' As the fisherman spoke, the ship had drawn nearer to the island. The bishop then left the group and sought out the captain. 'Captain, is it true that there are hermits who live there on that island?'

'So it's said, my Lord, but I don't know if it's true. Fishermen say they've seen them; but of course they may only be spinning yarns.'

'I should like to land on the island and see these men,' said the bishop. 'How could I manage it? Could I be rowed ashore?'

Releasing the Captive

The captain tried to dissuade him. 'We should lose much time. And if I might venture to say so to your Lordship, the old men are not worth your pains. I've heard it said that they're foolish old fellows, who understand nothing and never speak a word.' But the bishop insisted: 'I wish to see them, and I will pay you for your trouble and loss of time. Please may I have a boat?'

So the captain gave orders, and the ship's course was set for the island. When the ship could get no nearer to the island, a boat was lowered and the bishop was rowed ashore. The three old hermits bowed to the bishop, and he gave them his blessing, at which they bowed lower still. Then the bishop began to speak to them. 'I have heard that you're godly men who live here praying to our Lord for all people. I am an unworthy servant of Christ, but I am called by God's mercy to teach his flock, and I will to do what I can to teach you. Tell me now, how do you pray?'

'We pray in this way' said the oldest of the hermits: 'Three are ye, three are we, have mercy upon us!' And when the old man had said this, all three raised their eyes to heaven, and repeated: 'Three are ye, three are we, have mercy upon us!'

The bishop smiled. 'You've evidently heard something about the Holy Trinity, but you're not praying correctly. Listen, I will teach you.' And the bishop began explaining to the hermits how God had revealed himself to us, telling them of God the Father, God the Son, and God the Holy Spirit. 'God the Son came down to earth to save us, and this is how he taught us all to pray. Listen, and repeat after me: Our Father …

Reflections for the year of Mark

And the first old man repeated after him, 'Our Father,' and the second repeated, 'Our Father', and the third repeated, 'Our Father'. The bishop continued: 'Who art in heaven'. The first hermit repeated: 'Who art in heaven …' But the second blundered over the words, and the very old hermit, having no teeth, also mumbled indistinctly. And so it went on, all day long. The bishop laboured, saying a word twenty, thirty, a hundred times over, and the old men repeated it after him. They blundered, and he corrected them, and made them begin again.

It was getting dark and the moon was appearing over the water before the bishop rose to return to the vessel. When he took leave of the old men they all bowed down to the ground before him. He raised them, and blessed each of them, telling them to pray as he had taught them. Then he returned to the ship. As soon as the bishop had reached the vessel the anchor was weighed and the sails unfurled. The ship sailed swiftly away but the bishop could not sleep. He sat alone at the stern, gazing at the sea and thinking of the elderly hermits. He thought how pleased they'd been to learn the Lord's Prayer; and he thanked God for having sent him to teach and help such godly men.

Suddenly he saw something white and shining upon the waves. It must be seagull, or a boat sailing after us. But it's overtaking us rapidly. It was far away a minute ago, but now it's much nearer. It can't be a boat, because I can't see a sail; but whatever it is, it's following us and catching us up.' The captain also witnessed the sight, and let go of the helm in terror. 'Oh my God! The hermits are running after us on the water as though it were dry land!' All the passengers rushed onto the deck, and they saw the hermits coming along, hand in hand. All three were gliding upon the water as they approached the ship.

When the hermits reached the ship they all began to say with one voice: 'My Lord Bishop, we have forgotten the prayer you taught us. As long as we kept repeating it we remembered, but when we stopped saying it for a time, a word dropped out, and now it has all gone to pieces. We can remember nothing of it. Teach us again.'

The bishop bowed low before the old men, and said, 'Your own prayer will reach the Lord, you men of God. It is not for me to teach you. When you pray, say simply: "Three are ye, three are we. Have mercy upon us.'

And a light shone until daybreak on the spot where the three saintly hermits were lost to sight.

Reflections for the year of Mark

THE BODY AND BLOOD OF CHRIST

(YEAR B)

... he broke it and gave it to them. 'Take it,' he said, 'this is my body.'
(Mk 14:22)

Jesus took some bread, and giving it to his disciples he said, 'This is my body.' But what is the this he was referring to? 'Bread' you might answer. True, but not just bread – bread broken – *klomenon* in the Greek (1 Cor 11:24). The bread, broken and shared among his disciples, was a symbolic gesture. The very next day his body was to be 'broken' in death upon the cross.[213]

For most Catholics this insight is not obvious because the fraction rite (the breaking of the host) occurs some time after the consecration, accompanied by the Agnus Dei. It is interesting to note that the Anglican Book of Common Prayer directs the minister to break the bread as he says 'he brake it, and gave it to his disciples.'

By way of contrast, breaking the bread just prior to the consecration in the Mass of the Roman Rite has been deemed an abuse![214]

---

213 Tad Guzie, *The Book of Sacramental Basics*, Paulist Press, New York, 1981, p. 34.
214 'In some places there has existed an abuse by which the Priest breaks the host at the time of the consecration in the Holy Mass. This abuse is contrary to the tradition of the Church. It is reprobated and is to be corrected with haste.' *Redemptionis Sacramentum*, n. 55.

We venerate the consecrated bread and wine as a sacrament of the Body and Blood of Christ. But we also need to remind ourselves that the Christian community is the body of Christ. This fundamental insight is reflected in Matthew's gospel (25:40): 'In so far as you did this to one of the least of these brothers of mine, you did it to me.'

When St Paul, the fanatical persecutor of the early Christian community was travelling to Damascus, he heard the voice of the Lord asking, 'Saul, Saul, why are you persecuting me?' When Paul asked, 'Who are you?', the answer came: 'I am Jesus, whom you are persecuting' (Acts 9:5).

And who are the least of the Lord's brothers and sisters? In Australia, the least of the Lord's brothers and sisters must surely be the first inhabitants of this land, the aboriginal people. They are not 'least' in terms of their rich spirituality and cultural heritage.

But they are 'least' in the way they have been massacred and marginalised, dominated and disempowered, dispersed and dispossessed, ever since the Union Jack was first hoisted in Sydney Cove on 26 January 1788.

Our generation cannot play Pontius Pilate by seeking to wash our hands and absolve ourselves of all guilt. In the words of Michael McHugh, a former justice of the High Court of Australia,

> The dispossession of the Aboriginal peoples from their lands was a great wrong. Many people believe that those of us who are the beneficiaries of that wrong have a moral responsibility to redress it to the extent that it can be redressed.[215]

---

[215] *Western Australia v Ward (2002)* 213 CLR 1. p. 240-1. Transcript, 22 June 1998.

Reflections for the year of Mark

The reality is that past injustice continues to give rise to present injustices for indigenous Australians. Many of the disadvantages that Indigenous people now face stem from having had their land, their children, and their rights forcefully taken from them.

The assault upon Aboriginal people began around Sydney at the very beginning of white settlement. In 1789, an outbreak of smallpox introduced by the First Fleeters devastated the Aboriginal population in the Sydney area.[216] They never recovered. Even today the situation is appalling. Fr Frank Brennan cites health statistics 'where Aboriginal people live in fourth world conditions in a first world country.'[217]

The call to reconciliation has been part of our national agenda for some time. And what does reconciliation entail? In the words of Patrick Dodson, formerly chairperson of the Council for Aboriginal Reconciliation, 'Reconciliation is about acceptance, respect and recognition. It accepts the special place of indigenous peoples in the nation's history, respects indigenous cultures and recognises their human rights.'[218]

And like it or not, reconciliation must begin with acknowledging our guilt and saying 'Sorry'. On 16 March 1998, the Vatican expressed its 'repentance' for Christians who failed to resist the Nazi persecution and oppression of the Jews. The document was entitled

---

216 Jan Kociumbas, *The Oxford History of Australia, Volume 2*, 1770–1860, Oxford University Press, 1992, p. 52.
217 Interviewed by Ian Henschke on ABC Radio, 10 October 2003.
218 Quoted in *The Path to Reconciliation*, Canberra, Australian Government Publishing Service, 1997.

'We Remember: A Reflection on the Shoah' (*Shoah* is the Jewish term for the Holocaust, in which six million Jews died).[219]

This document acknowledged that 'the attitudes down the centuries of Christians towards the Jews' had a bearing on the failures of Christians to resist the Nazi attack on the Jewish people. It was Pope John Paul II's hope that this document would 'help to heal the wounds of past misunderstandings and injustices', and play a part in 'shaping a future in which the unspeakable iniquity of the Shoah will never again be possible.'[220] This Vatican document is, in its own words, 'an act of repentance'. It says that the Catholic Church 'desires to express her deep sorrow for the failures of her sons and daughters in every age.'

We Australians are called to a similar act of repentance that will help to heal the wounds of past misunderstandings and injustices towards the indigenous people of this land. Such an act of repentance is essential if we sincerely seek a future in which the iniquities of the past will never again be possible. On 13 February 2008, the then Prime Minister of Australia, Kevin Rudd, delivered an apology in the Australian parliament to the stolen generations, those Aboriginal and Torres Strait Islander children who were removed from their families, their communities and their country.

> To the mothers and the fathers, the brothers and the sisters,
> for the breaking up of families and communities, we say

---

219 'We Remember: A Reflection on the Shoah by the Commission for Religious Relations with Jews (16 March 1998)', in *The Pope Speaks*, vol. 43, no. 4 July/Aug 1998, pp. 243-6.
220 'Letter of Pope John Paul II to Cardinal Edward Cassidy' (12 March 1998), in *The Pope Speaks*, vol. 43, no. 4, July/Aug 1998, p. 246.

sorry. And for the indignity and degradation thus inflicted on a proud people and a proud culture, we say sorry.

We the Parliament of Australia respectfully request that this apology be received in the spirit in which it is offered as part of the healing of the nation.[221]

But some people seem to find it extraordinarily difficult to say 'Sorry'. The cartoonist Michael Leunig satirises our inability to say 'sorry'. A white Australian is seated on a chair, speaking to an Aboriginal sitting on a log: 'How do you expect me to say "sorry" if I don't feel sorry?'

'Perhaps', the Aboriginal replies, 'you could try compassion – or empathy. You could try to imagine the sorrow – how sad it is for a people to be outnumbered and persecuted and pounded – to lose their culture and their country.'

'That's not sad,' according to the white Australian. 'That's just plain bad luck! We won and you lost. You got trounced and you're just being a bad loser! In fact, I think you should do the decent thing and CONGRATULATE us for winning! Maybe if you said "congratulations" you'd be able to get on with life and stop sulking. You might be surprised how a few, simple words of acknowledgment can be very healing. I know it's not easy to say "congratulations" but perhaps you can begin by imagining just how much effort we put in, grinding you people into the dirt.'[222]

Jesus gave his disciples bread, broken – a symbol of his own body, broken in death. He passed them a cup of wine, a sacrament of his

---

[221] The full text of the speech may be obtained from http://news.ninemsn.com.au/national/379056/full-text-of-rudds-sorry-speech
[222] *The Sydney Morning Herald*, 31 May, 1997.

blood that was to be poured out in death. When we eat this bread, when we drink this wine, we proclaim his death. But in receiving this broken bread we also pledge to heal the weeping wounds in the body of Christ.

Reflections for the year of Mark

AUSTRALIA DAY

Set your hearts on his kingdom ... (Lk 12:31)

Watkin Tench, a member of the marine corps, sailed to Botany Bay with the First Fleet. As the fleet was about to set sail from England he wrote that the prisoners were in high spirits. 'Few complaints or lamentations were to be heard among them and an ardent wish for the hour of departure seemed generally to prevail.'[223] As they got clear of the Isle of Wight Tench strolled down among the convicts and noted that, with a very few exceptions, 'their countenances indicated a high degree of satisfaction, though in some the pang of being severed, perhaps forever, from their native land could not be wholly suppressed. In general, marks of distress were more perceptible among the men than the women.'[224]

The First Fleet set sail from England on 13 May 1787 under the command of Captain Arthur Phillip; it carried 1030 people. Seven hundred and thirty-six of them were convicts. Few of these prisoners were dangerous criminals by today's standards. They had been condemned to the new penal colony of Australia for offences that today would scarcely warrant a custodial sentence. The oldest of the

---

[223] Tim Flannery (ed.), *1788: Watkin Tench*, The Text Publishing Company, Melbourne, 1996, p. 17.
[224] Ibid., p. 19.

prisoners, Dorothy Handland, was eighty-two-years of age, a dealer in rags and old clothes. She had been sentenced to seven years for perjury. The youngest convict was a nine-year-old chimney sweep, John Hudson, sentenced to seven years for stealing some clothes and a pistol.[225] And so began a programme of mass exile in which more than 160,000 convicts would be exiled from Britain over the following seventy years. It was a Babylonian exile from which few returned.

On the afternoon of 26 January 1788, the fleet of eleven ships sailed into Sydney Harbour after a journey lasting more than eight months. This date was not the romantic beginnings of a new Jerusalem, such as the Mayflower pilgrims had sought two centuries earlier in America. As Australian writer Mark Tredinnick observes, 'Australia was not the child of nonconforming faith, nor of rebellion. It was an enactment of Britain, an attempt by that power to rid herself of people it wished gone. It began as a place of exile and became an unchosen home for many who could not leave.'[226] It was a convict settlement. In the first year of settlement five people were hanged and others were flogged repeatedly on the bare back.[227]

It is difficult to imagine the sense of desolation and abandonment that these convicts experienced in this ancient, yet alien, land. Few people in England at that time had travelled more than ten miles

---

225 Robert Hughes, *The Fatal Shore*, Pan Books, London, 1988, p. 73
226 Mark Tredinnick (ed.), *A Place on Earth*, University of New South Wales Press, Sydney, 2003, p. 41.
227 Geoffrey Blainey, *A Shorter History of Australia*, Mandarin, Port Melbourne, 1994, p. 28.

from their home. A 15,000-mile journey to the other side of the world was beyond their comprehension, an inconceivable distance.

Until comparatively recent times, home for most Australians was in England, in the Empire.

> We have stood here, farmed and cleared and built things here, but we have not grown native to the place. Our heads and hearts have been in the northern hemisphere. We took our models, looked for approval, found the syntax of our thoughts, the shape of our sentences, the grammar of our belongings, in England.[228]

After the first hundred years of European settlement most Australians still called a part of the British Isles home. 'The predominant view was that the most profound thing about being an Australian was that one was thereby a member of the British Empire.'[229]

The beginning of European settlement in Australia resonates with many themes from scripture. In the first chapter of the Bible we read that the earth was a formless void, and the divine wind swept over the waters. While not a 'formless void', there was little in this new settlement that had any place in the European imagination. Australia, as it came to be called,

> spoke to its settlers in a bafflingly foreign language – kangaroo and wombat; emu and platypus; cockatoo and kookaburra; eucalypt and waratah; aridity and sclerophylly; restrained seasonal variation; and being south of the equator, Christmas fell in summer. It is impossible to overestimate the sheer otherness of this place.

---

228 Mark Tredinnick, p. 43.
229 Edmund Campion, *Australian Catholics*, Viking, Ringwood, Vic., 1987, p. 59.

Releasing the Captive

It greeted its first white settlers 'with a landscape of bewildering and unrelenting foreignness, of scratchiness, hardness and aridity.'[230] And yet, the creation of the Australian nation emerged from the most inauspicious beginnings. In the words of today's first reading from the prophet Isaiah, 'then shall the wilderness be fertile land.... In the wilderness justice will come to live.' The Exodus story also resonates within the Australian story for they are both about people in chains being set free to build a nation.

And where was God in all of this: The first religious ceremony in the newly founded colony was held on Sunday, 3 February 1788. It was led by an Anglican minister, the Reverend Richard Johnson, under a large tree situated at what is now the intersection of Hunter, Bligh and Castlereagh Streets. With what can only have been unconscious irony he chose as the text for his sermon a verse from Psalm 116: 'What shall I render unto the Lord for all his benefits toward me?'[231]

One can imagine, writes Tom Frame, 'a variety of answers being muttered by his literally captive audience.'

Johnson ministered in the colony for the next few years, but found little interest among free settlers and convicts alike for prayer and worship. He left Australia in October 1800, returning to England a worn-out and disappointed man.[232] Patrick O'Farrell argues that

> Australia may best be understood as the first genuinely post-Christian society. Its founding fathers, in contrast with

---
230 Mark Tredinnick, p. 42.
231 Edmund Campion, *Rockchoppers*, Penguin Books, Ringwood, 1982, p. 44.
232 Tom Frame, *Losing My Religion*, University of New South Wales Press, Sydney, 2009, p. 41.

those of the American colonies, came from a society where religion was in decline and disarray, eroded by scepticism and indifference.[233]

Alfred George 'AG' Stephens, subeditor of *The Bulletin* and social commentator believed that 'the Australian environment is unfavourable to the growth of religion,' and that 'there is in the developing Australian character a sceptical and utilitarian spirit that values the present hour and refuses to sacrifice the present for any visionary future lacking a rational guarantee.'[234] The new colony was, it would seem, a child of the Enlightenment.

Many Australians claim that they are not religious, often meaning that they are not affiliated to any particular religion, or that they do not believe in God at all. However, 'worship' is an old English word that means 'to ascribe worth to', and in that sense every one is religious. People who ascribe ultimate worth to their job or their family, to money, possessions or sex, to music or some other art form, are in fact worshipping. The Bible would call such worship idolatry because it ascribes ultimate worth to something which is quite obviously finite.[235]

On the day that Cardinal Joseph Ratzinger was to be elected bishop of Rome, 18 April 2005, he presided and preached at the Mass *Pro Eligendo Romano Pontifice* (For the Election of the Roman Pontiff) in his role as dean of the College of Cardinals. In the homily,

---

233 Patrick O'Farrell, *The Catholic Church and Community in Australia*, Nelson, West Melbourne, 1977, p. 17.
234 Quoted in Tom Frame, p. 60.
235 Bruce Wilson, *Can God Survive in Australia?*, An Albatross Book, Sutherland, NSW, 1983, p. 204.

Ratzinger spoke about the 'dictatorship of relativism that does not recognize anything as definitive and whose ultimate goal consists solely of one's ego and desires.'[236]

Clive Hamilton, Executive Director of the Australia Institute, and Richard Denniss, Deputy Director of the same Institute, have published a political document, The Wellbeing Manifesto. They note that today's Australians are three times richer than their parents and grandparents were in the 1950s, but they are not happier. They conclude that Australians worry 'that we have become too selfish, materialistic and superficial and long for a society built on mutual respect, self-restraint and generosity of spirit.'[237]

Today's gospel warns us not to worry about our life and what we are to eat, nor about our body and how we are to clothe it. We are exhorted to set our hearts on God's kingdom, and all else will follow.[238] Even if many Australians are indifferent to religion and find it irrelevant to how they choose to live, our lives as disciples of Jesus are based upon on his words and works, and by the conviction that his death and resurrection have transformed human history. With Simon Peter we can say: 'Lord, to whom shall we go? You have the message of eternal life' (Jn 6:68).

---

236 Quoted in George Weigel, *The Cube and the Cathedral*, pp. 186-7.
237 Clive Hamilton and Richard Denniss, *Affluenza*, Allen & Unwin Crows Nest, NSW, 2005, pp. 217, 224.
238 The lectionary offers two gospel readings for Australia Day. I have chosen Lk 12: 22-32.

Reflections for the year of Mark

THE ASSUMPTION OF THE BLESSED VIRGIN MARY

And Mary said, 'My soul proclaims the greatness of the Lord and my spirit rejoices in God my Saviour.' (Lk 1:46)

The Abbey of the Dormition of the Virgin Mary dominates what today is known as Mount Zion, just south of the old city of Jerusalem. The present-day abbey was built in the early twentieth century for Kaiser Wilhelm II and was inspired by the cathedral in Aachen, Germany, where Charlemagne is buried. It commemorates the place of Our Lady's 'dormition' or 'falling asleep'.

The New Testament is silent about the death of Our Lady, but the first account of her burial comes from the *Transitus Mariae*, an anonymous work whose substance may be as early as the second or third centuries. In this document Mary is buried not on Mount Zion, but in a cavern in the Valley of Jehoshaphat (close by the Garden of Gethsemane). A church on that site – some distance from the present Dormition Abbey – had been built by the sixth century. This church was possibly destroyed by the Persians in 614, but it was rebuilt, because Arculf, writing in 670 AD, describes what he saw: 'It is a church built at two levels, and the lower part, which is beneath a stone vault, has a remarkable round shape. At the east end there is an altar, on the right of which is the empty rock tomb in which for a time Mary remained entombed.' This church was destroyed by the caliph Hakim in 1178, but by 1130 the Benedictines had rebuilt the double church. The superstructure of this church was destroyed by Saladin in 1187.

Another ancient tradition had Our Lady living, and dying, in Ephesus, where she lived with St John. It is still possible to visit the site of Mary's house in Ephesus. However in 451 Juvenal, the patriarch of Jerusalem, persuaded the emperor, Marcian, that Jerusalem had the better case.[239] But note, the Jerusalem church claimed only to be the place where Mary was buried, not where her body remained.

A narrative known as the *Euthymiaca Historia* (possibly written in the fifth century) relates how Emperor Marcian and his wife Pulcheria requested relics of the Virgin Mary from Juvenal while he was attending the Council of Chalcedon (451). According to the account, Juvenal replied that, on the third day after her burial, Mary's tomb was discovered to be empty, only her shroud being preserved in the church in Jerusalem. And that's a point worth pondering. There never has been a serious claim in Christian history about any site holding the mortal remains of Mary. Although the bodily assumption of Mary into heaven was only defined as an article of Catholic faith in 1950, it has long been accepted as part of Christian tradition.

Devotion to Our Lady has been an obstacle to Catholicism for many Protestants. But many Catholics have also struggled with Marian devotion. George Weigel, the biographer of Pope John Paul

---

[239] Jerome Murphy-O'Connor, *The Holy Land*, 1992, pp. 134-5.

II, tells us that 'Mary was also a bit of an obstacle at one point in the spiritual journey of a very Catholic young Pole named Karol Wojtyla, who grew up in a land of Marian piety and later became Pope John Paul II.' In *Gift and Mystery* the pope wrote of his struggle to discern his Christian vocation. He felt burdened by the traditional Marian piety of his birthplace: 'I began to question my devotion to Mary, believing that, if it became too great, it might end up compromising the supremacy of the worship owed to Christ.' It was through reading *True Devotion to Mary*, a work by the French theologian St Louis Grignion de Montfort (1673–1716), that he came to understand that all true Marian piety was Christ-centred. Mary was and remains a privileged vehicle for meeting her Son.[240]

Devotion to Our Lady is not an end in itself; she points us towards her Son. In fact, the last words of Mary recorded in the gospels are her instructions to the waiters at the wedding feast of Cana, recorded in the Gospel of St John. Her words say it all: 'Do whatever he tells you.' George Weigel puts it concisely:

> Mary is the unique witness who, from the moment of the Incarnation, always points beyond herself ... to her son. And because her son in the flesh is also the incarnate Son of God, by pointing us to her son Mary also points us into the heart of the Trinity.[241]

As the Dogmatic Constitution on the Church (*Lumen Gentium*) points out, quoting 1 Timothy 2:5-6, 'there is but one God and one

---

240 George Weigel, *Letters to a Young Catholic*, p. 55.
241 Ibid., p. 56.

mediator of God and men, the man Christ Jesus'. But Mary's role in the Christian story in no way 'obscures or diminishes this unique mediation of Christ, but rather shows its power.'[242]

Although the tomb of the Virgin near Gethsemane has better historical and archeological credentials for claiming to be the place where Our Lady was buried, I have always found the Dormition Abbey a far more compelling sacred space. In the crypt beneath the main church there is a life-sized statue of the Virgin, 'asleep,' carved from ivory and cherry wood. If you're lucky enough to spend some time there in silence, undisturbed by the constant procession of tourists and pilgrims, it is a beautiful place to ponder on Mary's place in the Christian story.

I invite you to look at Leonardo da Vinci's painting of the annunciation and Andy Warhol's adaptation of this ancient masterpiece, both of which are readily accessible on the internet.[243] Warhol has narrowed the scope of the original, portraying only the hands of Gabriel and Mary. He has, however, highlighted a distant mountain between these two figures that is barely noticeable in Leonardo's original painting.

The mountain in Judaeo-Christian iconography is the place of encounter with the divine, and so by making that more prominent Warhol has highlighted the essential message of the annunciation: the divine Word comes down 'from above' and becomes flesh in the womb of the Virgin.

---

242 *Lumen Gentium*, n. 60.
243 Cf. Gerald O'Collins and Mario Farrugia, *Catholicism*, Oxford University Press, 2003, p. 370.

Through Mary's fiat the transcendent becomes immanent and dwells among us, and in her acceptance of God's invitation we are given the pattern of Christian discipleship.

Mary is rightly acclaimed as first among the disciples, and so it is only fitting that she anticipates what God intends for all of us: 'A bodily resurrection to eternal life forever, within the light and love of the Trinity.' Mary's assumption is 'our destiny because we, too, have been configured to Christ, the son of Mary and the Son of God.' She is the 'first to experience the fullness of that which awaits all the saved.'[244]

So let us make Mary's fiat our own; let us heed her words to the servants at Cana: 'Do whatever he tells you.' Mary didn't look for an 'exit strategy', and nor should we. We are called 'to live in trust, not in calculation.' If we do as he tells us, as Mary asks us to do, we'll find 'the path to happiness, wholeness, and holiness that you will never find by keeping your options open.'[245]

---

[244] George Weigel, *Letters to a Young Catholic*, p. 58.
[245] Ibid., p. 62.

FEAST OF ALL SAINTS

I saw a huge number, impossible to count, of people from every nation, race, tribe and language. (Rev 7:9)

Pope John Paul II canonised 465 saints and was responsible for about 1300 beatifications. That exceeds all the canonisations and beatifications of the past four hundred years. One of the features of Pope John Paul's lengthy papacy was the way in which he revolutionised and dramatically speeded up the whole process of creating saints. The case of Mother Teresa, who died in 1997, is an obvious example; the late pope waived the customary period of five years that is supposed to elapse before the process can begin, and beatified her in 2003. Some time ago Pope Benedict was interviewed by four German broadcast journalists, one of whom raised the question of the huge number of canonisations under his predecessor. The pope responded diplomatically:

> In the beginning I also thought that the large number of beatifications was almost overwhelming and that perhaps we needed to be more selective; choosing figures that entered our consciousness more clearly.

The pope went on to say that he had decentralised beatifications

> in order to make these figures more visible in the specific places they came from. Perhaps a saint from Guatemala doesn't interest us in Germany and vice versa ... I've also

seen how these beatifications in different places touch vast numbers of people and that people say: 'At last, this one is one of us!' They pray to him and are inspired.²⁴⁶

Sadly, we don't always say, 'At last, this is one of us!' Instead, we're often tempted to say 'Oh, well, he or she could do those things because, after all, they were saints. But that's not for me.'²⁴⁷

Dorothy Day (1897–1980), an American convert to Catholicism was known for her social justice campaigns in defence of the poor, forsaken, hungry and homeless. She truly hungered for what is right. She is now a candidate for canonisation, but long before her death on 29 November 1980, many people already regarded her as a saint. She made it quite clear during her lifetime that she didn't want to become a saint: 'Don't call me a saint. I don't want to be dismissed so easily.' Dorothy Day

> didn't want people to think that what she did was extraordinary because what she did – loving God and neighbour – was in fact to be the ordinary way any Christian should live. She protested that loving God and neighbour wasn't meant to be unusual or artificially elevated to the stuff of sainthood, out of the reach of ordinary people. It was simply what everyday Christians were meant to do.²⁴⁸

A saintly life is not out of the reach of ordinary people. Saints are people who tried to embody the gospel message; people who

---

246 An edited version of the interview, broadcast on Vatican Radio on 13 August 2006, appeared in *The Tablet*, 19 August 2006, pp. 8-9.
247 William J. Bausch, *60 More Seasonal Homilies*, Twenty-Third Publications, Mystic, CT, 2003, p. 172.
248 Ibid.

responded to the call of God manifested through the 'signs of the times'; people who made the gospel come alive in their own day and in their own culture.

It is one thing to say that God is compassionate and loving; it is quite another thing altogether to experience God's love and compassion manifested in the life of someone like Dorothy Day. Not long after he was elected pope, John XXIII (now Blessed Pope John) visited Regina Coeli prison, telling the prisoners that since they couldn't come to see him, he had come to see them. He then told them that he had come from a poor family and explained, 'There are only three ways of losing money in Italy: farming, gambling, and women. My father chose the least interesting way.'

He went on to tell them that one of his brothers had been caught poaching, and an uncle had done time. 'These are the things that happen to poor people,' he said, and then added, 'But we are all children of God. And I; I am your brother.'

The audience, from priests to politicians, from convicts to jailers, wept openly. Suddenly, a murderer dared to approach the pope and ask: 'Can there be forgiveness for me?'

In answer, Pope John just took the murderer in his arms and hugged him, heedless of all danger to his person, let alone to his dignity.[249]

Saints are icons. The word icon is used rather loosely these days – almost anyone or anything, it seems, can become an icon – but in its

---

[249] William J. Bausch, *40 More Seasonal Homilies*, Twenty-Third Publications, Mystic, CT, 2005, p. 79.

original sense the word refers to a sacred image – painted according to certain stylised conventions – that functions as a window into the sacred. To be more precise, an icon is 'written', not 'painted', by an iconographer, for whom the work is both a vocation and a form of prayer.[250] We need people like Dorothy Day and John XXIII, whose lives were vibrant expressions of the gospel, whose lives gave us a glimpse into something greater.

But we also need to acknowledge that Catholics do not have an exclusive franchise on sanctity. Secular society also 'canonises' those whom they deem worthy. Consider the public outpouring of public emotion following the tragic death of Steve Irwin. Steve, the crocodile hunter, was an individual without guile, a man passionately devoted to wildlife and conservation. As the habitat for wildlife continues to decrease, Steve took a prophetic stance, buying huge tracts of land in Australia and overseas to protect and restore the habitat for native species. I doubt that Steve Irwin knew anything at all about the theology of ecology, but he certainly cared for the earth and its creatures.

Fred Hollows is another secular saint – a man of great compassion who worked tirelessly for people in third world countries. Thanks to his hard work and vision, more than one million people around the world can see today. In the 1970s, Fred dedicated three years to visiting indigenous communities in rural Australia with a team of colleagues to survey and provide eye-care services. He championed the treatment of trachoma and other eye diseases that were

---

250 George Weigel, *Letters to a Young Catholic*, p. 36.

prevalent among Aboriginal people. He visited over 465 Aboriginal communities and screened 100,000 people. His team treated 27,000 people trachoma and performed 1000 operations. In 1985 he turned down the Order of Australia in protest at the state of Aboriginal health. What motivated Fred? He explained it with his characteristic disdain for waffle: 'I believe that the basic attribute of mankind is to look after each other.' That sounds suspiciously similar to something in the gospels!

Jesus summed up the law and the prophets succinctly:

> Love God and your neighbour. This is not something over and above daily life, but the very kernel and heart of daily life, the springboard for our actions, the basis for our decisions, the grounding of our prayer life, the motivation of our careers, the purpose of our being here.[251]

It is the call to sanctity.

---

[251] William J. Bausch, *60 More Seasonal Homilies*, p. 172.

FEAST OF ALL SOULS

I am going now to prepare a place for you, and after I have gone and prepared you a place, I shall return to take you to myself, so that you may be with me where I am. (Jn 14:1-3)

Although the General Instruction of the Roman Missal and the *Order of Christian Funerals* do not condone[252] the eulogy, it has become part of the liturgical landscape. I believe there is a place within the funeral liturgy to reflect upon the life of the deceased, and that is best done by someone who has known the person well. *Order of Christian Funerals* makes provision for 'A member or a friend of the family' to speak 'in remembrance of the deceased before the final commendation begins.'[253]

A Christian funeral is about storytelling. Those attending the funeral liturgy are there because, in one way or another, the life of the deceased person has touched their own life, and through that love and friendship their human journey has been blessed and enriched.

---

[252] GIRM 382: 'At the funeral Mass there should, as a rule, be a short homily, but never a eulogy of any kind.' *The Order of Christian Funerals* repeats the prohibition: 'A brief homily based in the readings should always be given at the funeral liturgy, but never any kind of eulogy.' (n. 141).
[253] *The Order of Christian Funerals*, n. 171.

But even more importantly, in a Christian funeral the deceased person's story resonates within a far greater story, our faith story.

This was symbolised rather beautifully during the funeral of Pope John Paul II. The pope's pinewood coffin was placed directly on the ground and upon it, in accordance with his wishes, lay an open copy of the gospels. Here was a man who sought to live his life under the word of God, and now in death he lay, quite literally, beneath that word.

On the feast of All Souls we gather to pray for the dead. But we also gather to give thanks for lives that have embodied, however imperfectly, the word of God, and thereby given us fleeting glimpses of the transcendent. Since this applies to 'all saints' as well as to 'all souls', what is the difference between these two liturgical celebrations? An Anglican publication describes the differing emphasis of the two days in these words:

> psychologically and liturgically, there is a need for a day that is seen to be about our own departed, rather than the heroes of the faith, and that acknowledges human grief and fragility in a way that would hardly find a place when we celebrate the triumphs of the great ones on All Saints' Day.[254]

The former Anglican bishop of Durham, Tom Wright, argues that today's commemoration of all the faithful departed pulls the feast of All Saints 'out of shape.'[255]

He believes that these two days, celebrated back to back, split off 'so-called ordinary Christians from these so-called "great ones" in a

---

254 Quoted in N.T. Wright, *For All the Saints?* Morehouse Publishing, Harrisburg, PA, 2003, p. 48.
255 Ibid., p. 47.

way that the latter would have been the first to repudiate.' We have

> collectively forgotten just what a wonderful thing the gospel is: that our 'own departed' are themselves 'heroes of the faith' just as much as Peter, Paul, Mary, James, John and the rest. What makes the 'great ones' great is precisely that they, too, knew human grief and frailty.[256]

Bishop Wright has a point. The lives of the saints are inspiring, but our veneration can easily become 'a distant admiration of people who are not like us.'[257] It is often the faithful witness of people who will never be canonised that has the most profound effect upon us. My mother died from cancer at the age of 48.

I was a seminarian at the time, and I have kept all the letters that she wrote to me, from the day that I left home in 1965 until shortly before her death in 1969.

I grew up in Sydney, but completed most of my studies for the priesthood in Melbourne. My family drove me to the airport on 1 February 1965, and a day or two later I wrote home to let them know that I had arrived safely and that all was well. My mother's first letter, dated 6 February, begins thus:

> It was lovely to receive your letter and to hear that you had such a good trip. We stood and watched your plane out of sight and if you could have seen the sad household and known how much you were missed, you ego would have gone up several points. However, I have reached a happier frame of mind and am hoping we'll be able to get down (to Melbourne) in May.

---

256 Ibid., p. 49.
257 Ibid.

Mum's letters were full of family news, but very little else. They contain a week by week description of what my brothers were up to, and occasional news about old school friends. From reading these letters you wouldn't know which political party was in power at the time, or that Australia was involved in the Vietnam War.

Mum typed most of her letters but from 5 May 1969 onwards they are handwritten, and this was the first indication that something was wrong: 'I'm having a bit of trouble with my left arm and I can't type very well with it.'

The letter Mum wrote the following week contained ominous news. 'I went to the doctor who sent me to a specialist and it would seem that I have a tumour of some sort in my left breast.'

She died just over four months later. On the night before my mother died, my father and I were seated by her bedside at St Vincent's Hospital. Despite the great difficulty she had in breathing, I recall her removing her oxygen mask and saying quietly, 'I want to go home.'

We both knew that there was no likelihood of her returning home, but to comfort her, my father said, 'Don't worry, dear, we'll have you home in no time at all.' She replied, and these were the last words I remember my mother saying: 'No, I don't mean that home.'

At the end of her earthly pilgrimage my mother took shelter under the word of God. Jesus tells us, 'Do not let your hearts be troubled. You trust in God, trust also in me.' And he goes on to assure us, 'I am going now to prepare a place for you, and after I have gone and prepared you a place, I shall return to take you to myself, so that you may be with me where I am' (Jn 14:1-3). And where is that place? Jesus tells us that it is his 'Father's house' – his own home in heaven.

If my mother loved life in our family home, she will surely not be disappointed in what St Paul calls our true homeland in heaven (Phil 3:20).

BAPTISM OF THE LORD (FIRST SUNDAY IN ORDINARY TIME)

(YEAR B)

You are my Son, the Beloved; my favour rests on you. (Mk 1:11).

In the fourth episode of the television series Rome, centurion Lucius Voranus is accused of deserting the legion. He responds, 'I am no deserter. My time was served, I abided my sacrament.' The 'sacrament' (*sacramentum*, in the Latin) he referred to was the Roman soldier's oath of allegiance to his commander and to the gods of Rome. At some time during the second century Christians borrowed this term to describe the ceremonies by which one became a Christian. The three rituals of initiation – baptism, confirmation and eucharist – were similar to an oath of allegiance, not to a military commander or to pagan gods, but to Christ. We begin our Christian life by publicly proclaiming our allegiance to Christ through the sacrament of baptism. Unlike the Jewish tradition, where a person is born Jewish if their mother is Jewish, nobody is ever born a Christian.

Baptism is a Greek word. The verb baptise in (*baptisma* is the noun) means 'to dip in or under', 'to immerse', 'to bathe' or 'to wash'.[258] Originally baptism involved plunging a person right into the water, a practice known today as baptism by immersion. The first full description of the rite of baptism that we possess comes from Hippolytus's *Apostolic Tradition*, an early manual of church life and discipline that probably reflects the practice in Rome at the end of the second century. Adults and children go down into the water (naked!), and they are asked three questions. 'Do you believe in God the Father Almighty?' The catechumen (the candidate for baptism) replies 'I believe' and is then plunged beneath water. Upon emerging they are asked, 'Do you believe in Jesus Christ, the Son of God, who was born of the Holy Spirit and the Virgin Mary, who was crucified under Pontius Pilate, and died, and rose on the third day living from the dead, and ascended into heaven, and sat down at the right hand of the Father, the one coming to judge the living and the dead?' After answering 'I believe' they are immersed a second time. And finally, 'Do you believe in the Holy Spirit and the Holy Church and the resurrection of the flesh?' They are immersed a third time after answering 'I believe.'

An earlier church manual, *The Didache* (literally, 'The Teaching of the Twelve Apostles, (c. 100 or 120 AD) makes provision for cases where water is scarce:

> But with respect to baptism, baptize as follows ... (B)aptize in the name of the Father and of the Son and of the Holy Spirit,

---

[258] Gerhard Kittel & Gerhard Friedrich (eds) *Theological Dictionary of the New Testament*, abridged in one volume by Geoffrey W. Bromiley (William B. Eerdmans Publishing Company, 1985), pp. 92-4; Horst Balz and Gerhard Schneider, *Exegetical Dictionary of the New Testament, Volume 1*, William B. Eerdmans Publishing Company, Grand Rapids, MI, 1990, pp. 192-6.

in running water. But if you do not have running water, baptize in some other water. And if you cannot baptize in cold water, use warm. But if you have neither, pour water on the head three times in the name of the Father and Son and Holy Spirit.[259]

Sometimes symbolism has to be adjusted to physical necessity.

Jesus begins his public ministry when he is baptised by John in the waters of the Jordan. John preached 'a baptism of repentance for the forgiveness of sins.' (Lk 3:3). But why did Jesus, the sinless one, need to be baptised by John? Well, on one level, Jesus expressed his solidarity with sinful humanity. In the words of Pope Benedict: 'Jesus loaded the burden of all mankind's guilt upon his shoulders; he bore it down into the depths of the Jordan. He inaugurated his public activity by stepping into the place of sinners.'[260]

Going down into the waters of the Jordan, Jesus also symbolically enacted his future death and burial; emerging from the waters, he ritually proclaimed his rising from the tomb. He submitted himself entirely to his Father's will.[261] And that is precisely what happens to us at our baptism. St Paul told the Christians living in Rome,

> You have been taught that when we were baptized in Christ Jesus we were baptized in his death; in other words, when we were baptized we went into the tomb with him and joined him in death, so that as Christ was raised from the dead by the Father's glory, we too might live a new life. If in union with Christ we have imitated his death, we shall also imitate him in his resurrection (Rom 6:3-5).

---

[259] Bart D. Ehrman, *Lost Scriptures*, Oxford University Press, 2003, p. 211.
[260] Joseph Ratzinger (Pope Benedict XVI), *Jesus of Nazareth*, Doubleday, New York, 2007, p. 18.
[261] *Catechism of the Catholic Church*, n. 536.

During the Mass of Christian Burial the coffin is sprinkled with holy water, a powerful gesture, especially if the water is drawn from the baptismal font. Through the waters of baptism we were born again from the womb of the church. As our body awaits the tomb the same baptismal waters herald our entry into life eternal. At the end of our earthly pilgrimage we arrive where we started.

Baptism is also the sacrament, par excellence, for the forgiveness of sin. In the words of the *Catechism of the Catholic Church*, baptism, 'signifies and actually brings about death to sin and entry into the life of the Most Holy Trinity.'[262] While the plural 'sins' refers to sinful acts, the singular 'sin' refers to a sinful condition.[263]

St Paul experienced that condition as a civil war raging within. In his letter to the Romans (7:15-20) he writes:

> I do not understand my own behaviour ... Though the will to do good is in me, the power to do it is not: the good thing I want to do, I never do; the evil thing which I do not want – that is what I do.

The American monk Thomas Merton experienced this sinful condition as a false self:

> To say I was born in sin is to say I came into the world with a false self. I was born with a mask. I came into existence under a sign of contradiction, being someone that I was never intended to be and therefore a denial of what I am supposed to be.

---

262 Ibid., n. 1239.
263 Raymond E. Brown, *The Gospel According to John*, p. 56.

Life is therefore a lifelong pilgrimage, a quest for the authentic self.

> Every one of us is shadowed by an illusory person: a false self. ... My false and private self is the one who wants to exist outside the reach of God's will and God's love – outside of reality and outside of life. And such a self cannot help but be an illusion.[264]

Lucy demonstrates the same truth to Linus when she draws a picture of a heart, one side of which is shaded. 'This, Linus, is a picture of the human heart! One side is filled with hate and the other side is filled with love. These are the two forces which are constantly at war with each other.' 'I think I know what you mean,' replies Linus. 'I can feel them fighting.' Although we acknowledge what is good and right, like St Paul we often find ourselves unable to do it:

> I do not understand my own behaviour ... Though the will to do good is in me, the power to do it is not: the good thing I want to do, I never do; the evil thing which I do not want – that is what I do. (Romans 7:15-20).

Charlie Brown confides in Lucy: 'All it would take to make me happy is to have someone say he likes me.' 'Are you sure?' she replies. 'Of course I'm sure!' 'You mean you'd be happy if someone merely said he or she likes you? Do you mean to tell me that someone has it within his or her power to make you happy merely by doing such a simple thing?' Charlie is adamant. 'Yes! That's exactly what I mean!' Lucy seems almost won over. 'Well, I don't think that's asking too much ... I really don't. But you're sure now? All you want is to have

---

[264] Thomas Merton, *New Seeds of Contemplation*, Burns & Oates, London, repr. 2003, p. 33.

someone say, "I like you, Charlie Brown" and then you'll be happy?' 'And then I'll be happy!' Lucy turns and walks away: 'I can't do it!'[265]

This sinful condition – we've traditionally called it original sin – transcends the sinful acts of any individual. It seeps deep into the very fibre of a society, and over a period of time it warps our judgment and distorts our vision.

Take the case of slavery, for example. By the late 18th century over 11 million African men, women and children had been captured and taken as slaves to the West Indies and the American colonies. Great Britain was the superpower of the day, and much of its wealth was dependent upon slave labour. The slave trade was considered acceptable by all but a few.

The story of the abolition of slavery in the British Empire is powerfully told in *Amazing Grace*, a film that focuses upon the courageous battle waged by William Wilberforce and his associates. British ships carried black slaves from Africa, in terrible conditions, to the West Indies as commodities to be bought and sold. As Wilberforce courageously began his campaign against powerful and vested interests, the opposition seemed insurmountable, and for eighteen years he regularly introduced anti-slavery motions in parliament. In 1807, the slave trade was finally abolished, but this did not free those who were already slaves. Wilberforce retired from politics in 1825 and died on 29 July 1833, shortly after the act to free slaves in the British Empire passed through the House of Commons.

---

265 Charles Schulz, *The Complete Peanuts*, 1959 to 1960, Fantagraphics Books, Seattle WA, 2006, pp. 163, 272.

Releasing the Captive

In the movie's version of events, Wilberforce is influenced by John Newton, author of the well-known hymn *Amazing Grace*. After serving in the British navy, Newton joined the crew of a slave ship, and eventually became captain of his own vessel, also a slave trader. By this stage he had long since given up any religious convictions, but on a homeward voyage, while steering the ship through a violent storm, he experienced what he was to refer to later as his 'great deliverance'. He recorded in his journal that when all seemed lost and the ship would surely sink, he cried out, 'Lord, have mercy upon us.' Later in his cabin he reflected upon what he had said and began to believe that God had delivered him from the ravages of the storm and that grace had begun to work within him. He abandoned the slave trade and became an Anglican priest, although the fate of the 20,000 slaves he had transported over a period of twenty years continued to haunt him.

In a memorable scene from the movie, the aged and now blind Newton tells Wilberforce, 'I wish I could remember all their names, my 20,000 ghosts. They all had names, beautiful African names.' In tears he confesses, 'I'm a great sinner, and Christ is a great Saviour.' In the words of his best-known hymn:

> Amazing grace, how sweet the sound,
> That saved a wretch like me.
> I once was lost, but now I'm found
> Was blind, but now I see.

Wilberforce would undoubtedly have seen the abolition of slavery as a victory for God's amazing grace, granting sight to those who were blind, and finding those who were lost. It was the grace of baptism triumphant over the sin of the world.

Reflections for the year of Mark

SECOND SUNDAY IN ORDINARY TIME

(YEAR B)

'Rabbi, where do you live?' 'Come and see,' he replied. (Jn 1:38-39).

We are now in Year B of the church's liturgical calendar, the year of Mark. Since Mark's gospel is rather brief the gospel readings during the months of Ordinary Time will occasionally come from the gospel of John, as it does today.

The theme of today's readings is the call to discipleship. The first reading tells the story of the prophet Samuel's call and the gospel presents John's account of the call of Peter and Andrew. Next week we'll listen to Mark's version of the same incident.

The Lord called Samuel over a thousand years before Jesus called his disciples, and it happened like this. Samuel's mother, Hannah, had been unable to conceive, but when at last she gave birth to a son, she dedicated him to the Lord. The young Samuel therefore lived with Eli the priest at the shrine of Shiloh, where the Ark of the Covenant was kept.

While he slept in the holy place he heard a voice calling him by name, 'Samuel! Samuel!' Thinking it was Eli, he ran to the priest. 'Here I am, since you called me.' But Eli replied, 'I did not call you.

Go back to bed.' This happened a second and a third time. Eli then realised that it was the Lord who was calling the boy, so he said to Samuel, 'Go and lie down, and if someone calls say, "Speak, Lord, your servant is listening."'

And so, when the Lord called the boy again, he replied as Eli had instructed him, 'Speak, Lord, your servant is listening.'

God's call demands that we listen. That's a lesson I have yet to learn. More often than not, my prayer is, 'Listen, Lord, your servant is speaking!'

As John's gospel tells the story of Peter and Andrew, their call to discipleship goes through three stages. First, John's gospel tells us that Andrew and his unnamed companion are disciples of John the Baptist. If they were John's disciples they must have been seeking God's will, and that is the first step on any spiritual quest.

But then John directs them to someone else. As Jesus passes by, John says, 'Look, there is the Lamb of God.' When Jesus turns and sees Andrew and his friend following him, he asks, 'What do you want?' They ask, 'Where do you live?' and Jesus replies, 'Come and see.' They do, and their lives are transformed. This is the second step on our journey of faith – the Christian life is about meeting a person rather than finding answers.

A young man, a spiritual seeker, once journeyed into the desert to visit an elderly monk. He found the monk sitting by the entrance to his hermitage with his dog sprawled out lazily nearby. The young man asked the monk a question, 'Why is it, Abba, that some who seek God come to the desert and are zealous in prayer but leave after a year or so, while others, like you, remain faithful to the quest for a lifetime?'

The old man smiled and replied, 'Let me tell you a story: One day I was sitting here quietly in the sun with my dog. Suddenly a large white rabbit ran across in front of us. Well, my dog jumped up, barking loudly, and took off after the rabbit. He chased the rabbit over the hills with a passion. Soon, other dogs joined him, attracted by his barking. What a sight it was, as the pack of dogs ran barking across stony embankments and through thickets and thorns! Gradually, however, one by one, the other dogs dropped out of the pursuit, discouraged by the harsh terrain and frustrated by the chase. Only my dog continued to pursue the white rabbit. In that story, young man, is the answer to your question.'

The young man sat in confused silence. Finally, he said, "Abba, I don't understand. What is the connection between the rabbit chase and the quest for holiness?"

"You fail to understand," answered the old hermit, "because you haven't asked the obvious question. Why didn't the other dogs continue on the chase?"

And the answer to that question is, "They had not seen the rabbit."'

By way of analogy, Jesus is the rabbit (not lamb!) of God, and Andrew and his companion spent the remainder of the day with Jesus. What did he say that changed their lives? They were transformed by who Jesus was, not by what he said. We know this because when Andrew meets his brother Simon early the following morning he doesn't say, 'Let me tell you what I heard yesterday.' Rather, he takes Simon to Jesus. And here we come to the third step on the journey of faith – sharing that faith with others. Andrew can't wait to bring his brother to Jesus. It's interesting to note that the few times we meet Andrew in the gospels, he's bringing people to Jesus. Here it's his brother Simon; later we'll hear of him bringing the boy with the five barley loaves and two fish to Jesus (Jn 6:9), and later on he introduces a gentile delegation to Jesus (Jn 12:22).

Let me make some further observations about God's call. First, it is a call to use the gifts that God has given me, to be my authentic self. Jules Pfeiffer is an American playwright and satirical cartoonist. One of his cartoons features a teenager named Danny, who is thinking out aloud:

> Ever since I was a little kid I didn't want to be me. I wanted to be like Billy Whittleton, and Billy didn't even like me. I walked like he walked; I talked like he talked. I signed up for the same high school he signed up for. It was during high school that Billy Whittleton changed. He began to hang around with Herbie Vanderman. He walked like Herbie Vanderman; he talked like Herbie Vanderman. And then it dawned on me that Herbie Vanderman walked and talked like Joey Hamerlin. And Joey Hamerlin walked and talked like Corky Fabinson. So here I am, walking and talking like Billy Whittleton's imitation of Herbie Vanderman's version of Joey Hamerlin trying to walk and talk like Corky Fabinson. And who do you think Corky Fabinson is always walking and talking like? Of all people, dopey Kenny Wellington – that utter twit who tries to walk and talk like ... me![266]

---

[266] Quoted in William J. Bausch, *The Yellow Brick Road*, Twenty-Third Publications, Mystic, CT, 1999, p. 85.

Reflections for the year of Mark

There is, alas, something of James Thurber's Walter Mitty in all of us. Second, there is no statute of limitation on God's call. In 1958 Angelo Roncalli was elected pope at the age of 78. It is difficult to know for certain what the College of Cardinals had in mind, but some have suggested that Roncalli was elected to be a mere caretaker pope. John XXIII was anything but a caretaker pope; by summoning the Second Vatican Council he inaugurated a great era of renewal within the church. Roncalli had kept a journal for most of his adult life and it has been published under the title, *Journal of a Soul*. One entry in his journal was written during a retreat he made at the Benedictine abbey of Solesmes during Holy Week of 1945. He was then aged 64. The journal entry reads:

> I must not disguise from myself the truth: I am definitely approaching old age. My mind resents this and almost rebels, for I still feel so young, eager, agile and alert. But one look in my mirror disillusions me.[267]

It was to be another 13 years before Angelo Roncalli was elected pope, at the age of 78, taking the name John XXIII. As Pope John XXIII he instigated a monumental period of renewal in the church. And let us also remember Pope Benedict XVI, also elected to the papacy at the age of 78, several years beyond the mandatory retirement age for bishops.

As Cardinal Joseph Ratzinger, he had been Prefect of the Sacred Congregation for the Doctrine of the Faith and President of the Pontifical Biblical Commission from 1981 until the death of Pope

---

267 Pope John XXIII, *Journal of a Soul*, Geoffrey Chapman, London, 1965, p. 264.

Releasing the Captive

John Paul II in 2005. With the pope's death I'm sure he was looking forward to retirement and the opportunity to complete a major study on Jesus that he had begun writing in 2003.

The God of surprises had other ideas, and the greatest challenge of his ministry now lay ahead of him as the newly-elected bishop of Rome. The call to discipleship doesn't have a use-by date.

Reflections for the year of Mark

THIRD SUNDAY IN ORDINARY TIME

(YEAR B)

Come after me and I will make you into fishers of people. (Mk 1:17)

The first reading from the prophet Jonah and today's gospel are stories about a call. Jonah is called to preach repentance to the Ninevites, and Jesus calls Simon and Andrew, and James and John. The book of Jonah is really a parable, a didactic tale, written for Jews in the wake of their return from exile in Babylon. Still scarred by the memory of exile, Jews of the time were inward-looking and hostile to foreigners. The prophecy of Jonah rejects this narrow nationalism and proclaims that God's mercy extends even to Israel's enemies. Nineveh is the capital city of Assyria, a nation that has always been hostile and cruel to Israel. Jonah received a divine call to preach repentance to the people of Nineveh, but he despised the Ninevites and longed for their destruction. If he preached repentance they might repent and be spared. And so, to escape the divine call, Jonah defiantly headed off in the opposite direction, boarding a vessel sailing for Tarshish – in Spain.

Here we have a perennial theme – escaping the call. The English poet Francis Thompson (1859–1907) describes the attempt to escape in his best known poem, *The Hound of Heaven*:

> I fled Him, down the nights and down the days;
> I fled Him, down the arches of the years;
> I fled Him, down the labyrinthine ways
> Of my own mind; and in the mist of tears
> I hid from Him, and under running laughter.[268]

But Jonah's attempt to escape is futile. A great storm arose and the sailors cast lots to discover the culprit. The lot pointed to Jonah. At Jonah's instigation the sailors cast him overboard and at once the sea subsided. Jonah was then swallowed by a huge fish, and he remained in the belly of the fish for three days and three nights. The fish then spewed Jonah out upon the dry land, and a second time he heard the word of the Lord, 'Go to Nineveh.' This is where today's first reading commences.

Jonah preached repentance, and much to his dismay the Ninevites renounced their evil ways and God relented. The point of this short parable – it's only about three pages long in most translations of the Bible – becomes clear only when we read the conclusion. God spared the Ninevites and Jonah leaves the city, sulking. In fact, the Bible says 'he fell into a rage'.

Feeling really sorry for himself he prays, 'So now Lord, please take my life, for I might as well be dead as go on living.' Jonah sits

---

[268] Francis Thompson, *The Poems of Francis Thompson*, Oxford University Press, London, 1937, p. 89.

down to rest, and God ordains that a castor-oil plant should grow up over Jonah to 'give shade for his head and soothe his ill-humour.' Jonah was delighted with the castor-oil plant. However, the next day God ordained that a worm should attacks the castor-oil plant and it dies, much to Jonah's dismay. Jonah is left exposed to a scorching east wind and the full blast of the sun's rays. Here is the lesson. God reprimands Jonah for being upset over the castor-oil plant, but totally oblivious to the fate of more than 120,000 Ninevites. Jonah must learn to see differently. The Ninevites are not enemies to be destroyed, but misguided people to be saved.

Jesus began his public ministry with the call, 'Repent, and believe the Good News.' The Greek word for repentance in Mark's gospel is *metanoia*, which means literally 'a change of mind'. *Metanoia* is ultimately about a new way of seeing. Writing to the Christians of Rome, St Paul exhorted them, 'Do not model your behaviour on the contemporary world, but let the renewing of your minds transform you ...' (12:2). *Metanoia* is not about seeing anything different; it is about seeing differently, and there are many filters that distort our view of reality. There are many reasons why we fail or refuse to see things as they are. We may be afraid of change; we may have too much invested in the status quo; we may simply fall prey to ingrained prejudices.

In 1888 a man picked up a French newspaper and, somewhat startled, read his own obituary. It was, of course, a mistake; it was his brother who had died, and the newspaper had run the wrong obituary. Nevertheless, he was curious to read what people wrote about him. The obituary stated '*Le marchand de la mort est mort*' (The merchant of death is dead) and went on to describe him as a person 'who became rich by finding ways to kill more people faster than ever before, died yesterday.' As he read on he was taken aback by the description of himself as a 'merchant of death', a person who had amassed a huge fortune by manufacturing weapons of mass destruction.

This was a moment of *metanoia*, an hour of conversion. This was not the legacy he wished to leave behind. From then onwards this person devoted his time, energy and money to the cause of peace. Today he is best remembered not as a 'merchant of death', but as the founder of the Nobel Peace Prize, Alfred Nobel.[269]

Metanoia is not about seeing anything different; it is about seeing differently, and there are many filters that distort our view of reality. There are many reasons why we fail or refuse to see things as they are. We may be afraid of change; we may have too much invested in the status quo; we may simply fall prey to ingrained prejudices.

Consider the example of sliced bread. We often describe something new as 'the best thing since sliced bread'. An American amateur inventor Otto Rohwedder started work on a bread-slicing machine in 1912, but he encountered significant opposition from bakers who said nobody would buy sliced bread because it would dry out. It wasn't until May 1928 that he was able to put his bread-slicing machine to commercial use, but according to David Dale's

---

[269] Adapted from Brian Cavanaugh, *The Sower's Seeds*, Paulist Press, Mahwah, NJ, 1990, pp. 44-5.

fascinating book *The 100 Things We Loved about the 20th Century*, Australian bakers resisted.

'In 1942', according to Dale, 'Melbourne bakers voted to prohibit slicing and wrapping machines, apparently feeling the process was unnatural.' How they had misjudged the market. By the end of the 20th century Australians were spending $359 million a year on sliced bread.[270]

Stephen Covey, author of *The 7 Habits of Highly Effective People*, offers an example of seeing a situation differently. One Sunday morning he was traveling on a subway in New York.

> People were sitting quietly – some reading newspapers, some lost in thought, some resting with their eyes closed. It was a calm, peaceful scene. Then suddenly, a man and his children entered the subway car. The children were so loud and rambunctious that instantly the whole climate changed. The man sat down next to me and closed his eyes, apparently oblivious to the children. The children were yelling back and forth, throwing things, even grabbing people's papers. It was very disturbing. And yet, the man sitting next to me did nothing. It was difficult not to feel irritated. I could not believe that he could be so insensitive as to let his children run wild like that and do nothing about it, taking no responsibility at all. It was easy to see that everyone else on the subway felt irritated, too. So finally, with what I felt was unusual patience and restraint, I turned to him and said, 'Sir, your children are really disturbing a lot of people. I wonder if you couldn't control them a little more?' The man lifted his gaze as if to come to a consciousness of the situation for the first time and said softly, 'Oh, you're right. I guess I should do something

---

[270] David Dale, *The 100 Things We Loved about the 20th Century*, Pan, Sydney, 1999, pp. 35-6.

about it. We just came from the hospital where their mother died about an hour ago. I don't know what to think, and I guess they don't know how to handle it either.'

Covey reflects upon this situation:

> Can you imagine what I felt at that moment? My paradigm shifted. Suddenly I saw differently, I thought differently, I felt differently, I behaved differently. My irritation vanished. I didn't have to worry about controlling my attitude or my behaviour; my heart was filled with the man's pain. Feelings of sympathy and compassion flowed freely.[271]

The call is in the first place a call to repentance; it is also a call to 'follow me.' The call of the disciples emphasises an important point – it is Jesus who seizes the initiative in calling people to follow him. Jesus issues 'a peremptory call to follow him, a call addressed to people who have not taken the initiative of asking to follow him.'[272]

When Jonah was called, he headed off in the opposite direction. What thoughts might have run through the minds of Simon and Andrew, James and John? Your livelihood is fishing, your family depends upon you; what will become of them? Who is this wandering healer and exorcist that you would give up everything to follow him? Is he mad? His family certainly thinks he is! You hypocrite! Is a sinful man like you worthy enough? You'll be the laughing stock of every village around the lake. What do you know about preaching?

---

[271] Stephen R. Covey, *The 7 Habits of Highly Effective People*, The Business Library, Melbourne, 1989, pp. 30-1.
[272] John P. Meier, *A Marginal Jew: Companions and Competitors, Volume III*, Doubleday, New York, 2001, p. 50.

Reflections for the year of Mark

Or what might the father of James and John have said? 'Boys, this business will be yours one day. You can't walk off and leave me after all I've done for you. I'm your father.'

It was a courageous step because following Jesus

> was not simply a metaphor for absorbing and practising his teachings. Jesus called individuals to follow him literally, physically, as he undertook various preaching tours of Galilee, Judea, and surrounding areas.[273]

Nor was this a temporary calling:

> It did not set any time limit on the obligation to follow him. There was no course of studies, the completion of which would release a disciple from constant attendance upon Jesus.

This contrasted with the relationship between a rabbinic student and his teacher, the whole point of which was to learn the rabbi's interpretation of the Torah and then leave to undertake one's own career as a rabbi. By contrast, Jesus does not call disciples to learn Torah, but 'to experience and proclaim the kingdom of God.'[274]

For the disciples 'this is a long adventure and one that they did not expect. It is a following filled with misunderstandings, failures, suffering, and finally hope.'[275]

---

273 Ibid., p. 54.
274 Ibid., p. 55.
275 John Shea, *Eating with the Bridegroom*, p. 47.

FOURTH SUNDAY IN ORDINARY TIME

(YEAR B)

In their synagogue just then there was a man possessed by an unclean spirit ... (Mk 1:23)

Each of the evangelists offers us a distinctive insight into the identity and mission of Jesus – who he is and what he is called to do. Like a symphonic overture, their insight is announced through the set piece that each of them places at the outset of Jesus' public ministry. The set piece with which Matthew leads his gospel off is the Sermon on the Mount; for Luke it is the inaugural sermon in the Nazareth synagogue, and for John it is the wedding feast at Cana (Mt 5-7; Lk 4:16-30; Jn 2:1-11). In Mark's gospel it is the story we have just heard, an exorcism. 'The whole mission of the Markan Jesus is encapsulated in the implicit affirmative response to the demon's question, 'Have you come to destroy us?' (1:24).'[276] Mark portrays Jesus as 'the Stronger One (1:7; 3:27) who sets human beings free from demonic control'.[277]

The episode is set in Capernaum, an ancient fishing town located on the northern shore of the Sea of Galilee. It was the closest to a

---

276 Joel Marcus, *Mark 1-8*, Doubleday, New York, p. 2000, p. 190.
277 Brendan Byrne, *A Costly Freedom*, St Paul's, Strathfield, NSW, 2008, p. xi.

permanent base that Jesus had during his Galilean ministry; in the gospels of Matthew and Mark it is referred to simply as 'his own city' (Mt 9:1; Mk 2:1). Since 1968 excavations have revealed some remains of the city from the time of Jesus, including the synagogue and the house of St Peter. The Spanish pilgrim Egeria visited Capernaum sometime between 381 and 384 and noted that 'In Capernaum the house of the prince of the apostles has been made into a church, with its original walls still standing … There also is the synagogue where the Lord cured a man possessed by the devil. The way in is up many stairs, and it is made of dressed stone.'[278] The remains of the synagogue today's pilgrim sees at Capernaum date from the late fourth or early fifth century, but it was built on the foundations of the synagogue of the Roman centurion.[279]

Today's gospel tells us that Jesus entered the synagogue on the Sabbath[280] and began to teach. A man possessed by an unclean spirit begins to shout: 'What do you want with us Jesus of Nazareth? Have you come here to destroy us?' Jesus then commands the unclean spirit to come out of the man. In ancient cultures it was widely believed that 'evil spirits could not only inflict suffering on people from without (demonic obsession) but could even invade and take over their bodies (demonic possession).'[281] Despite the plethora of horror

---

278 Quoted in Jerome Murphy-O'Connor, *The Holy Land*, p. 224.
279 Virgilio C. Corbo, 'Capernaum', in David Noel Freedman (ed.), *The Anchor Bible Dictionary, Volume 1*, Doubleday, New York, 1992, pp. 866-9.
280 The Sabbath commences at sunset on Friday and continues until sunset on Saturday.
281 John P. Meier, *A Marginal Jew: Rethinking the Historical Jesus: Mentor, Message, and Miracles, Volume II*, Doubleday, New York, 1994, p. 405.

Releasing the Captive

movies and TV shows that feature demons, vampires, werewolves, zombies, witches, wizards and ghosts, we remain sceptical about devils. In the ancient world, however, the universe 'was perceived as being peopled by a wide variety of spirits, most of them threatening; in fact, humans occupied only a small part of this universe.' In the Greco-Roman world popular religion 'was very much concerned with liberation from these malevolent powers.' Apocalyptic Judaism 'thought of the world as locked in a lethal struggle between God and the power(s) of evil.' Exorcism, therefore, was not uncommon.[282] However strange it might sound to us in the twenty-first century, Jesus was, among other things, a first-century Jewish exorcist.[283] He no doubt saw exorcisms 'as part of his overall ministry of healing and liberating the people of Israel from the illness and other physical and spiritual evils that beset them.'[284]

In Mark's gospel this exorcism in the synagogue at Capernaum 'opens up and sets the pattern for the entire ministry of Jesus that has now begun to unfold.'[285] What is that saying to us? Before answering that question, let us ask a more basic question: What is the essential meaning of demonic possession? The Australian biblical scholar Brendan Byrne explains it in this way: 'In essence the demonic has to do with control. People in the ancient world generally and the biblical world in particular spoke of demonic possession when they felt

---

282 Donahue and Harrington, *The Gospel of Mark*, p. 83.
283 John P. Meier, *A Marginal Jew: Rethinking the Historical Jesus: Mentor, Message, and Miracles, Volume II*, p. 406.
284 Ibid., p. 407.
285 Brendan Byrne, *A Costly Freedom*, p. 46.

themselves held captive from within by forces and compulsions over which they had no control – transpersonal forces that robbed them of freedom of choice, stunted their human growth, and alienated them from God, from life in community, and from their own individual humanity.'[286] Let us look, then, at a modern story of exorcism – not quite the casting out of unclean spirits in the literal sense, but the destruction of forces that keep people bound and oppressed, forces that rob them of freedom, forces that stunt and alienate them.

The demon to be exorcised in this story is world poverty. Of the six million people living on our planet today, two billion live on $2 a day; one billion live on $1 a day, in what is described as extreme poverty.[287] Caught in a cycle of poverty, education is a luxury many families in developing countries cannot afford. The World Bank estimates that across the globe, more than a hundred million primary age children are not in school. Secondary school attendance rates are even lower. For many, enrolling in high school would be unheard of.[288]

The story begins with *metanoia* – a new way of seeing. David Bussau, brought up in an orphanage in New Zealand, came to Australia in 1966. At the age of fifteen, with only a few dollars and little else, he set up his first hot dog stand at a local football ground. By thirty-five he was a multi-millionaire and the owner of a highly

---

286 Ibid., p. xii.
287 Figures taken from David Bussau's 2006 Australia Day Address, obtainable at http://www.australiaday.com.au/whatson/australiadayaddress2.aspx?AddressID=5
288 Information taken from Insight, the Summer 2008 newsletter of Opportunity International, obtainable at http://www.opportunity.org.au/home.asp?pageid=D4348B7A25DCB012

successful construction company in Sydney. It was Kerry Packer, then Australia's richest man, who triggered David's metanoia. Early in 1976 one of David's three construction companies had a contract to restore Kerry Packer's Bellevue Hill mansion. Among other jobs the restoration involved building gun cases and cocktail cabinets. One evening, when the project was almost completed, Kerry Packer phoned David at home. David was in the midst of bathing his two young daughters, but in language a little too spicy for a Sunday homily, Packer ordered him to get over to his place immediately. A catch on one of the cocktail cabinets wouldn't close and he was holding a party that evening. 'I'm embarrassed this beautiful cocktail cabinet won't close.'

David went, but he was indignant that Packer had that kind of power over him. 'That triggered in my life this sense that I wasn't on the planet to pamper to the rich and famous, and maybe I'd lost my way in terms of what my purpose was.' David explained his change of outlook in terms of the 'economics of enough'. In other words, he already had 'enough' for a comfortable lifestyle. Which begs the question, how much is enough? It varies, of course, with each individual, but when Rockefeller was asked that question he replied, 'Just a little bit more.'

David began to wind down his businesses, and the family decided to move to Darwin to assist with reconstruction in the wake of Cyclone Tracy. The church that David attended in Darwin had a relationship with an Indonesian church located in an area that had been devastated by an earthquake. So David volunteered help rebuild a small village of about a thousand people, most of whom were tenant rice farmers. It was here that David hit on the idea of microfinance. It happened like this. One of the rice farmers told him that his wife was expecting their third child, but his first two children, aged about six and seven, had already been mortgaged to loan sharks and land owners. As is typical in a situation like this, the person who made the loan takes the children away to work in a carpet factory or a cigarette factory as a way of repaying the loan that the parents had taken out – a loan that they had to take out just to survive between the rice harvests. It was bondage, a forced slavery. David asked the farmer what he was good at, apart from rice farming, and he replied that his wife could sew very well. David offered to loan the farmer some money to buy a sewing machine so that his wife could make a few clothes and sell them at market. They signed a contract, agreeing that this was a loan, a simple commercial transaction. They bought a sewing machine, and the farmer's wife went to work. Within nine months they had bought a second sewing machine and employed another person from the village to work for them. Within eighteen months the rice farmer had repaid all the money he had borrowed from the loan shark and could redeem his children. The family had been set free from bondage; a demon had been exorcised.

In 1979 David founded Opportunity International with a likeminded counterpart in the USA. Like the mustard seed, David's project started out very small – one family in a small village. Now, thirty years later, Opportunity International has 1.25 million loans to people in twenty-three countries averaging $220 per loan. The organisation employs 9800 people in 28 countries around the world, but they also create a job every thirty seconds of the day. They have a 97.5 per cent repayment rate.[289]

What is the lesson to be learnt from the synagogue at Capernaum? Our standard of living in Australia is among the highest in the world. According to the World Bank, Australia contains four of the world's top ten most livable cities.[290] It is within our power, as a nation and as individuals, to help set the downtrodden and oppressed free. That is what exorcism is all about. Pope Benedict concluded his 2009 World Day of Peace message with these words:

> At the start of the New Year, then, I extend to every disciple of Christ and to every person of good will a warm invitation to expand their hearts to meet the needs of the poor and to take whatever practical steps are possible in order to help them. The truth of the axiom cannot be refuted: 'to fight poverty is to build peace.'[291]

---

289 I have taken David's story from an interview with Richard Fidler broadcast by the ABC on 23 January 2009. You can listen to the interview at http://mpegmedia.abc.net.au/local/brisbane/200901/r332830_1503409.mp3 Additional material came from http://www.news.com.au/perthnow/story/0,21598,23110658-948,00.html

290 David Bussau's 2006 Australia Day Address.

291 The full text of the pope's message can be accessed at http://www.vatican.va/holy_father/benedict_xvi/messages/peace/documents/hf_ben-xvi_mes_20081208_xlii-world-day-peace_en.html

FIFTH SUNDAY IN ORDINARY TIME

(YEAR B)

And the fever left her and she began to wait on them. (Mk 1:31)

In this first chapter of Mark's gospel we have something like a typical day in the life of Jesus. Today's gospel is set in Capernaum, a commercial centre beside the lake of Galilee, a home to fishermen, farmers, merchants, tax-collectors and soldiers. This village was the centre of Jesus' ministry in Galilee. After leaving the synagogue he went straight to the house of Simon and Andrew where he healed Simon's mother-in-law. Peter was therefore a married man.

What became of his wife once Peter left his nets and his livelihood to follow Jesus? Was she left at home to look after the children and extended family, including her mother? The gospels are silent, but St Paul isn't. In his first letter to the Corinthians, written about twenty years after the death of Jesus, Paul tells us that Peter was accompanied by his wife, as were the other apostles. The gospels and the Acts of the Apostles tell us a good deal about the ministry of the apostles, but unfortunately they are silent about the wives who supported their husbands in their ministry – Mrs Peter, Mrs Andrew, Mrs James and Mrs John!

Releasing the Captive

The synagogue is, literally, just across the road from Peter's house where, in the course of time, a church was built over the site. The fourth-century pilgrim Egeria noted that 'the house of the prince of the apostles has been made into a church, with its original walls still standing', and in the sixth century the Piacenza pilgrim noted that 'the house of St Peter is now a basilica.'[292] The present church built over the ruins of the house was constructed in 1990 and its design is somewhat evocative of a flying saucer.[293]

Jesus is told that Simon's mother-in-law had gone to bed with a fever, so upon entering the house he heals her, and immediately she begins to wait upon them. It's worth noting that in the world view of the gospel physical illness is just as much a mark of the rule of Satan as demonic possession.[294] So again we have Jesus setting someone free.

Here we also have another key theme: As soon as Simon's mother-in-law had been healed she began to serve them. Now that she is well again she is able to offer hospitality, but something more important is happening. This woman has become a paradigm of Christian discipleship, which it not ambitious for positions of honour or prestige.

Later in the gospel, when James and John approach Jesus seeking to sit one at his right hand and the other at his left when he comes into his glory, he has to remind all the disciples that 'The Son of Man

---

[292] Quoted in Jerome Murphy-O'Connor, *The Holy Land*, p. 224.
[293] For a look at the inside of the church, go to http://www.3disrael.com/north/the_modern_church.cfm
[294] Brendan Byrne, *A Costly Freedom*, p. 46.

himself came not to be served but to serve' (Mk 10:45). The most poignant expression of that service occurs in John's gospel when Jesus washes the feet of his disciples.

One further things needs to be said about this woman's cure. There is a difference between being cured and being healed. Richard Alpert had been a professor of psychology at Harvard. His bestseller *Be Here Now* sold two million copies and tells the story of his journey to India and a transformation that turned him from a 'neurotic Jewish overachiever' to a white-robed yogi who found inner peace. He is now known as Ram Dass, a name meaning 'servant of God.'

In 1997, aged 65, he suffered a massive stroke. The doctors said that the cerebral haemorrhage had been so massive that he probably wouldn't survive. News passed from friend to friend: 'Ram Dass had a stroke. He can't move or speak and may not live.' He did survive, although still affected by the stroke.[295] Reflecting on what had happened to him he said,

> While cures aim at returning our bodies to what they were in the past, healing uses what is present to move us more deeply to Soul Awareness.... (A)lthough I have not been cured of the effects of my stroke, I have certainly undergone profound healings of mind and heart.[296]

Jesus didn't dash around Palestine as a one-man medical emergency unit, curing everyone who was sick. His cures were a sign of

---

295 Sara Davidson, *The Dass Effect*, http://www.nytimes.com/library/magazine/home/20000521mag-ramdass.html
296 Ram Dass, *Still Here: Embracing Aging, Changing, and Dying*, ed. by Mark Matousek and Marielle Roeder Riverhead Books, 2000, p. 67, quoted in William J. Bausch, *Once Upon a Gospel*, Twenty-Third Publications, Mystic, CT, 2008, pp. 171-2.

a deeper healing, a healing of the human spirit that made people whole. One can be physically cured but remain unhealed.

There is a final lesson to be learnt from today's gospel. After a hectic day, Jesus rises early the next morning and goes off to a lonely place to pray. Jesus needed that time in prayer to reclaim the true direction of his mission and to focus on where it was taking him. The inescapable rhythm in Jesus' ministry is a balance between time with others and time alone. The German Protestant theologian Dietrich Bonhoeffer (1906–1945) who was murdered by the Nazis in 1945 wrote a book called *Life Together*. It grew out of his experience of preparing people for ministry in the German Confessing Church. One chapter is entitled 'The Day with Others'; another chapter is called 'The Day Alone'. These two 'days' are essential ingredients in the life of every Christian, indeed of every human being.

Some of us, by temperament, seek company; others of us seek solitude. The Desert Fathers and Mothers sought refuge in the desert during the early centuries of Christianity. The desert taught them wisdom and enabled them to discover the true self. Their insights have been collected in a volume called the *Verba Seniorum*. An excellent English edition has been edited by Benedicta Ward and is called *The Sayings of the Desert Fathers*.

One story concerns Abba Arsenius and Abba Moses. Arsenius was a highly educated and cultivated man; he had been a tutor to the imperial family and a senior civil servant in Constantinople before becoming a monk. He was renowned in the desert for his humility, but also for his silence and seclusion. Abba Moses the Ethiopian was a converted highwayman. A certain brother came to see Abba Arsenius at Scetis. He arrived at the church and asked the clergy if he could visit Abba Arsenius. 'Have a bite to eat,' they said, 'before you go to see him.' 'No,' he replied, 'I shan't eat anything until I have met him.' Arsenius' cell was a long way off, so they sent a brother along with him. They knocked on the door, went in and greeted the old man, then sat down; nothing was said. The brother who had escorted the visitor said, 'I'll leave you now; pray for me.' But the visitor didn't feel at ease with the old man and said, 'I'm coming with you.' So off they went together. Then the visitor said, 'Will you take me to see Abba Moses, the one who used to be a highwayman?' When they arrived, Abba Moses welcomed them happily and enjoyed himself thoroughly with them until they left.

The brother who had escorted the visitor said to him, 'Well, I've taken you to see the foreigner and the Egyptian; which do you like the better?' 'The Egyptian (Moses) for me!' he said.

One of the fathers overheard this and prayed to God saying, 'Lord, explain this to me. For your sake one of these men runs from human company and for your sake the other receives them with open arms.'

Then two large boats were shown to him floating on the river. In one of them sat Abba Arsenius and the Holy Spirit of God in perfect quiet. And in the other boat was Abba Moses with the angels of God: they were all eating honey cakes.[297]

---

[297] Slightly adapted from Rowan Williams, *Silence and Honey Cakes*, A Lion Book, Oxford, 2003, pp. 42-3.

Some of us abide with the Holy Spirit of God in perfect silence, and others of us make merry with the angels eating honey cakes. But of course, it is not a matter of either silence or honey cake. Those of us more inclined to silence must make an effort to eat honey cake; and those of us who prefer honey cake must learn the lessons that silence would teach us.

Amidst the busyness of life we are easily distracted and disoriented. Have you ever heard of Carl Perkins? He was an American pioneer of what is known as rockabilly music, and the composer of a song that Elvis Presley made famous – *Blue Suede Shoes*. Despite the fact that his songs were recorded by artists like Elvis, the Beatles, Dolly Parton and Johnny Cash, Carl never achieved superstar status. Perhaps he was aware of the price of stardom. In a 1996 interview he said,

> I never envied Elvis, his mansion and all that. All those boys – Elvis, Jerry Lee Lewis, Roy Orbison – they all lost their wives, their families. People say to me, 'What happened to you, Carl? All of them went to superstardom. Where'd you go?' I say, 'I went home. And that's a good place to be.'[298]

That is a lesson we can learn from today's gospel: We need some quiet time to find our true home, to come to terms with our true identity and the mission that God has entrusted to each of us.

---

298 Jon Pareles, 'Carl Perkins dies at 65' http://query.nytimes.com/gst/fullpage.html?res=950CEFD81338F933A15752C0A96E958260&sec=&spon=&pagewanted=3

Reflections for the year of Mark

SIXTH SUNDAY IN ORDINARY TIME

(YEAR B)

A leper came to Jesus and pleaded on his knees: 'If you want to,' he said, 'you can cure me.' (Mk 1:40)

The Jesus we meet in Mark's gospel is the one who has come to set us free. Over the past two weeks I've spoken about David Bussau, the story of a modern 'exorcist' – not someone who casts out demons in the literal sense, but a person who exorcises the unclean spirits of poverty and ignorance. It all began in a small Indonesian village where people were oppressed and alienated by debt. Bussau devised a simple but effective strategy to set them free.[299] Today we meet a man, a leper, who seeks to be set free from exile and alienation and to be reunited with family and friends.

We know leprosy today as Hansen's disease, named after the Norwegian physician Gerhard Henrick Armauer Hansen who discovered the bacillus mycobacterium leprae in 1868. But the disease called leprosy that we read about in the gospels covered a wide range of skin conditions that are not associated with the deadly bacillus

---

299 David Bussau's story is told by Philippa Tyndale in *Don't Look Back*, Allen & Unwin, Sydney, 2000.

Hansen discovered.[300] People suffering from psoriasis, eczema, or any fungal infection of the skin would have been diagnosed as lepers.[301] Such a diagnosis had heartbreaking consequences. Not only did such people suffer from a discomforting skin condition, but they were deemed to be unclean and banished from society, as the book of Leviticus makes clear: 'Anyone with a contagious skin-disease will wear torn clothing and disordered hair; and will cover the upper lip and shout, 'Unclean, unclean.' As long as the disease lasts, such a person will be unclean and, being unclean, will live alone and live outside the camp' (Lev 13:45-46).

The Jerusalem Bible translation of today's gospel tells us that Jesus 'felt sorry' for the leper who approached him, and the New American Bible and the New Revised Standard Version translation says that Jesus was 'moved with pity'. However, the Greek word that Mark uses is more accurately translated as 'anger', not 'feeling sorry' or 'moved with pity'.

Anger tells us that something is wrong. It is an important and valuable emotion. Anger in itself is neither good nor bad. It's what we do with our anger that determines its morality. Some of us sit on our anger and stew; perhaps dream up strategies for revenge. Others gain energy from their anger to right the wrong. No wonder Jesus was angry when he encountered a man with leprosy. He is also con-

---

300 The lectionary published by Geoffrey Chapman uses the (1966) Jerusalem Bible translation. The New Jerusalem Bible (1985) replaces 'leper' with 'A man suffering from a virulent skin-disease'. The New American Bible uses 'leper'.
301 Cf. John Dominic Crossan, *Jesus: A Revolutionary Biography*, HarperSanFrancisco, 1994, p. 78.

fronting a social system that robbed people of their human dignity, and religious laws that robbed them of hope. One could argue that this was done for the greater good, to prevent widespread contagion. But how many people with harmless skin conditions were also cast into oblivion?

If exorcism is essentially about oppression, leprosy is surely about ostracism and exile. If David Bussau is a contemporary 'exorcist', where might we find an example of a person healing today's lepers? As I was listening to Richard Fidler's radio programme *The Conversation Hour* the answer leapt out at me. Richard was interviewing Kat Armstrong, a founding member of Women in Prison Advocacy Network (WIPAN).[302] WIPAN represents women in prison, but it also supports women who are released from prison, many of whom have lost their children, their home, their family and their partner. They are ostracised from the community, condemned to isolation and exile like the leper in biblical times.

Many women in prison are victims of domestic violence and sexual abuse, and they turn to drugs or alcohol to numb the pain. A recent Australian study of women in prison found that

> 87 per cent of incarcerated women were the victims of sexual, physical or emotional abuse in either childhood (63%) or adulthood (78%). The majority were victims of multiple forms of abuse.[303]

---

302 To hear the interview, go to http://www.abc.net.au/local/stories/2009/02/13/2490805.htm
303 Holly Johnson, *Drugs and Crime: A Study of Incarcerated Female Offenders* (Research and Public Policy Series, no. 63. Australian Institute of Criminology, 2004), p. 16. The study can be downloaded from http://www.aic.gov.au/publications/rpp/63/

Releasing the Captive

Kat's parents married when her mother was seventeen and her father nineteen. Her father was drafted and served in Vietnam for eighteen months, an experience that left him angry and disturbed. Her parents constantly fought and she experienced extreme levels of domestic violence. The marriage eventually ended in divorce. At the age of fifteen Kat socialised with an older group of teenagers, and before long she was using recreational drugs and alcohol to help block the painful side of life. It was a form of escapism and she felt best when she was high. She dropped out of school in year twelve, left home and lived in shared accommodation where she began using amphetamines on a daily basis and began dabbling with heroin. She entered the workforce as a trainee accounts clerk, and to finance what was an increasingly expensive habit she began stealing money from the company's petty cash. It wasn't long before she was found out and asked to leave. She fell pregnant, but the father denied paternity and wanted nothing to do with the child. By the time the baby was born he was engaged to someone else. During the pregnancy Kat kicked the heroin habit and began to get her life together. Sadly, things went downhill rapidly after the birth of her daughter. She suffered postnatal depression and began injecting heroin again. It was not long before she was physically and mentally addicted. She resorted to crime to finance her drug habit, and was arrested eventually arrested for credit card fraud. Because of the amount of money involved she was jailed, the first of three stints in prison for crimes that became increasingly serious. She would end up spending ten years in prison.

Reflections for the year of Mark

Kat's wake-up call came during her third stint in prison. Her daughter, then aged eleven, refused to speak with her, and told her mother by letter not to contact her again. It was a completely devastating experience, a life-altering moment. Here we have the modern leper – ostracised by society and almost no hope that life will get better. Kat had to make a decision. Would she remain a prisoner of leprosy (drug abuse), or begin to take responsibility for the direction of her life? In prison she commenced a law degree by correspondence, and began to assist other prisoners with their legal problems. She has now been out of prison for six years and clean from drugs for ten. 'I believe anyone and everyone can change,' she told Richard Fidler.

Kat's life now is that of healing the 'leper'. She was a founding member of WIPAN, an organisation that grew out of the sad reality that little was being done for women once they were released from prison. At this point in their lives they are most vulnerable. Many of them do not have a home to go to; they must confront the difficult task of finding a job; and many of them no longer have easy access to their children. They need support and counselling, especially if there is a danger of relapse; they need to be welcomed back into the community that has ostracised them. Without that support many of these women are in danger of re-offending.[304]

David Bussau founded Opportunity International, an organisation that now assists over 1.25 million people world wide through

---

[304] See the report by Debbie Kilroy, *When Will You See the Real Us? Women in Prison*, a paper presented at the Women in Corrections: Staff and Clients Conference, 31 October–1 November 2000. The paper can be downloaded from http://www.awipn.org.au/research.htm

small loans. Kat Armstrong became a founding member of Women in Prison Advocacy Network. They are both remarkable people, but you and I are not called to be them. Perhaps, though, in our own sphere of influence we might allow some of Jesus' anger to take hold of us.

What can I do to set the oppressed free, how can I welcome the leper? When a parishioner recently told me of his work with Alcoholics Anonymous I thought immediately of Jesus casting out an unclean spirit – in this case, the spirit of addiction. Another parishioner told me about her work as a primary school teacher specialising in the area of reading recovery. The young children she works with see the printed page as nothing but indecipherable squiggles. They are exiled from the world of education, information and imagination encoded in the written word. Like Jesus healing the leper, she also is reaching out to the exile.

It is also heartening to read about people who have volunteered to become foster parents. Nationwide there are 36,000 children in out-of-home care, living with relatives or in foster homes. Writing about foster-parents Greg Bearup notes that the young people living in foster homes 'are overwhelmingly the children of junkies, severe alcoholics, schizophrenics, mentally disabled parents and the extreme poor who inhabit the fringes of our affluent society.'

The children who are rescued from the wreckage of these families 'are damaged, sometimes beyond repair'.[305] There are 8050 foster carers across Australia, a task they undertake out of love. This, too, is a reaching out to the leper.

---

305 Greg Bearup, 'Hope lives here', in *Good Weekend*, 9 April 2011, p. 12.

Reflections for the year of Mark

During the Vietnam War a man by the name of Bob Considine was accompanying an infant Vietnamese orphan to the United States so that the child could be adopted. At one point during the long flight he noticed that the baby's eyes overflowed with tears, but the child wasn't making a sound. He asked the flight attendant if she knew what the problem might be. She replied that she had seen a number of war orphans, and this condition was not unusual. She explained, 'The reason they don't make a sound when they cry is because they've learned from experience that no matter how loud they might cry, nobody will come.'[306]

May the lepers among us and those possessed by unclean spirits not find it so!

---

[306] Adapted from William J. Bausch, *Once Upon a Gospel*, Twenty-Third Publications, Mystic, CT, 2008, p. 176.

SEVENTH SUNDAY IN ORDINARY TIME

(YEAR B)

He was preaching the word to them when some people came bringing him a paralytic carried by four men. (Mk 2:3)

The roof of a Palestinian house was flat and regularly used as a place to relax. An outside staircase or wooden ladder gave easy access. The roof consisted of flat beams laid across from wall-to-wall, about a metre apart. The space in between the beams was filled with reeds, matted layers of thorns, and several inches of clay.[307] Often a flourishing crop of grass grew on the rooftop. It was fairly easy to dig out the filling between two of the beams, and the damage done was easily repaired. So, the paralytic's friends dug out the filling between two of the beams and lowered him right at the feet of Jesus. Bishop Tom Wright suggests that it was probably Jesus' own house, since he had moved to Capernaum from Nazareth.[308]

Jesus must surely have smiled at the persistence and ingenuity of the paralytic's friends, even if they had made a hole in his roof, and

---

[307] Joseph A. Fitzmyer, *The Gospel According to Luke I-IX*, The Anchor Bible, New York, 1970, p. 582.
[308] Tom Wright, *Mark for Everyone*, SPCK, London, 2001, p. 16.

the gospel tells us that he saw their faith.[309] But his first words are not, 'Pick up your stretcher and walk.' Jesus tells the man that his sins are forgiven. You can imagine what the paralytic was thinking: 'I haven't come here for absolution; I've come to be healed.' But a contemporary audience wouldn't have found those words of Jesus so strange in the circumstances. There was a longstanding belief, and humanity has never quite thrown it off, that sin and sickness go hand in hand. Most of the people present in that crowded house would have assumed that the paralytic's physical condition was the direct result of sin.[310]

However much we attempt to dismiss the link between sin and sickness as a primitive and superstitious relic from a less enlightened age, it remains deeply engrained within the human psyche. Many Westerners have uncritically adopted the concept of karma, a term used in several Eastern religions to refer to the law of cause and effect in the ethical realm. Karma implies that every volitional action is followed by its due effect, or, in colloquial terms, what goes around comes around. Sin may indeed affect us profoundly (depression, eating and sleeping disorders, nightmares, anger, shame, guilt, prolonged grief, emotional numbness, alienation from God, and loss of self-esteem), but Christianity steadfastly rejects the belief that sin and physical infirmity are inexorably linked. For several years I was

---
[309] Cf. William Barclay, *The Gospel of Mark*, The Saint Andrew Press, Edinburgh, repr. 1971, pp. 39-40.
[310] John R. Donahue and Daniel J. Harrington, *The Gospel of Mark*, The Liturgical Press, Collegeville, MN, 2002, p. 93.

the Catholic chaplain at Sydney's Royal Hospital for Women when it was located at Paddington. A distressing part of that ministry was supporting families following a neo-natal death. On more than one occasion I recall a tearful mother telling me that she was certain that the death of her baby was God's punishment for an abortion she'd had several years earlier.

Philip Yancey writes of a close friend, Claudia, who was diagnosed with Hodgkin's disease. Drastic surgery and cobalt treatment took their toll on Claudia's body.

> Beauty fled her almost overnight. She felt and looked weary, her skin darkened, her hair fell out. Her throat was raw, and she regurgitated nearly everything she ate. A deacon from her local church advised Claudia to reflect on what God was trying to teach her. 'Surely something in your life must displease God ... Somewhere, you must have stepped out of his will. These things don't just happen. God uses circumstances to warn us, and to punish us. What is he telling you?'[311]

As Rabbi Harold Kushner observes,

> One of the ways in which people have tried to make sense of the world's suffering in every generation has been by assuming that we deserve what we get, that somehow our misfortunes come as punishment for our sins.[312]

That assumption leaves us spiritually paralysed and alienated from God and the church. Jesus has returned home to Capernaum after

---

[311] Philip Yancey, *Where Is God When It Hurts?: Disappointment with God*, Zondervan Treasures, 1996, pp. 16-17.
[312] Harold S. Kushner, *When Bad Things Happen to Good People*, Pan Books, London, 1981, p. 17.

preaching in nearby villages. Over the past few weeks we have heard stories about him casting out an unclean spirit and healing a leper. Today he heals a paralytic. If, as I've recently suggested, David Bussau is an example of a contemporary 'exorcist', and Kat Armstrong is working to heal today's 'lepers', where might we find someone healing the paralytic?

In 2009 Caritas Australia's Lenten appeal, Project Compassion, featured the story of a Ugandan woman by the name of Teopista. Her story is that of a family paralysed – paralysed in the sense that they were the victims of forces beyond their control; they had neither the awareness nor the expertise to raise themselves up.

Five years ago she and her husband Fred worked hard to provide for their seven children. She explained,

> My family ate one meal a day. Sometimes we went without food when we had no money and nothing to cook. We couldn't afford school fees so sometimes the children were sent home from school.

Over 80 per cent of Ugandans are subsistence farmers, and poor land management, environmental degradation and unpredictable weather conditions have all taken their toll. Pests and diseases have further threatened their staple food crops.

In 2003 Teopista's family joined the Sustainable Agriculture Project sponsored by Caritas Australia. This project supports nine hundred subsistence farmer families by teaching them to manage their land and resources sustainably, improve their household's food security and increase their income.

Teopista explains:

> Through on-farm training we have learnt to improve our farm yields organically, to harvest rainwater, and about basic nutrition and hygiene. My family can now eat three meals a day and better plan for periods of scarcity. With money for school fees, my children are now able to attend local schools.[313]

Who healed the paralytic? Well, Jesus did, of course. But the paralytic might never have been healed had it not been for the persistence and ingenuity of his four friends. They didn't heal him, but they laid him at the feet of someone who could. This is where we come into the story. I will probably never travel to Uganda, nor indeed to any of the other places where Caritas sponsors projects. And even if I did, I certainly don't have the expertise to help subsistence farmers with sustainable agriculture. But other people do have those skills, and organisations such as Caritas invite us to assist them. Where am I in today's gospel? Hopefully, I'm one of the four.

---

[313] Information contained in the 2009 Project Compassion Kit, *An Environment to Grow In*.

EIGHTH SUNDAY IN ORDINARY TIME

(YEAR B)

New wine, fresh skins. (Mk 2:22)

No one sews a piece of unshrunken cloth on an old cloak, and nobody puts new wine into old wineskins. What on earth is Jesus talking about? Well, on one level, he is giving commonsense advice. You can't use unshrunken cloth to patch a garment because when the garment gets wet the new patch will shrink and tear the fabric. In Palestine, wine was kept in wineskins, and new skins had a greater elasticity. As skins grow old they became unyielding because they have already stretched as far as they can. New wine is still fermenting and therefore gives off gases that cause a build up of pressure. If the wineskin is new it will yield to the mounting pressure, but if it's old and hard it will explode as the pressure builds up. So, if you have new wine, you need new wineskins.[314]

Rabbi Harold Kushner reminds us that

> Religion is not primarily a set of beliefs, a collection of prayers or a series of rituals. Religion is first and foremost a way of seeing. It can't change the facts about the world we live in, but it can change the way we see those facts, and that in itself can often make a difference.[315]

---

314 Cf. William Barclay, *The Gospel of Mark*, pp. 55-6.
315 Quoted in William J. Bausch, *The Yellow Brick Road*, p. 281.

But it's a constant challenge to see things as they are and not as we would like them to be. A beautiful actress became greatly perturbed about her looks as she got on in years. Her photographer in particular began to feel the brunt of her temperamental moods. One day she was very unhappy over a set of photos taken of her, and she was furious with the photographer. 'What's happened to you?' she cried. 'These pictures are awful. Where is that fine technique you had 20 years ago when you first started photographing me?' The tactful photographer replied, 'Well, you must remember, I am 20 years older now!'

Jesus had encountered closed minds, unwilling to change; minds that had become fixed and settled in their ways and unable to contemplate new ways, uncomfortable with a new vision. In other words, what Jesus is doing 'can't be fitted in to the existing ways of thinking and living. If people try to do that they'll have the worst of both worlds. At the time, this meant that Jesus' powerful kingdom-ministry couldn't be fitted into the ways of thinking that his fellow first-century Galileans already had.' They needed to think and see differently, to get new wineskins for the new wine he had to offer. 'Most people are threatened by that kind of challenge.'[316]

The philosopher Immanuel Kant (1724–1804) said that all human beings experience reality through filters. In other words, we never know things as they really are; we only know things as they appear to us. St Thomas Aquinas expressed this same idea in these words: 'Things known are in the knower according to the mode of

---

[316] Tom Wright, *Mark for Everyone*, p. 23.

the knower.'³¹⁷ All experience is interpreted experience. Kant called things as they really are the noumena. He called reality as it appears to us the phenomena. We can never know the noumena, only the phenomena.³¹⁸ The Jewish Talmud put it slightly differently: We never know things are they are. We only know things as we are. Consider this analogy. A person wearing rose-tinted spectacles can only see the world with a rose-coloured tint. Now while we can take off the tinted spectacles, there are certain filters inbuilt into us as human beings that cannot be removed. Such filters colour our way of seeing the world, of perceiving reality. A lady recently rang up the editor of her daily newspaper and told him she was cancelling her subscription, since the paper had run some anti-Catholic articles. She added: 'And note that this is the fourth time I have cancelled my subscription because of your sectarianism.'

We only see things as we are. A man who felt deeply depressed about his obesity consulted a psychiatrist. As a diagnostic procedure, the psychiatrist decided to show the man certain pictures and ask him to say the first thing that came into his mind. The psychiatrist showed the man the picture of a camel. The patient then said: 'It reminds me of food.' 'Why food?' the psychiatrist asked. 'Are things so bad where you live that you have to eat camel?' But the patient replied, 'Doctor, everything reminds me of food.'

The same psychiatrist tried a similar technique with another patient. 'I'm going to show you certain geometric patterns. I want

---

317 *Summa Theologica*, II/II Q1, art. 2.
318 See T.D. Weldon, *Kant's 'Critique of Pure Reason'*, 2nd edn, Clarendon Press, Oxford, 1958, pp. 190-1.

you to tell me the first thing that comes into your mind.' And so the psychiatrist showed the man the diagram of a square: 'That reminds me of sex.' He showed him the diagram of a circle: 'That reminds me of sex.' Likewise, when he showed the patient diagrams of a rectangle, a triangle, a pentagon – they all reminded the patient of sex. 'It seems quite obvious to me,' said the psychiatrist, 'that you are obsessed with sex.' But the patient replied, 'I'm not the one obsessed with sex. You're the one showing me all those sexy drawings.'

In other words, if you see the world through the filters of food, all things remind you of food; if you see the world through the filters of sex, all things remind you of sex. We never see things are they are. We only see things as we are. However, we are often totally oblivious to these inbuilt filters, many of which are culturally conditioned. Language itself is a system of interpretation. English, for example, is the language of a white, patriarchal society, and that is probably why it is so awkward to use inclusive language without becoming inelegant or cumbersome. The South African Anglican archbishop, Desmond Tutu, once observed that you don't realise how 'white' the English language is until you're a black person speaking it. 'Could you imagine me,' he said, 'being tickled pink?'

The opponents of Jesus were probably not evil people. They simply had closed minds. They had all the answers they needed, so what could this teacher from Galilee possibly teach us. When the devil saw a seeker of truth enter the house of a saintly teacher he was determined to do everything in his power to turn him back from his quest. So he subjected the seeker to every form of temptation – wealth, lust, prestige – but the seeker brushed aside these temptations quite easily. But when he entered the teacher's house he was somewhat taken aback. There was the teacher sitting in an upholstered chair with many disciples sitting at his feet. 'That man certainly lacks humility, the principal virtue of saints,' he thought to himself. Then he observed other things about the master that he did not like. For one thing, the teacher virtually ignored him. 'I suppose that's because I don't fawn over him like the others do,' he thought to himself. He also disliked the kind of clothes the teacher wore, and the somewhat conceited way that he spoke. All of this led him to the conclusion that he had come to the wrong place and must continue his quest for wisdom elsewhere. As he walked out of the room the teacher, who had seen the devil seated in the corner of the room, said, 'You need not have worried, tempter. He was yours from the very first, you know.'[319]

New wine, fresh skins. To be a disciple of Jesus is not just adding a few bits and pieces to our lives, like sewing a patch onto a garment. 'Discipleship calls for a total transformation of life. We probably continue to do much that we have always done; we live and work with the same people, we enjoy many of the same things, but as disciples all is completely new. It is like a marriage commitment that colours our entire lives. A fundamental change takes place when we marry; we are the same people, and yet we are radically different.'[320]

---

319 Adapted from William J. Bausch, *The Yellow Brick Road*, p. 26.
320 Dianne Bergant and Richard Fragomeni, *Preaching the New Lectionary*, Year B, p. 261.

Releasing the Captive

NINTH SUNDAY IN ORDINARY TIME

(YEAR B)

'Stretch out your hand.' He stretched it out and his hand was better.
(Mk 2:5)

The Jewish Sabbath begins at Friday sunset and ends on Saturday sunset. It is a badge of Jewish identity. The Torah forbids work on the Sabbath, and Jewish tradition, codified in the Mishnah, listed 39 key activities that were forbidden on the Sabbath. While walking through some cornfields on a Sabbath day the disciples are obviously hungry, so they pick some ears of corn. However, in the eyes of the Pharisees that is tantamount to reaping, an activity forbidden on the Sabbath. After appealing to an incident from the life of King David, Jesus reminds the Pharisees that 'the sabbath was made for man, not man for the sabbath.' This becomes an argument about a correct understanding of the Torah, and many liberal rabbis of the time would have agreed with Jesus. A well-known rabbinic principle put it this way: 'The sabbath is delivered unto you and you are not delivered to the sabbath.'[321]

---

[321] D.E. Nineham, *Saint Mark*, Penguin Books, Harmondsworth, 1963, pp. 106-7.

Reflections for the year of Mark

Christians transferred observance of the Sabbath to Sunday, and in many Christian countries it was observed strictly. Tom Wright writes about Sabbath observance in England, and it would have been much the same in Australia:

> When I was young, everybody kept Sunday as a very special day. Just a few decades ago, in the average English town, there were no shops open on Sundays; there was no professional sport – yes, no football, no racing; everything was very, very quiet.

He cites a cartoon of the time that sums up the attitude, and perhaps some of the ambivalence:

> An anxious father, worried about what the neighbours may say, tells his little girl she mustn't play with her hoop in the street on Sunday. She should go into the back garden. 'Isn't it Sunday in the back garden?' asks the girl.[322]

Although Sabbath observance is a quaint memory for Christians, Pope Benedict makes an observation:

> How salutary it would also be for our society today if families set aside one day a week to stay together and make their home the dwelling place and the fulfillment of communion in God's rest.[323]

The second incident in today's gospel, the healing of a man with a withered hand, is another clash with the Pharisees over the Sabbath. The rabbis were clear about the fact that saving life overrules the Sabbath, but this man did not have a life-threatening condition. The

---
322 Tom Wright, *Mark for Everyone*, p. 29.
323 Joseph Ratzinger (Pope Benedict XVI), *Jesus of Nazareth*, Doubleday, New York, 2007, pp. 108-9.

Pharisees could well have asked, 'Why can't this healing wait until tomorrow?' We're now reading from Chapter 3 of Mark's gospel, and already it's clear that Jesus is on a collision course with the self-appointed guardians of ancestral traditions. They refuse to recognise that Jesus is God's agent, and that he has come to set people free from the reign of evil. For Jesus the battle against evil is already raging, 'and on that battlefield every human action either strikes a blow for life or wields one for death; the cautious middle ground, upon which one might wait for a few minutes before doing good, has disappeared.'[324]

Jesus' healing of this man's hand is yet another sign that God's kingdom is crushing demons and disease. Let us digress for a moment to consider miracles, for they play an important role in the gospel of Mark and constitute almost half of Mark's account of Jesus' public ministry. What do we make of miracles? It's interesting that the gospels never use the word 'miracle' when referring to something like the healing of a withered hand.

In the synoptic gospels such deeds are usually referred to as *dynameis*, which can be translated from the Greek as 'deeds of might (or power)'. John's gospel uses the word *erga* (works) or *semeia* (signs). Perhaps the word 'signs' points us in the right direction because it 'immediately shifts our attention from them as deeds that might transcend what has been called the laws of nature to their religious value and significance, which is invariably found in the gospel-stories that recount them.'[325]

---

[324] Joel Marcus, *Mark 1-8*, Doubleday, New York, 2000, p. 252.
[325] Joseph A. Fitzmyer, *A Christological Catechism*, Paulist Press, New York, 1981, pp. 34-5.

God usually works in and through the skill of doctors and nurses to restore people to health, but can or does God intervene in human affairs through extraordinary or miraculous means? We have inherited the legacy of the Age of Reason, and that means we expect a rational explanation for all that happens. Miracles leave us perplexed because they don't have a rational explanation that can be tested scientifically or empirically verified.

Many scholars refuse to accept the possibility of miracles. Marcus Borg, a well-known biblical scholar says 'I do not and cannot believe that God is an interventionist.'[326] John Shelby Spong, the retired Episcopal bishop of Newark, USA, is adamant that we live in a world 'that has no reason to believe that any danger has ever subsided, any sickness been cured, any natural disaster averted, or any war won in response to the prayers of human beings.' To believe otherwise, he argues, is 'naïve at best and unbelievable at worst.'[327] The famous German scholar Rudolf Bultmann concluded that the miracles were not historical on the general philosophical principle that modern people do not believe in miracles.[328]

Before proceeding, let's ask: What is a miracle? John Meier offers a useful working definition: 'A miracle is (1) an unusual, startling, or extraordinary event that is in principle perceivable by any interested and fair-minded observer, (2) an event that finds no reasonable

---

326 Marcus J. Borg, *The Heart of Christianity*, HarperSanFrancisco, 2003, p. 196.
327 John Shelby Spong, *Why Christianity Must Change or Die*, HarperSanFrancisco, 1998, p. 140.
328 Raymond E. Brown, *Responses to 101 Questions on the Bible*, Paulist Press, New York, 1990, p. 65.

explanation in human abilities or in other known forces that operate in our world of time and space, and (3) an event that is the result of a special act of God, doing what no human power can do.'[329] Do such miracles occur? A Gallup opinion survey published in 1989 found that about eighty-two per cent of Americans polled believed that 'even today, miracles are performed by the power of God.' Only six percent completely disagreed with the proposition.[330]

Any objective observer can answer the first two points of Meier's definition, but only faith enables us to answer 'Yes' to the third point. Consider a contemporary example of healing. At the shrine of Lourdes in France there is a medical bureau that is made up of doctors of different faiths and no faith.[331]

Their task is to examine supposed miraculous cures to ascertain where there is any medical or scientific explanation for the cure they have been asked to examine. Members of this medical bureau examine the patient's records to establish that a serious condition did exist. They further ascertain that the cure occurred without any medical intervention, that the cure was instantaneous or of baffling rapidity, and that the condition hasn't reoccurred within a year, and finally that there is no indication of fraud or psychological delusion.

If they are satisfied that these conditions exist they refer the case to what is called the International Medical Committee, located

---

329 John P. Meier, *A Marginal Jew: Mentor, Message, and Miracles, Volume II*, Doubleday, New York, 1994, p. 512.
330 George Gallup, Jr, and Sarah Jones, *100 Questions and Answers: Religion in America*, Princeton Religion Research Center, 1989, quoted in John P. Meier, pp. 520-1.
331 The material on Lourdes may be found in Meier, pp. 515-17; 528.

in Paris. This committee conducts a further study and draws up a detailed report. If all the evidence satisfied the committee it may declare that the cure is 'medically inexplicable'. The doctors involved in this process distinguish between 'medically inexplicable' cures and those that are considered unusual but not beyond all possible scientific explanation. They avoid using the word 'miracle'.

Two doctors, both members of the medical team, one a committed Catholic and the other an atheist, might agree that a particular cure has no medical or scientific explanation. But how will each of them interpret that fact? The Catholic doctor may conclude, 'Surely God has cured this patient; it is a miracle.' The atheist will see things differently: 'Whatever the ultimate explanation, there is no miracle here because there is no God to cause miracles.' In neither case is the doctor speaking as a doctor, but as a person with a particular world view.

Between 1948 and 1993 there have been 1300 alleged cures at Lourdes, only eighteen of which have been accepted as miracles by church authorities. That simply means that only eighteen cures have met the very strict criteria adopted by the International Medical Committee. Let us be wary, therefore, of a peculiarly modern mindset that dismisses miracles because they defy the laws of nature. Raymond Brown warns that

> a modern philosophical understanding of reality is not to be assumed as one-hundred-percent correct and normative for what might have been. Nor is it really certain that modern people do not believe in miracles. Despite the put-down that those who do are not modern, I suspect that if one counted heads, more would believe in the miraculous than disbelieve.[332]

---

[332] Raymond E. Brown, op. cit., *Responses to 101 Questions on the Bible*, p. 66.

Demons are certainly a manifestation of the kingdom of evil in the gospels, but so are sickness and affliction. In Mark's gospel miracles are signs of the decisive victory over forces that oppose God's reign, signs that the long-awaited time of liberation is at hand.

These miracles, or mighty works as the New Testament calls them, herald the sovereign and healing rule of Israel's God. They announce 'that the kingship of God is now breaking anew into human history and into that of Palestinian Judaism in particular. They are the concrete evidence that a new understanding of God's kingship is authentic.'[333]

---

333 Joseph A. Fitzmyer, op. cit., *A Christological Catechism*, p. 35.

Reflections for the year of Mark

TENTH SUNDAY IN ORDINARY TIME

(YEAR B)

The snake tempted me and I ate. (Gen 3:13)

The Book of Genesis tells us about the creation of the world, and about the creation of man and woman. But it didn't take place exactly as the Book of Genesis tells us it happened. What really happened was this. God created man, but he soon became lonely. So God created the animals and paraded them past the man. But none of them took the man's fancy. And so God said, 'Look, I can fashion a creature for you, I'll call it 'woman', and she will cook, wash and iron and look after all the housework. She'll never answer back or nag, and be totally subservient.'

'Wow', said the man. 'What will that cost me?'

'That will cost you an arm and a leg,' replied God.

'Gee, that's pretty expensive. What would I get for just a rib?'

I love book sales, and only recently, while rummaging through a table of discounted books at a sale in the Pocket Book Shop I came across a gem. It was entitled the *Oxford Book of Villains*, edited by John Mortimer, the creator of Rumpole. It is an anthology of the great villains of English literature. Mortimer has categorised his villains under the following headings: Master Crooks, Minor Crooks, Murderers, Seducers and Cads, Con Men, Hypocrites, Traitors and Spies, and Tyrants. In the introduction he notes that the difficulty in preparing a book of villains is that the field stretches towards infinity. 'The world may be short of many things, rain forests, great politicians, black rhinos, saints and caviar, but the supply of villains is endless.'[334]

The fact of the matter is, though, that if villainy hadn't existed it would have been necessary for the creators of the world's literature to invent it. In most stories, villains provide the plot and make virtue interesting. Hamlet without the prince would be difficult, but Hamlet without Claudius would be impossible. Imagine the tedium of Snow White without the witch, or Little Red Riding Hood without the wolf. Could you imagine the story of Robin Hood without the Sheriff of Nottingham, or Cinderella without the ugly sisters.[335]

Malcolm Muggeridge once suggested that if God is the great dramatist, he knew that the serpent and his descendants were essential characters, and the cast list would be incomplete without them. And so, in today's first reading from the Book of Genesis, we meet the serpent.

What is this story all about, and how should we interpret it? Must we understand it literally? Does today's first reading describe an event that took place in a specific geographical location – the Garden of Eden? Was it an event that took place at a specific moment

---

[334] John Mortimer (ed.), *The Oxford Book of Villains*, Oxford University Press, Oxford, 1993, p. vii.
[335] Ibid., pp. vii-viii.

in human history? Biblical scholars would call this story a myth. Let me dwell for a moment on that word 'myth'. The term 'myth' has acquired pejorative connotations in our day-to-day language. Like the term 'old wives' tale' the word 'myth' is generally used to describe a fanciful story, or an explanation for something, that seems plausible at first, but ultimately proves to be false.

Weekly magazines like *Woman's Day* or *New Idea* regularly explode what they call 'myths'. An article in a recent edition of the British magazine *Harpers & Queen* asked a panel of health and beauty experts to examine 'the strange world of beauty myths'. Their task was 'to discover the truth (and destroy more than a few myths)'. 'Myth', as used in the article, is synonymous with 'pure fiction'. And so we learn that it is 'totally untrue' that 'Eating jelly will strengthen the nails'. The proposition 'Waxing doesn't hurt' is summarily dismissed as 'Myth!', and 'If you stop exercising, your muscle turns to fat' is a 'real myth'.[336]

In its more technical sense, the word 'myth' has quite a different meaning. Myth is a sacred story that seeks to express profound truths about the human condition, but the meaning and truth of the mythic story is not equivalent to its scientific and historical accuracy.[337] Is the Bible myth?

Well, the Bible is not really a single book. It is a library. In a library, you have books of every kind: fiction and fantasy; fact and fable. So it is with the Bible. And so, some parts of the Bible are

---

336 Newby Hands, 'True Lies', *Harpers & Queen*, November 1995, pp. 95-8.
337 John Shea, *Stories of God*, The Thomas More Press, Chicago, IL, 1978, p. 48.

myth, as understood in the technical sense of the word. But that does not mean that they are untrue. It simply means that the truth is not always to be found at the narrative level. That is true, of course, of the parables. Think of parables like the Prodigal Son and the Good Samaritan. Was Jesus telling us about events that had actually happened? Maybe they did, but that's irrelevant. Jesus told these stories, perhaps he made them up, to give us an insight into God and his kingdom. To argue about whether there really was a prodigal son or a good Samaritan would completely miss the point.

A fundamentalist makes the mistake of wanting to interpret the whole of the Bible as if it were literally true at the narrative level. In 1993, the Biblical Commission of the Catholic Church published a document entitled *The Interpretation of the Bible in the Church*. This Vatican document has a preface written by the then prefect of the Congregation for the Doctrine of the Faith, Cardinal Ratzinger (now Pope Benedict XVI). The preface says this about fundamentalism: The fundamentalist approach is dangerous, for it is attractive to people who look to the Bible for ready answers to the problem of life. Cardinal Ratzinger warns that 'the Bible does not necessarily contain an immediate answer to each and every problem', and he adds that

> fundamentalism actually invites people to a kind of intellectual suicide. It injects into life a false certitude, for it unwittingly confuses the divine substance of the biblical message with what are in fact its human limitations.[338]

---

338 Pontifical Biblical Commission, *The Interpretation of the Bible in the Church*, St Paul Book & Media, Boston, 1993, p. 75.

Reflections for the year of Mark

I have called the story in today's first reading a myth. In other words, it is a sacred story about the nature of evil in this world, using the metaphors of a garden, forbidden fruit and a wily serpent. The Genesis myth explores the nature of sin as rebellion, as a rejection of our divine destiny, as a loss of innocence, as alienation and exile from the harmony symbolised by the garden. The myth is set 'in the beginning' – in the time before time. It is a story about every time.

The story from Genesis is therefore not about a particular man and woman, Adam and Eve. Adam (a name meaning of the ground) and Eve (life-giving) are like Everyman, a character in a medieval morality play of that name. Plays such as *Everyman* were overtly didactic, more in the nature of an animated sermon.[339] They were an effective means of catechesis in a predominantly illiterate society.

The central character of the play, Everyman, represents all of humanity, as is clearly indicated by his name. God summons Death, his mighty messenger, and commands him:

> Go thou to Everyman,
> And show him, in my name,
> A pilgrimage he must on him take,
> Which he in no wise may escape.[340]

Everyman pleads that he is unready, and Death allows him time to find a companion for the journey beyond the grave. Virtues, vices, relationships and human faculties such as discretion, strength, and beauty are all personified and meet with Everyman to listen to his

---

[339] A.C. Cawley (ed.) *Everyman and Medieval Miracle Plays*, J.M. Dent & Sons, London, 1956.
[340] *Everyman*, line 65, in Cawley, p. 209.

plight. One by one, they desert him until Good Deeds alone undertakes to accompany him. 'All fleeth save Good Deeds.'[341]

The moral of the play is clear and unambiguous; Everyman's experience is true for all of us. Likewise in the Book of Genesis, Adam and Eve are not two individuals who once lived in a specific time and place. The man and the woman of Genesis transcend map and calendar.

They are every man and every woman who has ever existed, and their story is also the story of our own struggle with the forces of evil in the world.

---

341 *Everyman*, line 873, in Cawley, p. 232.

ELEVENTH SUNDAY IN ORDINARY TIME

(YEAR B)

What can we say the kingdom of God is like ... It is like a mustard seed ...
(Mk 4:30-31)

What is a parable, because we're told that Jesus would not speak to the people except in parables. 'Parable' comes from two Greek words, *para*, meaning next to, and *ballein*, meaning to throw, and so 'parable' means literally 'to throw next to'. A parable attempts to explain something that is mysterious to us; in today's gospel it's the kingdom of God (or God's reign or rule).

We know little or nothing about God's kingdom, so let's place (or throw up) alongside it something we are familiar with (a mustard seed) and allow it to throw light on what we don't know. The parable proceeds from the known to the unknown. It's a brain teaser and often, it must be said, has a sting in the tail. God's kingdom is like a mustard seed. We're told that the mustard seed at the time of its sowing is the smallest of all the seeds on earth, yet it grows into the biggest shrub of them all. What does that tell us about God's kingdom? Well, that it has the tiniest of beginnings and grows into something great. Let's see how that works.

Releasing the Captive

In the 1950s in Montgomery, Alabama, buses were racially segregated, but if the white section of the bus filled up, black people were supposed to give up their seats to the whites. On the evening of December 1, 1955, Rosa Parks, aged 42, was sitting in the front seat of the coloured section of a bus and all the seats reserved for whites had filled up. The bus driver said, 'Let me have those front seats.' But nobody moved, including Rosa. She was tired of giving in to white people. The driver spoke up a second time: 'Y'all better make it light on yourselves and let me have those seats.'[342]

Rosa explained how she felt:

> For half of my life there were laws and customs in the South that kept African Americans segregated from Caucasians and allowed white people to treat black people without any respect. I never thought this was fair, and from the time I was a child, I tried to protest against disrespectful treatment. But it was very hard to do anything about segregation and racism when white people had the power of the law behind them.[343]

So Rosa refused to budge from her seat. The driver threatened her. 'I'm going to have you arrested.' Two white police officers boarded the bus and escorted her to a squad car.

That small gesture of defiance ignited the American Civil Rights movement. A bus boycott was organised, with the result that Montgomery city buses were practically empty. When the boycott finally ended a year later, segregation on buses was ruled unconstitutional.

---

342 Rosa Parks (with Jim Haskins), *Rosa Parks: My Story*, Puffin Books, New York, 1992, p. 115.
343 Ibid., p. 2.

Reflections for the year of Mark

And that was only the beginning! Rosa could have been tempted to think that nothing that she could do would make the slightest bit of difference, but how wrong she would have been. I'm reminded of something Anita Roddick said (quoting Betty Reese): 'If you think you are too small to be effective, you have never been in bed with a mosquito.'

Muhammad Yunus is a Bangladeshi banker and economist and founder of the Grameen Bank. The Grameen Bank is a unique organisation established for the sole purpose of extending microcredit to the poorest of the poor in Bangladesh. In 2006 Muhammad Yunus and the Grameen Bank jointly won the Nobel Peace Prize for their efforts to create economic and social development from below.

Again, it's a story of small beginnings and it began almost thirty years ago. After returning to Bangladesh from the USA with a brand-new PhD, Yunus began teaching at the University of Chittagong. But all around him people were dying of hunger as the country suffered from a severe famine. As an economist he felt helpless and frustrated. There was nothing in his economist's tool box that could help him to fix the situation. When he went to see how people lived in the village next door to the university campus he was overwhelmed by the extent of the problem, but he resolved to do something. 'I don't have the capacity to make a permanent contribution in any way. But definitely I have the capacity to help one person for one day.' Here we have the mustard seed falling into the ground.

Yunus soon discovered that money lenders in the village were destroying people's lives. He met a woman who was making bamboo

Releasing the Captive

stools, but she earned only a few cents each day. 'I couldn't believe anybody could work so hard and make such beautiful bamboo stools yet make such a tiny amount of profit. She explained to me that because she didn't have the money to buy the bamboo to make the stools, she had to borrow from a trader, and the trader imposed the condition that she had to sell the product to him alone, at a price that he decided.'

The woman had virtually become a slave labourer for the trader, for such a small amount of money. When Yunus asked her how much the bamboo cost she said, 'Oh, about 20 cents.' He realised that 'People suffer for 20 cents and there is nothing anyone can do about it.' He wanted to give some money to people like this woman so that they would be free from the moneylenders and able to sell their products at market prices, which were much higher that the pittance they received from traders. He debated whether he should give her twenty cents, but came up with another idea. He decided to make a list of people in the village who needed that kind of money.

With one of his students he went around the village for several days and came up with a list of 42 people who were in the same predicament as the woman making bamboo stools. When he added up the total amount of money these 42 people needed he was astounded. It added up to 27 dollars. He felt ashamed of himself for being part of a society which could not provide even 27 dollars to 42 hard working, skilled human beings.

Yunus' first response was to give the 27 dollars to those 42 people, telling them they can pay him back whenever they were able to. This

Reflections for the year of Mark

would enable them to sell their products wherever they could get a good price. But why couldn't a bank do this? 'I went to the bank and proposed that they lent money to the poor. The bankers almost fell over.' They came up with one excuse after another. 'They are not creditworthy; they cannot offer collateral; such a tiny amount is not worth lending; they will never pay it back.'

It was then that the mustard seed began to germinate. 'Finally, I had the thought, Why am I trying to convince them? I am totally convinced that poor people can take money and pay it back. Why don't we set up a separate bank?' It took Yunus two years to convince the government, but it finally happened on 2 October 1983. Now the Grameen Bank works in more than 46,000 villages in Bangladesh, through 1267 branches and over 12,000 staff members. They have given loans to five million people, and the repayment rate stands at 98 per cent.

Yunus believes that his greatest challenge 'has been to change the mindset of people. Mindsets play strange tricks on us. We see things the way our minds have instructed our eyes to see.'[344]

What can come of a mustard seed? It is the smallest of seeds. 'The seed itself may be quite inconsequential, but deep within itself it possesses great potential,' and although this potential 'unfolds before the eyes of human beings, the secrets of its growth are really

---

[344] My information on Muhammad Yunus and the Grameen Bank comes from a number of interviews available on the internet, but also from the transcript of an interview with Yunus in Stephen R. Covey, *The 8th Habit*, Free Press, New York, 2004, pp. 6-9. See also the interview (and transcript of the interview) with Andrew Denton on the ABC programme *Elders* http://www.abc.net.au/tv/elders/transcripts/s2757468.htm

beyond human comprehension. Human beings plant the seed, watch it grow, and harvest its yield, but the seed works in its own mysterious ways.'[345] How often are we tempted to do nothing because, we argue, our paltry efforts would achieve nothing? What difference can I make? The parable of the mustard seed encourages us to use the little we have in the service of God's kingdom, and to allow its potential to unfold in ways that are beyond human fathoming.

---

345 Dianne Bergant and Richard Fragomeni, *Preaching the New Lectionary*, Year B, p. 280.

Reflections for the year of Mark

TWELFTH SUNDAY IN ORDINARY TIME

(YEAR B)

> *Then it began to blow a gale and the waves were breaking into the boat so that it was almost swamped. But he was in the stern, his head on the cushion, asleep.* (Mk 4:38)

'I am plagued by doubts,' writes Woody Allen. 'What if everything is an illusion and nothing exists? In that case, I definitely overpaid for my carpet. If only God would give me some clear sign! Like making a large deposit in my name at a Swiss bank account.'[346]

Perhaps we've all, at one time or another, expressed sentiments similar to those of Woody Allen. In difficult times we feel confused, unsure of where we're going. We want a sign, but the Lord is nowhere to be found. We feel abandoned. Today's story about the apostles crossing the Lake of Galilee is the gospel's response to our feelings of abandonment. Jesus was asleep in the stern of the boat, worn out from his ministry. It was then that a fierce storm suddenly blew up. The apostles were overwhelmed with fear, and aroused their sleeping master. 'We're sinking; don't you care?' And Jesus rebuked the wind

---

346 Woody Allen, *Complete Prose*, Picador, London, 1997, p. 10.

and said to the sea, 'Quiet now! Be calm!' And the wind dropped, and all was calm again. 'Ah', we might say. 'If only it were like that in real life! If only the Lord would intervene when I am caught in the middle of some storm, and with a simple command, restore calm to my troubled life!'

Well, perhaps God is present, but we're not aware of it at the time. Consider for a moment that epic event we know as the Exodus. The explicit intervention of God, as recorded in the book of Exodus, may strain the credibility of contemporary readers.

Rabbi Harold Kushner tells the story of a youngster who returned home from Sunday school where he had just learnt the story of the Exodus. When his mother asked him what he'd learnt, he told her: 'The Israelites got out of Egypt, but Pharaoh and his army chased after them. They got to the Red Sea and they couldn't cross it. The Egyptian army was getting closer. So Moses got on his walkie-talkie, the Israeli air force bombed the Egyptians, and the Israeli navy built a pontoon bridge so the people could cross.' When the shocked mother asked if that was really the way the story was taught, the lad replied, 'Well, no, but if I told it to you the way they told it to us, you'd never believe it.'[347]

Looking back over their flight from slavery in Egypt, the Israelites realised that God was truly present among them, even if it hadn't seemed so at the time. The Bible's account of the Exodus makes explicit what only became obvious in hindsight. 'You'd never believe it!' A society that demands scientific analysis and empirical verifica-

---

[347] Harold S. Kushner, *When Bad Things Happen to Good People*, p. 64.

tion constantly attempts to edit out our sense of the sacred. When Alexander Solzhenitsyn received the Templeton Prize for Progress in Religion in 1983 he observed that

> The great crisis of humanity today is that it has lost its sense of the invisible. We have become experts in the visible, particularly in the West.[348]

In Greek drama an apparently insoluble crisis was often resolved through the intervention of a god, a role played by an actor who was lowered onto the stage by a crane. Such a dramatic ploy was known by the Latin phrase *deus ex machina*, literally 'god from the machine'. *Deus ex machina* came into English usage from Horace's *Ars Poetica* where he instructs poets that they must never resort to a god from the machine to solve their plots. Few modern works feature deities lowered onto stage by a crane, but the term deus ex machina describes situations where an author resorts to an artificial or improbable (and often clumsy) plot device to work his or her way out of a difficult situation. When the cavalry comes charging over the hill or when the impoverished hero is relieved by an unexpected inheritance, it's often called a *deus ex machina*.

The *deus ex machina* would be a handy kind of god to have – a deity ready to intervene whenever we are imperiled by the storms of life. But our experience of God is often quite different. In 1940 C.S. Lewis wrote *The Problem of Pain*, a reflection on suffering from a purely theoretical point of view. Lewis writes about pain as a detached spectator. Some twenty years later he wrote another book on pain,

---

348 *The Tablet*, 14 May 1983.

A Grief Observed, published under a pseudonym. *A Grief Observed* was written after his beloved wife, Joy Davidman, had died of cancer in the third year of their short-lived marriage. He is no longer the detached spectator; now he is an actor, intimately involved in the drama of human suffering. 'You never know how much you really believe anything,' Lewis wrote, 'until its truth or falsehood becomes a matter of life and death to you.'[349]

When the storm of despair seems set to overwhelm us, we cry out, 'Where is God?' In the midst of his grief Lewis wrote,

> When you are happy, so happy that you have no sense of needing Him, if you turn to Him then with praise, you will be welcomed with open arms. But go to Him when your need is desperate, when all other help is vain and what do you find? A door slammed in your face, and a sound of bolting and double bolting on the inside. After that, silence. You may as well turn away.[350]

We are wrestling here with an ancient mystery, known in more recent times as theodicy, a term coined by one of the great philosophers and mathematicians of the seventeenth century, Gottfriend Wilhelm Leibniz (1646–1716). Theodicy struggles with the tension between belief in an all-powerful and all-loving God on the one hand, and the reality of human suffering on the other. The book of Job seeks to unravel the mystery of human suffering but, in the end, Job is forced to acknowledge that his 'ignorant words' cannot fathom

---

349 Quoted in Philip Yancey, *Where is God When It Hurts?: Disappointment with God*, p. 20.
350 Quoted in Yancey, *Where is God When it Hurts?: Disappointment with God*, p. 15.

that which is beyond him. (cf. Job 42:3). A verse from the Bengali poet Rabindranath Tagore (1861–1941) comes to mind:

> The water in a vessel is sparkling;
> the water in the sea is dark.
> The small truth has words that are clear;
> the great truth has great silence.[351]

In April 2011 Pope Benedict responded to a question asked by Elena, a seven-year-old Japanese girl in the wake of a devastating earthquake and tsunami. She told the pope, 'I am very frightened because the house where I felt safe really shook a lot and many children my age have died. I cannot go to play in the park. I want to know: why do I have to be so afraid? Why do children have to be so sad?'

The pope told Elena that we do not have the answers, 'but we know that Jesus suffered as you do, an innocent, and that the true God who is revealed in Jesus is by your side. This seems very important to me, even if we do not have the answers, even if we are still sad; God is by your side and you can be certain that this will help you.'[352]

Threatened by the dark and tempestuous sea we instinctively seek a *deus ex machina* to extricate us immediately. 'Beam me up, Scotty!' But the great truth confronts us with silence; there are no small truths from the heart of the tempest. Today's gospel does not solve

---

351 'Stray Birds', CLXXVI, in *Collected Poems & Plays of Rabindranath Tagore*, Macmillan, London, 1962, p. 309.
352 http://www.catholicnewsagency.com/news/in-historic-tv-qa-pope-benedict-speaks-about-suffering-comatose-persons-persecution/

the problem, because it is not a problem to be solved. We are grappling here with a profound mystery, and the gospel leaves us with an image that help us see into the mystery – the beautiful image of Jesus with us, his head on the cushion, asleep in the stern.

When we are fearful and overwhelmed by the waves; where do we place our faith? In the power of the mighty storm, or in the one whom even the wind and the sea obey? Such a faith does not mean certainty; it means the courage to live with uncertainty. In the words of Rabbi Jonathan Sacks, such a faith 'does not mean having the answers, it means having the courage to ask the questions and not let go of God, as he does not let go of us.'[353].

---

353 Jonathan Sacks, *To Heal a Fractured World: The Ethics of Responsibility*, Continuum, London, 2005, p. 199.

THIRTEENTH SUNDAY IN ORDINARY TIME

(YEAR B)

My daughter, your faith has restored you to health;
go in peace and be free from your complaint. (Mk 5:34)

Today's gospel has sometimes been called a Markan sandwich, a reference to a technique that Mark uses several times – framing one story with another.[354] The idea is that each story helps to interpret the other or, to sustain the culinary image, 'the flavour of the outer story adds zest to the inner one; the taste of the inner one is meant in turn to permeate the outer one.'[355]

The outer story is about the raising of the daughter of Jairus, while the inner story is about a woman suffering from a haemorrhage. Mark links the women in a number of ways: neither of them is named, but they are both referred to as 'daughter'; the older woman has been suffering from her affliction for twelve years, and that is the age of the younger girl; the contrast of the older woman needing to touch Jesus to be healed, and Jesus touching the younger girl to bring her back to life

---

354 This technique of storytelling is also called intercalation, or simply A-B-A.
355 Tom Wright, *Mark for Everyone*, p. 58.

Releasing the Captive

Jairus is a synagogue official and almost certainly a prominent and respected man in the village. His office involved leading the worship services and overseeing the physical condition and financial well-being of the synagogue.[356] Like the woman whom we shall meet in a moment, Jairus has faith in the power of Jesus to heal. Throwing himself at the feet of Jesus he earnestly beseeches him to come and lay his hands upon her so that she might be saved and have life.

Here, at least, is one Jewish leader who is not hostile to Jesus. Jesus then sets out to see the girl, followed by a large crowd. Enter the woman with the haemorrhage. Some commentators regard the woman with a flow of blood as being ritually unclean, but the text of the gospel never mentions uncleanness. Nor is the gospel text explicit about the location of the haemorrhage, although most commentators conclude that the flow is uterine or vaginal. Even if the haemorrhage were uterine, there is nothing in the purity laws of the Pentateuch (cf. Lev 15:25-30) that would socially ostracise this woman, nor is there a prohibition against her touching anyone.[357]

The American biblical scholar John Meier concludes that 'the issue of contracting ritual impurity does not seem to be on the mental horizon of the evangelists as they tell the story of the woman with the flow of blood. It is later commentators, starting with the Fathers of the Church, who read the problem into the text.'[358]

---

356 Cf. Joel Marcus, *Mark 1-8*, p. 355; Donahue and Harrington, *The Gospel of Mark*, p. 173.
357 Amy-Jill Levine, 'Discharging Responsibility: Matthean Jesus, Biblical Law, and Hemorrhaging Woman', in Amy-Jill Levine (ed.), *A Feminist Companion to Matthew*, Pilgrim Press, Cleveland, OH, 2004, p. 77; John P. Meier, *A Marginal Jew: Law and Love, Volume IV*, Yale University Press, New Haven, 2009, p. 409.
358 John P. Meier, *A Marginal Jew: Law and Love, Volume IV*, p. 409.

This woman has lived with a distressing condition for twelve years and she is desperate. Having spent all her money on long and painful treatments under various doctors she was none the better for it; in fact she was getting worse. She had probably tried all the treatments available to women with her problem. The Talmud lists no fewer than eleven treatments for menstrual disorders. Some of these treatments are tonics and astringents, but others leave us dumbfounded: 'carrying the ashes of an ostrich-egg in a linen rag in summer and a cotton rag in winter; or carrying a barley corn which had been found in the dung of a white she-ass.'[359]

In faith she reached out and touched Jesus' cloak, 'and immediately something like an electric shock courses through her body'[360], and the flow of blood stopped immediately. This is the only miracle story in the gospels where Jesus does not initiate the cure. Of her own accord this woman reached out and snatched the power of God. 'Your faith has restored you to health,' Jesus tells her.

Jesus then continues his journey to Jairus' house, but the young girl is dead by the time he arrives. Jesus exhorts Jairus to have faith. One who is stronger than death has arrived. This means that Jairus and his household 'must resist the way death parades as ultimate and not be carried away by weeping and wailing or cowed by ridicule.'[361]

The faith that Jesus requires, *pistis* in the Greek text, has just been manifested so beautifully in the story of the woman's healing. It 'implies not just intellectual assent but emotional involvement and

---

359 William Barclay, *The Gospel of Mark*, p. 128. Cf. b.Sabb. 110ab.
360 Joel Marcus, *Mark 1-8*, p. 367.
361 Ibid., p. 360.

commitment and is sometimes better translated by "trust".'[362] This faith or trust is tested in times of adversity. How many times during those twelve years of suffering with a haemorrhage did this woman reach the brink of despair? Perhaps it made her bitter, but today's gospel story suggests that it also made her better. The woman's haemorrhage brought her to this turning point in her life, this moment of faith. How difficult was it for Jairus, a synagogue leader, to reach out in faith to Jesus? Whatever personal reservations he might have had about Jesus, he is desperate because his daughter is close to death.

Today's gospel invites us to ask ourselves how we have handled failures and disappointments. Have they crushed us, or have they become instruments of self-transcendence?

The Australian movie *The View from Greenhaven* is about a retired couple, Dot and Dash, who live in an idyllic coastal town. Dash McGregor, the husband, has become an irascible and grumpy hermit, spending most of his time in the backyard shed and hurting the feelings of those who love him the most.

On the occasion of their 40th wedding anniversary Dot and Dash receive the gift of a mystery train trip from their adult daughter. Dash reluctantly accompanies his wife but he can't enter into the spirit of the adventure, especially when the mystery destination turns out to be the very town in which they live. Dot and Dash's relationship reaches a crisis point when Dot decides to leave him. She tells Dash, 'You live in paradise. You've got everything – a beautiful family, a beautiful home, a wife who loves you, but you can't see it, so I can't

---

[362] Ibid., p. 360

stay.' Dash is devastated: 'Stay because I love you.' As Dot turns to board the train she replies, 'When was the last time you showed me?' Dash is forced to face the demons of his past and to act decisively, and he does. But nothing would have changed had not Dot trampled on his heart. Dash is set free from a prison of his own making.

Suffering can crush the human spirit, but it can also become an agent of transcendence. I am reminded of a memorable scene from Goethe's play, *Faust*. Faust, the seeker after truth, is disturbed in his study by Mephistopheles, who is, in fact, the devil, disguised as a wandering scholar. In the course of the conversation, Faust asks, 'Who art thou?' He receives an enigmatic reply, 'I am part of that spirit which always wills evil, but always creates good.'[363] In other words, people so often rise above themselves and are transformed through their suffering. As Darryl Reanney points out,

> It is precisely because Beethoven was going deaf that he was driven to write some of his greatest music; precisely because Demosthenes had a speech impediment that he went on to become one of the greatest orators in ancient Athens; precisely because Helen Keller was born blind that she was able to "see" the inner workings of human sorrow in such clear outline.[364]

William Bausch calls today's gospel 'a gospel of invitation.' It invites us to ask 'How have the failures made you a better person? How have the disappointments brought you to your knees? How have the hurts at least given you a certain humility – to know that

---

363 Quoted in Darryl Reanney, *The Death of Forever*, Longman Cheshire, Melbourne, repr. 1993, p. 232.
364 Ibid., p. 233.

ultimately everything's in God's hands anyway? How have the troubles and the addictions, the broken hearts, given you a better sensitivity with humankind?'[365]

---

[365] William J. Bausch, *Timely Homilies*, Twenty-Third Publications, Mystic, CT, 1990, p. 101.

FOURTEENTH SUNDAY IN ORDINARY TIME

(YEAR B)

A prophet is only despised in his own country among his own relations and in his own house. (Mk 6:4)

After listening to what Jesus had to say the people of Nazareth ask in amazement, 'This is the carpenter, surely?' 'Carpenter' is a translation of the Greek word *tektōn*, a term that could be applied to any worker who plied his trade 'with a hard material that retains its hardness throughout the operation, e.g., wood and stone or even horn or ivory.'[366] The word often referred to a woodworker, and some of Jesus' work would certainly have been carpentry in the narrow sense of the word. It was a calling that involved 'a wide range of skills and tools', and while it demanded a fair level of technical skill it 'also involved no little sweat and muscle power'. Fr John Meier observes, 'The airy weakling often presented to us in pious paintings and Hollywood movies would hardly have survived the rigors of being

---

[366] Richard A. Batey, 'Is Not This the Carpenter?' NTS 30 (1984), pp. 249-58, quoted in John P. Meier, *A Marginal Jew: The Roots of the Problem and the Person*, Volume I, p. 281.

Nazareth's *tektōn* from his youth to his early thirties.'[367] John Dominic Crossan warns against interpreting *tektōn* in modern terms 'as a skilled, well-paid, and respected member of the middle class'.[368]

The upper and lower classes within the Roman Empire were separated by an abysmal gulf.

> On the one side of that great divide were the Ruler and the Governors, who together constituted one per cent of the population but owned at least half of the land. Also on that same side were three other classes: the Priests, who could own as much as 15 per cent of the land; the Retainers, ranging from military generals to expert bureaucrats; and the Merchants, who probably evolved upward from the lower classes but who could end up with considerable wealth and even some political power as well.' On the other side of the divide was the vast majority of the population, the peasants, who lived at subsistence level if they were lucky. About two-thirds of their annual crop went to support the upper classes. About five percent of the population belonged to the artisan class – below the peasants in social class 'because they were usually recruited and replenished from its disposed members. Beneath the artisan class were 'the Degraded and Expendable classes – the former with origins, occupations, or conditions rendering them outcasts; the latter, maybe as much as 10 percent of the population, ranging from beggars and outlaws to hustlers, day laborers, and slaves.[369]

As a *tektōn* Jesus belonged to the artisan class, and that perhaps explains why the people of his hometown were so bewildered by his learning. 'Where did the man get all this?' As so often happens,

---

[367] John P. Meier, *A Marginal Jew, Volume I*, p. 281.
[368] John Dominic Crossan, *Jesus: A Revolutionary Biography*, p. 24.
[369] Ibid., p. 25.

those who know us the best understand us the least. But perhaps his teaching unsettled them.

> The kind of kingdom Jesus was talking about was not the sort of kingdom his contemporaries wanted to hear about. When the good folk of Nazareth had such an excuse for rejecting him, they took it with both hands. They didn't need to believe such a dangerous message; they could dismiss it as 'Oh, he's just the local handyman'. As if that made any difference.[370]

They were unwilling to see beyond his apparent ordinariness and that was their way of containing the challenge. G.K. Chesterton once wrote that 'the greatest of all illusions is the illusion of familiarity.'[371] Fr Ronald Rolheiser makes the observation that

> familiarity is also the death of respect, wonder, and awe. When our minds, hearts, and imaginations are no longer poised for surprise and astonishment, when we feel that we have already understood something, then we no longer have a healthy fear of God or indeed of each other. A healthy fear of God means living in such a way that nothing becomes too familiar to us.[372]

We hear what we want to hear; we see what we want to see. A class of children was taken on a bushwalk by their teacher. She explained to them that, during the walk, they were to observe the various plants, insects, animals and birds in the bush. When they returned to their classroom they were to make a list of what they'd seen. At the end of the excursion one young boy, Michael, had writ-

---

370 Tom Wright, *Mark for Everyone*, p. 66.
371 A paraphrase of G.K. Chesterton, *The Everlasting Man*, 26-28, quoted in Ronald Rolheiser, *The Shattered Lantern*, p. 107.
372 Ronald Rolheiser, *The Shattered Lantern*, p. 107.

ten: 'No kangaroos'. That was the sole record of his observations. The teacher acknowledged that neither he nor any of the other children had observed any kangaroos in the bush, and she sympathised with Michael in his disappointment. But she urged him to think about what else he might have seen during the walk, and to record that on his project sheet. Michael replied: 'But I was only looking for kangaroos.'

The 2006 movie *Colour Me Kubrick* is the story of Alan Conway (played by John Malkovich), an English con artist who deceived a surprising number of people into believing that he was the famous film director Stanley Kubrick. What made this deception all the more amazing was that Conway didn't resemble Kubrick in the slightest, nor did he know a great deal about Kubrick or his movies. Conway's success, it would seem, lay in that fact that because people were enamoured by the mystique attached to Kubrick's name, they wanted to believe that he was Kubrick. We see what we want to see.

In the 1972 movie *Butterflies are Free*, Don Baker is a young man, blind from birth. Don (played by Edward Albert), moves into a Greenwich Village apartment and becomes acquainted with his scatty next-door-neighbour, a 19-year-old actress named Jill Tanner (played by Goldie Hawn). Jill seems totally incapable of forming a lasting relationship. Like a butterfly flitting freely from one flower to the next, she drifts from one romantic involvement to another.

Jill and Don become emotionally involved, but she puts the relationship in the 'too-hard basket' – because, she tells him, 'you can't see'. To which Don replies, 'There are none so blind as those who will not see.' Ironically, he who was blind was far more perceptive in seeing into the workings of the human heart.

A certain man who used to meet his brother every Friday afternoon for a few drinks after work was transferred by his company to New York. Bidding him farewell at the airport, the brother said: 'Make sure you have a drink for me every Friday afternoon.' And so, religiously, every Friday in New York the man would go to the same bar and order two large Scotches.

This went on, week after week, for several years. Until on one occasion the man approached the bar and ordered only one Scotch. The bartender looked concerned. 'Gee, I hope this doesn't mean that something has happened to your brother.' To which the man replied, 'No, No, No. My brother's fine. But just the other day I visited the doctor and he was seriously concerned about my liver. He told me I had to give up drinking, and I have. From now on I'm just having one for my brother.' We hear what we want to hear!

The people of Nazareth could not or would not see; they were asking the right questions – Where did he get all this? What is this wisdom that has been granted him, and these miracles that are worked through him? But they immediately supplied their own answers – he's the carpenter, he's the son of Mary, the brother of James and Joset and Jude and Simon. Theirs is 'the premature answer to the challenge of Jesus of Nazareth that brooks no further enquiry.'[373] Jesus is rejected 'by those who knew (him) the best but

---

373 Robert Crotty and Gregory Manly, *Commentaries on the Readings of the Lectionary*, Pueblo Publishing Company, New York, 1975, p. 248

apparently understood him the least – a situation not uncommon for those who have been drawn by God from out of the group to speak God's word to that group.'[374]

The folk of Nazareth failed to see, they failed to hear, and because of their lack of faith Jesus could work no miracle there. In the words of William Barclay, 'There is laid on us the tremendous responsibility that we can either help or hinder the work of Jesus Christ. We can open the door wide to Him – or we can slam it in His face.'[375]

---

[374] Dianne Bergant and Richard Fragomeni, *Preaching the New Lectionary, Year B*, p. 296.
[375] William Barclay, *The Gospel of Mark*, p. 141

FIFTEENTH SUNDAY IN ORDINARY TIME

(YEAR B)

Jesus summoned the Twelve and began to send them out in pairs. (Mk 6:7)

Jonathan Sacks is Chief Rabbi of Britain and the Commonwealth and in one of his recent books, *To Heal a Fractured World*, he writes about the ethics of responsibility. Reflecting upon the word 'responsibility' Rabbi Sacks makes an obvious point – it's made up of two words: 'response' and 'ability'. What is my ability to respond to the fractured world in which I live?

He tells the story of a young British university student who was halfway through an undergraduate course in philosophy. His studies had challenged his faith and he had many questions that he needed to discuss. While on vacation he travelled to the United States of America and sought out rabbis whose writings he had read.

Throughout his travels one name kept coming up in conversation. Time and time again he was told that he must meet one of the most revered leaders of the Jewish world, Menahem Mendel Schneersohn, known as the Rebbe of Lubavitch. When he visited Rabbi Schneersohn's centre in Brooklyn he told one of his disciples that he would like to meet the rabbi. The man laughed. 'You and thousands of others! Every moment of the rabbi's day is full.' The young British student was not deterred and he left a contact number in the hope that he might be able to arrange a meeting before he returned home. Three weeks later a phone call came. 'The rabbi can see you.'

When he was finally admitted to the rabbi's presence the student was surprised. He had imagined that the rabbi would be a powerful, charismatic leader, but instead he met an unassuming and quietly spoken man who gave the student the impression that he was the most important person in the room. The rabbi responded to the student's questions, but then he turned the tables and began to ask the student questions: What was he doing to strengthen Jewish life in the university where he was studying? Was he befriending other students and drawing them close?

The student was taken by surprise. He had never thought of himself as a leader, nor had he ever wanted to be one. He had sought out the rabbi in the hope that he might resolve certain questions about faith and religion. Instead, it seemed as though the rabbi was attempting to recruit him to a religious task. The rabbi became insistent. He was inviting this British student to get involved, to take the initiative and accept responsibility.

The effect of the meeting was not immediate and the student returned home to continue his studies. But the rabbi's words continued to echo in his mind. In a nutshell the rabbi had said 'Things are going wrong. Are you willing to be one of those who helps to put them right?' The question continued to trouble him, and years later the young man began theological studies and eventually became a rabbi, and then a teacher of rabbis, then a chief rabbi. Yes, Rabbi Jonathan Sacks was telling his own story. He had been called and challenged by a saintly rabbi who was more than a leader; he was someone who created leadership in others.[376]

Jesus has called his disciples, and now he sends them out on their first missionary journey. He instructs them to taken nothing with them on their journey – no bread, no haversack, no coppers for their purses, not even a second tunic.

'Journey' is a translation of the Greek *hodos*, and that word in Mark's gospel means more than just a trip from one place to another; it also connotes the 'way of discipleship'.[377] Jesus is about to teach his disciples a fundamental lesson in trust. They are to depend upon the hospitality offered to them. If they are not welcomed they are to move on.

These are not instructions solely for this mission; they are symbolic of the demands of discipleship. They are to trust both God and their neighbour. John Dominic Crossan contrasts the instructions that Jesus gave his disciples as he sent them out with the rather different approach of the Cynics.

Cynicism was a Greek philosophical movement founded by Diogenes of Sinope in the fourth century before Christ. The Cynics challenged society's material values, but they always carried a simple knapsack slung over their shoulders. 'What it symbolized for the Cynics was their complete self-sufficiency.'[378] The disciples of Jesus

---

376 Jonathan Sacks, *To Heal a Fractured World*, pp. 254-6.
377 Donahue & Harrington, *The Gospel of Mark*, p. 190.
378 John Dominic Crossan, *Jesus: A Revolutionary Biography*, p. 118.

are not self-sufficient and must depend upon the generosity and hospitality of others.

In the second year of the Jesuit novitiate in Australia, Jesuit novices undergo an experience that teaches this lesson. They are dropped about 140 kilometres from the Jesuit house at Sevenhill in South Australia and they have eight days to walk the distance home, begging for food and accommodation. They are not allowed to tell anyone who they are or what they are doing. Reflecting on this experience one Jesuit wrote,

> It's the only time in my life I've been remotely in what we could call a wilderness and the first time I've known real hunger. I experienced many knock backs, but there were a few occasions when people were extraordinarily generous. We were told that we couldn't trade off being a Jesuit, but if we were invited into someone's home we could tell them who we were so they wouldn't be afraid that they might have welcomed Jack the Ripper to stay the night. If, however, a person offers the garage and a sandwich we are not allowed to use our being a Jesuit to get an upgrade from economy to first class! One woman welcomed me into her home and questioned me at length about where I was from, where I was going, and how I got to her place. Then she declared, 'I think I can trust ya.' She then invited me into the house, offered a meal that night, breakfast the next morning, and the use of a comfortable guest room. Just before I left I thanked her for her extraordinary generosity and told her who I was. 'Well listen sunshine,' she said, 'let's face it, I knew you were OK 'cause you're the most beautifully spoken, articulate beggar I've ever met'.[379]

---

379 Richard Leonard, http://www.liturgyhelp.com Homily for the first Sunday of Lent, 2004.

Reflections for the year of Mark

Jesus sends the disciples out to heal a fractured world. You and I also have the ability to respond but, sadly, not always the inclination. 'Why me?' When the American West was being settled the stagecoach was the major means of transportation until the advent of rail. What is not commonly known, however, is that the stagecoach had three different kinds of ticket: first-, second- and third-class. Now how on earth, you may ask, could you have three separate classes when all the passengers sat together in a single cabin?

The difference between first-, second- and third-class tickets was this: if you had a first-class ticket, you could remain seated during the entire trip no matter what happened. If the stagecoach got stuck in mud, or had trouble making it up a steep hill, or if a wheel fell off, you could remain seated because you had a first-class ticket. If you had a second-class ticket, you could also remain seated – until there was a problem. In that case, you had to get out and stand to one side and watch while other people worked. You didn't have to get your hands dirty, but you weren't allowed to stay on board. When the stagecoach was fixed you could get back on board and take your seat.

If you had a third-class ticket, you had to get off if there was a problem, and you had to help fix it. You had to assist repairing a broken wheel, or push the coach if it got bogged down or had difficulty negotiating a steep incline.[380] Needless to say, if too many of us travel with first-class tickets very little will get done.

---

380 Adapted from William J. Bausch, *The Total Parish Manual*, Twenty-Third Publications, Mystic, CT, 1994, p. 19.

Releasing the Captive

Rabbi Sacks refers to a psychological phenomenon known as the Genovese Effect. It takes its name from Kitty Genovese, a young woman who was stabbed to death by a serial rapist and murderer in a New York suburb in 1964. Many people heard her cries but no one came to assist her. The Genovese or Bystander Effect was researched by two social scientists, John Darley and Bibb Latané, in 1968. They staged a number of emergencies and then measured how long it took before participants did something about it, or if they intervened at all. These experiments, frequently replicated, showed that a lone bystander was far more willing to intervene than a group of bystanders. People in a group all think that someone else should act. 'Why me?' 'Why should I intervene?'[381]

Jesus sent the disciples out to preach and heal, just as you and I are called and sent. Why me? Well, as Rabbi Sacks points out, there is no life without a task; no person without a talent; no moment without its call.

God whispers our name, and the greatest reply is that of Abraham: 'Here am I.' I am ready to heed your call, to mend a fragment of your all-too-broken world.[382]

---

[381] Jonathan Sacks, *To Heal a Fractured World*, p. 253. See also http://en.wikipedia.org/wiki/Bystander_effect
[382] Ibid., 262.

Reflections for the year of Mark

SIXTEENTH SUNDAY IN ORDINARY TIME

(YEAR B)

He took pity on them because they were like sheep without a shepherd.
(Mk 6:34)

Last Sunday's gospel told us about Jesus sending out the disciples in pairs. They preached repentance and healed many sick people. Now they've returned, tired and weary, but excited at what God has done through their ministry. In contemporary jargon they needed to debrief; they needed R&R. So Jesus invites them to come away to a deserted place to rest for a while. Unfortunately, things don't quite work out that way because people guessed where they were going and arrived at the place ahead of them. When Jesus stepped ashore he saw a large crowd waiting for him and he took pity on them. 'Pity' is a rather insipid translation of the Greek verb *splanchnizomai*, which comes from the noun *splanchna*. *Splanchna* refers to what were known as the 'nobler viscera', that is, the heart, the lungs, the liver and the intestines. These were considered to be the seat of the emotions, especially of anger, anxiety, desire, fear, and even of love. It refers, therefore, to the 'seat of feelings or sensibilities.' Instead of saying that Jesus was moved to pity, it would be a more accurate translation if we were to say that he was moved to the very depth of his being. 'Pity' sounds so limp and effete; 'compassion' would be closer to the mark.[383]

In his encyclical *Caritas in Veritate* (Love in Truth),[384] Pope Benedict is profoundly moved by the 'scandal of glaring inequalities', the gulf between the ostentatious wealth and profligacy of rich people and countries, and the acute deprivation of millions of others.[385] Here's an example of that gap. According to Jack de Groot, Chief Executive Officer of Caritas Australia, one billion people will go to bed hungry tonight.[386] The World Bank has set the poverty line at US$1.25 per day. The number of people whose income puts them under the poverty line is 1.4 billion.[387] According to UNICEF, nearly 10 million children under five years of age die each year from causes related to poverty.[388] As one man in Ghana, told a researcher from the World Bank:

> Take the death of this small boy ... The boy died of measles. We all know he could have been cured at the hospital. But

---

[383] Gerhard Kittel and Gerhard Friedrich (eds), *Theological Dictionary of the New Testament*, Abridged in one volume by Geoffrey W. Bromiley, William B. Eerdmans Publishing Company, Grand Rapids, MI, 1985, pp.1067-8; William Barclay, *New Testament Words*, SCM Press, London, 1964, pp. 276-80.
[384] http://www.vatican.va/holy_father/benedict_xvi/encyclicals/documents/hf_ben-xvi_enc_20090629_caritas-in-veritate_en.html
[385] Pope Benedict (*Caritas in Veritate*, p. 22) is quoting from Paul VI, Encyclical Letter, *Populorum Progressio*, p. 9
[386] http://www.adelaide.catholic.org.au/sites/SouthernCross/opinions?more=12626
[387] Peter Singer, *The Life You Can Save*, Text Publishing, Melbourne, 2009, p. 7.
[388] Ibid., p. 4.

the parents had no money and so the boy died a slow and painful death, not of measles but out of poverty.[389]

But consider some examples from the other side of the wealth divide. The co-founders of Google, Larry Page and Sergey Brin, reportedly bought a Boeing 767 and spent millions of dollars fitting it out for their private use. And what about the Iranian-American telecommunications entrepreneur, Anousheh Ansari, who paid a reported $20 million for eleven days in space?[390] According to Dr Timothy Jones, an archaeologist who led a US government-funded study of food waste, 100 billion dollars of food is wasted in the United States every year.[391] There are some good news stories, though. Warren Buffett, one of the most successful investors in history and ranked by Forbes as the second richest person in the world with an estimated net worth of approximately $37 billion, has pledged to give away eighty-five per cent of his fortune to the Gates Foundation.[392] Bill and Melinda Gates have already given $29 billion and are planning to give more.[393] Gates began his charitable outreach when he read that half a million children die every year from rotavirus. I must confess that I've never heard of rotavirus, nor had Bill Gates, but it's the most common cause of severe diarrhoea in children. He asked himself, 'how could I never have heard of something that kills

---

389 Donal McNeil, 'Child mortality at record low: further drop seen', *New York Times*, 13 September 2007, cited in Singer, p. 4.
390 Peter Singer, p. 10.
391 Lance Gay, 'Food waste costing economy $100 Billion, study finds', Scripps Howard News Service, 10 August 2005. Quoted in Singer, p. 12.
392 http://en.wikipedia.org/wiki/Warren_Buffett
393 Peter Singer, op. cit., p. xii.

half a million children every year?' In developing countries millions of children die from diseases that have been eliminated from first world countries. As Gates tells the story, he and his wife Melinda 'Couldn't escape the brutal conclusion that – in our world today – some lives are seen as worth saving and others are not'. This led Gates to set up his foundation and to endow it with an initial gift of $28.8 billion.[394]

When Jesus saw the crowd, he was moved to the very depth of his being. When, on 3 January 2007, Wesley Autry saw a young man suffer a seizure and fall from a Harlem station platform onto the railway tracks he didn't hesitate. As an oncoming train approached Autry jumped down to the tracks and pushed the man into a drainage trench between the rails, covering him with his own body. The train passed inches above Autry's head, but neither man was harmed. When he was later praised by the president of the United States for his bravery, he downplayed his actions: 'I don't feel like I did something spectacular. I just saw someone who needed help. I did what I felt was right'.[395]

Wesley Autry saved a life and was rightly acclaimed as 'the subway hero'. But what if I told you that you can save a life, without having to jump into the path of an oncoming train? Have you bought a bottle of water recently? If you're paying for bottled water when perfectly safe drinking water comes out of the tap, you're spending money on something you don't really need. Around the world there

---

394 Ibid., p. 168.
395 Ibid., ix.

are over a billion people who are struggling to survive on less than you paid for that bottle of water.[396] As I think about how I should respond to hunger and poverty I recall that during the past week I bought a coffee at Gloria Jeans, and I shared a bottle of wine over lunch with a friend. Those two items alone cost about $25, and I didn't really need either. If there were a poor and destitute family from a third world country actually here at Mass with us today I'm sure that we'd respond generously to their plight. But the same family faraway in another country is a different matter.

I've already mentioned the Genovese or Bystander Effect and the research undertaken by social psychologists John Darley and Bibb Latané.[397] Kitty Genovese was a young woman who was stabbed to death by a serial rapist and murderer in a New York suburb in 1964. Many people heard her cries but no one came to assist her. Darley and Latané staged a number of emergencies and then measured how long it took before participants did something about it, or if they intervened at all. These experiments, frequently replicated, showed that a lone bystander was far more willing to intervene than a group of bystanders. In one such experiment Darley and Latané invited students to participate in a market research survey. The students went to an office where a young woman gave them a questionnaire to fill out. She then went into an adjacent room that was separated from the office by a curtain. After a few minutes the students completing the questionnaire heard the woman cry out. She had obviously

---

396 Ibid.
397 B. Latané and J. Darley, *The Unresponsive Bystander: Why Doesn't He Help?* Appleton-Century-Crofts, New York, 1970.

climbed onto a chair to get something from a shelf, and the chair had fallen over: 'Oh, my God, my foot ... I ... I ... can't move ... it. Oh, my ankle. I ... can't ... can't ... get ... this thing off ... me.' Her moaning went on for another minute. How did the students react? When the experiment was conducted with only one student in the room, seventy per cent offered to help. When there was a second student present in the room completing the questionnaire (someone who was in fact a stooge, and who did not respond to the calls for help), only seven per cent offered help. Even when there were two genuine students in the room the proportion who offered to help was much lower than when there was only one student.[398] Which just goes to show that people in a group all think that someone else should act. 'Why me?' 'Why should I intervene?'[399]

In the words of Pope Benedict, 'Feed the hungry (cf. Mt 25: 35, 37, 42) is an ethical imperative for the universal Church, as she responds to the teachings of her Founder, the Lord Jesus, concerning solidarity and the sharing of goods.'[400] Over a billion people will go to be hungry tonight; millions of children will die of preventable disease. 'They' ought to do something about it – the government, the church, the United Nations, the World Bank, UNICEF, the Bill and Melinda Gates Foundation – and thankfully, they are. But what can I do? Hopefully my life will amount to more than consuming products and generating garbage. Will this world be a better place for my having been here?

---

398 Peter Singer, op. cit., 57.
399 Jonathan Sacks, *To Heal a Fractured World*, p. 253.
400 *Caritas in Veritate*, n. 27

SEVENTEENTH SUNDAY IN ORDINARY TIME

(YEAR B)

There is a small boy here with five barley loaves and two fish; but what is that between so many? (Jn 6:9)

Some well-known gospel stories are recorded by only one of the evangelists. The parable of the Good Samaritan, for example, is found only in Luke's gospel; we read about Jesus changing water into wine at the wedding feast of Cana only in the gospel of John; and it's only in Matthew's gospel that we hear of the magi or wise men paying homage to the infant Jesus. Today's gospel story of the feeding of the multitude is the only miracle recorded in all four gospels. In fact, Mark and Matthew offer two versions of this miracle; it must therefore be saying something very important to us.

I've called the feeding of the multitude a miracle, but John's gospel prefers the word 'sign'. And what does John mean by calling this incident a sign? The feeding of the multitude is not merely an act of compassion – Jesus' feeding a hungry and weary multitude that had followed him over some considerable distance. It is certainly that, but much more besides. It is a sign that points firstly to Jesus.

A favourite storytelling technique used by the evangelists is to take significant events from the Old Testament and repeat or echo them in a different context. They do this to show that Jesus has assumed the role that was previously filled by the great figures of the Hebrew scriptures, such as Elisha or Moses.[401] A Jewish audience hearing the story of the loaves and fishes would have been familiar with the story about Elisha that we heard today from the second book of Kings. Note the obvious parallels. A man offers Elisha some food, and Elisha tells him to give it to the people to eat. The small amount of food is obviously inadequate to feed one hundred men, but Elisha insists, 'Give it to the people to eat.' They eat, and there is food left over. Elisha, the man of God, feeds one hundred men, and there is food left over. Jesus feeds 5000 and there are twelve hampers of food left over. If a great man of God miraculously feeds a hundred, what conclusion can we draw from someone who miraculously feeds a far greater multitude?

John's gospel also wants us to hear the feeding of the multitude against the background of yet another story. He offers us a fairly explicit clue when he tells us that the feeding of the multitude took place shortly before the Jewish feast of Passover. We are immediately invited to listen to this story against the background of the great story of the Exodus. Matthew and Mark make the same point by telling us that this occurred in a desert place. When the Jews escaped from slavery in Egypt they wandered for forty years in the desert, and of course, God fed them with a bread-like substance they called

---

401 Richard Holloway, *Doubts and Loves*, Canongate, Edinburgh, 2005, p. 150.

manna. God fed the Israelites in the wilderness; Jesus fed the multitude in a deserted place. Here is the beginning of a new Exodus, a new liberation from slavery.

The story of the loaves and fishes is also a sign pointing to us. Jesus takes the offering of a small boy – five barley loaves and two fish. A child in first century Palestine had no rights, and we can see in the small boy a person without power or influence. Yet he brings the little he has, and Jesus does great things with it. Isn't it a perennial temptation, when confronted by what seem to be insurmountable obstacles, to throw up our arms in despair? My contribution won't make the slightest difference, we tell ourselves. The American statesman Benjamin Franklin responded to just such a predicament with this verse:

> For want of a nail the shoe was lost,
> for want of a shoe the horse was lost,
> for want of a horse the rider was lost,
> for want of a rider the army was lost,
> for want of the army the battle was lost,
> for want of the battle the war was lost,
> for want of the war the kingdom was lost,
> and all for the want of a little horseshoe nail.

When Pope John Paul II visited Scotland he challenged the young people to do what the small boy of today's gospel did:

> You feel conscious of your inadequacy ... But what I say to you is this: place your lives in the hands of Jesus. He will accept you and bless you ... beyond your greatest expectations.[402]

---

[402] Quoted in Mark Link, *Vision 2000*, Tabor Publishing, Allen, TX, 1992, p. 127.

Releasing the Captive

On one level this miracle is about feeding hungry people. I must admit that I have never experienced true hunger. The Russian writer and historian Alexander Solzhenitsyn fought in the Second World War, but was imprisoned in a Soviet forced-labour camp (or *gulag*) for eight years between 1945 and 1953 for commenting unfavourably on Stalin's conduct of the war. Solzhenitsyn began his writing career when he was released from prison, and was awarded the Nobel Prize for Literature in 1970.

One of his most moving books, written in 1973, is *The Gulag Archipelago*, a factual account of the reign of terror under Stalin. As a result he was arrested and exiled. He lived in the United States until he was free to return to Russia in 1994. Solzhenitsyn writes of the intense hunger prisoners experienced in the gulag. All that a starving prisoner could think of was food. Hunger forced an otherwise honest person to become a thief. It made the most unselfish person look towards his neighbour to see if his ration was bigger that his own.

Hunger darkens the mind so much that it refuses to dwell on anything else but food. Severe hunger turns a person into an insomniac. Even when one does manage to fall asleep, food is still present, for even one's dreams are concerned with it. He writes,

> If you were to ask a wartime camp inmate what his highest, supreme, and totally unattainable ambition was, he would reply without a second's hesitation: 'To eat just once a bellyful of black bread – and then I could die happy.'[403]

---

[403] Quoted in Flor McCarthy, *Sunday & Holyday Liturgies: Cycle B*, Dominican Publications, Dublin, 1983, p. 163.

Reflections for the year of Mark

A billion people go to bed each night hungry. I have never known such hunger or poverty. In some ways I'm like a rich young girl who began her essay thus: 'There was a poor family. The father was poor, the mother was poor. The children were poor. The butler was poor ...'[404]

Today's story of the young boy's seemingly insignificant offering of five loaves and two fish is saying something important to us. When Peter Singer teaches the course called Practical Ethics he asks his students to think about this hypothetical situation:

> On your way to work, you pass a small pond ... It's early in the morning, so you are surprised to see a child splashing about in the pond. As you get closer you see that it is a very young child, just a toddler, who is flailing about, unable to stay upright or walk out of the pond. You look for the parents or babysitter, but there is no one else around. The child is unable to keep his head above water for more than a few seconds at a time. If you don't wade in and pull him out, he seems likely to drown. Wading in is easy and safe, but you will ruin the new shoes you bought only a few days ago, your suit will get wet and muddy, and you'll be late for work. What should you do?

Most people would almost assuredly say, 'Rescue the child.' Ruining a new pair of shoes, getting your trousers wet, and being late for work aren't as important as saving a child's life. In this scenario the young child is in difficulty right before our eyes. We can see the child struggling; we can hear the cries of distress. We'd like to think that we'd do all we could to save the child. But

---

[404] A story Timothy Radcliff attributes to Sr Helen Prejean in Timothy Radcliff, *Why Go To Church?*, Continuum, London, 2008, p. 184.

what about the ten million children under five years of age who, according to UNICEF, will die of poverty-related causes this year? Because we can see them struggling and we can't hear their cries of distress it's easy to put them out of our mind.

We're good at making excuses for not acting. In 2007 something resembling Peter Singer's hypothetical situation occurred near Manchester, England. A ten-year-old young boy by the name of Jordon Lyon leapt into a pond to save his eight-year-old stepsister Bethany who had slipped in. He struggled to support her in water about two metres deep but went under himself. Some nearby fishermen managed to pull Bethany out, but by then Jordon could no longer be seen. When the alarm was raised two community support officers soon arrived, but they refused to enter the pond to find Jordon. He was later pulled out, but attempts at resuscitation failed. At the inquest on Jordon's death, the officers' refusal to act was defended on the grounds that they had not been trained to deal with such situations. The mother responded: 'If walking down the street and you see a child drowning you automatically go in that water. You don't have to be trained to jump in after a drowning child.'[405] Most of us would agree with the mother's statement, but keep in mind those ten million children under five years of age who will die this year from causes related to poverty. By donating a relatively small amount of money, you and I could save a child's life.

Can't afford much? That's all right. Just bring the five loaves and two fish that you have!

---

405 Peter Singer, *The Life You Can Save*, Text Publishing, Melbourne, 2009, pp. 3-4; For an account of Jordon Lyon's death, see http://news.bbc.co.uk/2/hi/uk_news/england/manchester/7006412.stm

EIGHTEENTH SUNDAY IN ORDINARY TIME

(YEAR B)

What sign will you give to show us that we should believe in you? What work will you do? (Jn 6:30)

Last Sunday we heard St John's account of the miracle of the loaves and fishes, although John's gospel prefers the word 'sign' rather than 'miracle'. This Sunday, and for the next three weeks, we will be reflecting on the meaning of that sign. John provides us with an interpretative key to the meaning of this sign when he tells us, 'It was shortly before the Jewish feast of Passover.' He wants us to listen to the story of the loaves and fishes against the backdrop of the story of Passover, and that's what we'll do today, not because we're students of ancient history, but because the Passover story sheds light on our own journey of faith. Today's first reading from the book of Exodus is an appropriate backdrop for today's gospel because it tells the story of God providing food for his people in the wilderness.

Passover is a story of liberation from slavery and entry into the Promised Land. During a time of severe famine, Joseph and his sons seek food in Egypt, and they remain there under the protection of their brother Joseph, a high official in Pharaoh's government. With the passing of generations, the Jewish people become 'fruitful and prolific' in Egypt, and a new king who had never heard of Joseph feels threatened by a people who have become so 'numerous and powerful' in the land (Ex 1:7-8). The Israelites are enslaved, their lives made miserable with hard labour, but they continue to increase and spread. Pharaoh then orders the Hebrew midwives to kill all baby boys as they are born, but they disobey him. In desperation Pharaoh commands his subjects to cast every newborn Jewish boy into the Nile (Ex 1:22). When Moses is born his mother hides him for three months, but when it is no longer possible to keep his birth a secret she places her baby inside a papyrus basket coated with bitumen and pitch and laid it among the reeds at the edge of the river. Pharaoh's daughter notices the basket when she goes down to the river to bathe. She feels sorry for the baby and decides to keep him. His mother is employed as the child's nurse, and when the boy has grown up he is presented to Pharaoh's daughter who treats him like a son (Ex 2: 1-10).

Now an adult, Moses goes to visit his kinsmen. As he watches their forced labour he sees an Egyptian strike a Hebrew. No one is around, so he kills the Egyptian and hides his body. When, on the following day, he tries to break up a fight between two Hebrews he is reproached by one of them: 'Do you intend to kill me as you killed the Egyptian?' Realising that the matter had come to light and his own life was now in peril because he had killed an Egyptian, Moses flees into Midianite territory. Here, he marries Zipporah, the daughter of a Midianite priest.

At this point we come to the first lesson that I would like to draw from the Passover story. Moses is looking after his father-in-law's flock close to Mount Horeb when he sees a bush on fire, but the bush is not devoured by the flames. As he draws closer a voice coming from the burning bush orders him to remove his shoes for he is standing on holy ground. When he asks the voice for its name, he receives the enigmatic reply: Ehyeh-Asher-Ehyeh. Any commentary on this text will tell you that the precise meaning of these Hebrew words is uncertain. It could be translated as 'I will be who I will be', or 'I am who I am' or 'I am what I am.'[406] What are we to make of that? It's telling us that God cannot be contained in human words or ideas. Richard Holloway makes the observation:

> The trouble with all thinking about God is that it is an unavoidably human process, and one of the things we know about ourselves is that we inescapably project something of ourselves onto whatever we think about. Or, to use another metaphor, everything we encounter is filtered through the lens of our own complex selfhood, with inevitably distorting results.[407]

The Christian tradition speaks of two interdependent and inseparable paths to knowing God: the apophatic way (via negativa), which speaks of God as essentially unknowable and inexhaustible, and the kataphatic way (via positiva) which emphasises God as knowable. But we are not talking about an 'either-or' because there is a 'paradoxi-

---

406 Cf. Richard Holloway, *How to Read the Bible*, W.W. Norton & Company, New York, 2007, p. 30.
407 Ibid., p. 16.

cal necessity of both presence and absence' in our quest for God.[408] Medieval theology knew this as 'the contradiction of opposites'. All things come in pairs: sun and moon, night and day, hot and cold, up and down, man and woman – so we should not be surprised that our quest for God involves presence and absence. Morton Kelsey describes these two different ways of leading people on the spiritual pilgrimage:

> The first is the sacramental method, in which we try to mediate the divine through images, pictures, symbols and rituals. Often this results in confusing the image with the reality and can lead to idolatry ... The second way is based on the idea that we can best find the divine through emptying ourselves of all images and contents. This point of view stresses the fact that all descriptions and pictures of the holy are inadequate.[409]

The ambivalence in our approach God is captured in the story about a group of Jews in the concentration camp at Auschwitz who decided to put God on trial.

> They charged him with cruelty and betrayal. Like Job, they found no consolation in the usual answers to the problem of evil and suffering in the midst of this current obscenity. They could find no excuse for God, no extenuating circumstances, so they found him guilty and, presumably, worthy of death. The Rabbi pronounced the verdict. They he looked up and said that the trial was over: it was time for the evening prayer.[410]

---

408 Bernard McGinn, *The Foundations of Mysticism*, Crossroad, New York, 1991, p. xviii.
409 Quoted in Alan Jones, *Soul Making*, pp. 24-5.
410 Karen Armstrong, *A History of God*, Mandarin, London, 1993, p. 431.

The second lesson that I would like to draw from the Passover story is this: Ehyeh-Asher-Ehyeh, the God who cannot be conveniently contained, is not calling Moses (and us!) to belief but to action. Moses is told: 'I am sending you to Pharaoh, for you are to bring my people the Israelites out of Egypt' (Ex 3:10). Holloway puts it this way:

> God is an imperative voice calling us to a particular kind of action, not an object calling us to a particular kind of belief. In other words, it is not what you believe, but how you act that matters.[411]

Jesus was moved with compassion when he saw the enormous crowd that had followed him. His first concern was to feed them, not to teach them. 'Where can we buy some bread for these people to eat?' (Jn 6:5). I come back to a point that I've stressed over the past two weeks: What is our response to the fact one billion people will go to bed hungry tonight?[412] What is our response to the fact that according to UNICEF, nearly 10 million children under five years of age die each year from causes related to poverty?[413] Perhaps ours is the frightened human response of Moses. Who am I to do this? Suppose they will not believe me or listen to my words? I have never been eloquent; send someone else. A poem by Kadya Molodovsky expresses the Jewish anguish at being God's chosen people, but it could equally express our own anxieties at being called to action:

---

411 Richard Holloway, *How to Read the Bible*, op. cit., p. 30.
412 http://www.adelaide.catholic.org.au/sites/SouthernCross/opinions?more=12626
413 Peter Singer, *The Life You Can Save*, Text Publishing, Melbourne, 2009, p. 4.

Releasing the Captive

> O God of Mercy
> For the time being
> Choose another people.
> We are tired of death, tired of corpses,
> We have no more prayers.
> For the time being
> Choose another people.[414]

In 2009 I led a pilgrimage from Egypt into the Holy Land. One of the highlights of our time in Egypt was to climb Jebel Musa, the second highest peak in the Sinai and the place which an ancient tradition identifies as the mountain on which Moses received the tablets of the Law. We reached the top of the mountain in the dark of night and remained to watch the sunrise. Later that morning we visited St Catherine's monastery at the base of the mountain.

> The monastery is built around the traditional site of the burning bush and, believe it or not, the bush is still there after three thousand years! I couldn't help smiling, though, when I saw a fire extinguisher located only two or three metres away from the base of the bush! That image says it all – who can live with a bush that might erupt into flame and summon us into action yet again?[415]

The final lesson I would like to take from the Passover story is symbolised by that strange bread-like substance that God sends to nourish his people in the wilderness. It is called manna, a word that comes from the Hebrew expression the people mutter when they first see it: *man hu*, 'What is it?' When the artist Paul Gauguin heard

---

414 From a poem by Kadya Molodovsky, translated from the Yiddish by Irving Howe, *The Penguin Book of Yiddish Verse*, 1987, quoted in Holloway, op. cit., p. 34.
415 Bruce Feiler, *Walking the Bible*, HarperCollins, New York, 2001, p. 229.

news of his daughter's death from pneumonia in 1897 he produced a massive painting that was a cry of pain at the mystery of existence. He wrote three questions on a corner of the canvas (in French): Where do we come from? What are we? Where are we going?[416] These are bruising questions indeed and, in the words of Emily Dickinson,

> they are like a 'Tooth
> That nibbles at the soul.[417]

Australian psychotherapist Peter O'Connor argues that we need to believe. 'We find it very difficult to sustain ourselves in a state of uncertainty. Believing in something, in anything, is necessary for psychological survival, otherwise we are subject to the most profound feelings of despair.'[418]

In the face of this relentless quest for meaning the gospel offers us the image of Jesus, the bread of life. Manna nourished the body, but not the spirit. Here we have manna of a different kind that satisfies the deepest longings and yearnings of the human heart. Whoever eats this bread will never hunger.

---

416 Richard Holloway, *Between the Monster and the Saint*, Canongate, Edinburgh, 2008, p. 57.
417 Emily Dickinson, 'This World is not Conclusion', *The Complete Poems*, Little, Brown and Company, Toronto, 1960, poem 501.
418 Peter O'Connor, in John Marsden (ed.) *This I Believe*, Random House, Sydney, 1996, p. 253.

NINETEENTH SUNDAY IN ORDINARY TIME

(YEAR B)

Anyone who eats this bread will live for ever. (Jn 6:51)

Our story defines who we are, and our story consists of all the people, places and events that make each of us a unique individual. William Bausch writes that

> every people, nation, and community have stories and myths that preserve and prolong the traditions that give them their identity. When a nation is in trouble, it often returns to its traditional stories to look for direction and healing, to regain a sense of what made it great in the past and what will nurture it into the future ... Individuals, families, and communities also have their identifying stories that link them to who they are, to their culture. They tell the story over and over again of their spouse's death, what happened in our town twenty or thirty years ago that people will never forget. A region or a nation has its story concretized in shrine, statue, museum. A person without a story is a person with amnesia. A country without its story has ceased to exist. A humanity without its story has lost its soul.[419]

---

419 William Bausch, *Storytelling, Imagination and Faith*, Twenty-Third Publications, Mystic, CT, 1984, p. 33.

Central to the Jewish story is that epic journey that we know as the Exodus. With mighty hand and outstretched arm the Lord led his people out of slavery in Egypt. For 40 years they wandered in the desert, and on Mt Sinai they received the Law. The Lord fed his people with manna from heaven, and at last led them to the Promised Land.

All of this happened over 3,000 years ago, yet every year devout Jews retell the story during the celebration of Passover. On the night of the first full moon of spring (in the Northern Hemisphere) the family gathers around the dinner table for a festive meal. The youngest one at table asks, 'Why is this night different from all other nights?' The father, reading from the Haggadah, tells the story: 'We were slaves to Pharaoh in Egypt. and the Lord our God took us with a strong hand and an outstretched arm …'[420]

When Jewish people gather to celebrate Passover, it is not an exercise in nostalgia, a longing for bygone days. They remember the past because it tells them who they are, but more importantly, it assures them that God who rescued them in the past will rescue them again.

In John's gospel the interpretive key that unlocks the meaning of the miracle of the loaves and fishes is the Exodus story. Remember, though, that John's gospel never uses the word 'miracle', preferring instead the word 'sign'. In other words, the feeding of the multitude is a wondrous act that reveals who Jesus really is. At the beginning

---

[420] Ben-Ami Scharfstei (trans.) *Passover Haggadah*, Shilo Publishing House, 1959, pp. 13, 15.

of Chapter 6 we're told that 'The time of the Jewish Passover was near' (6:4), and there are constant references to the Exodus story throughout the chapter. In today's gospel Jesus tells the people,

> Your fathers ate the manna in the desert and they are dead; but this is the bread that comes down from heaven, so that a man may eat it and not die. I am the living bread which has come down from heaven (6:49-50).

Manna is prominently mentioned in the liturgy of the Passover meal,[421] and it has been argued that Chapter 6 of John's gospel reflects 'a medley of themes drawn from the synagogue readings at Passover time.'[422] It is worth noting that John's lengthy account of the Last Supper (Chapters 13 to 17) does not include the institution of the eucharist, but many commentators suggest that Chapter 6 is John's account of the institution of the eucharist.[423] Exodus and eucharist are intimately linked, and the eucharistic overtones that resonate throughout this chapter invite us to see our reception of holy communion as a participation in a new Exodus, an invitation to eat the bread of life and satisfy our spiritual hunger.

God nourished Elijah in the wilderness; he fed his people with manna in the desert; and in the eucharist we are invited (in the words of today's responsorial psalm) to 'taste and see that the Lord is good.' Exodus, Elijah and eucharist – each is a story of food given at a time of crisis to people who were grumbling or dispirited. Elijah was fleeing the wrath of Jezebel after the slaughter of her prophets on

---

421 Raymond E. Brown, *The Gospel According to John I-XII*, p. 245.
422 Brown cites the research of Aileen Guilding. Brown, pp. 278-9.
423 Robert Kysar, *Preaching John*, p. 185.

Reflections for the year of Mark

Mt Carmel; the people were rebellious in the wilderness; and today's gospel tells us that the Jews were complaining because Jesus had said that he was the bread that came down from heaven.

Rabbi Sir Jonathan Sacks, Chief Rabbi of the United Hebrew Congregations of the Commonwealth, tells of an interesting phenomenon he read about in James Surowiecki's *The Wisdom of Crowds*. The American naturalist William Beebe came across a strange sight in the jungle of Guyana.

> A group of army ants was moving in a huge circle. The ants went round and round in the same circle for two days until most of them dropped dead. The reason is that when a group of army ants is separated from its colony, it obeys a simple rule: follow the ant in front of you. The trouble is that if the ant in front of you is lost, so will you be.'

By contrast Rabbi Sacks reflected upon a wonderful tutor he has recently acquired – a satellite navigation system. It's a marvellous device, but he suspects that its inventor had never met a Jewish driver.

> What happens is this. Once the machine has worked out the route, a polite lady's voice tells you something along the lines of: 'Keep straight for 300 yards, then turn right.' Normally, this would suffice. But as anyone who has shared a journey with a Jewish driver knows, the response is likely to be: 'What does she know? I've been driving this car for 20 years. I know the neighbourhood like I know my own mother. Anyone knows that in 300 yards, you turn left.' What happens then? Well, 'it goes silent for a few moments ... It then sends up a signal: 'Recalculating the route.' Seconds later it provides you with a new set of instructions, based on wherever you have landed up as a result of going left when you should have gone right.'[424]

---

[424] Jonathan Sacks, 'The prophets are our unflappable sat-nav, not the lost car in front', *The Times*, 4 February 2006.

Releasing the Captive

What a marvellous metaphor for God's untiring guidance. The Jewish people wandered for forty years in the wilderness, led by the first navigation system – a pillar of cloud by day and a pillar of fire by night. And whenever they rebelled, God simply recalculated the route. When our endless cycles of folly and fractiousness lead us to the verge of starvation on our own Exodus, the Lord offers a route to salvation and bread for the journey.

TWENTIETH SUNDAY IN ORDINARY TIME

(YEAR B)

I am the living bread which has come down from heaven. (Jn 6:51)

In today's first reading from the book of Proverbs, Wisdom (*sophia* in Greek) invites the ignorant and foolish to eat her bread and drink the wine she has prepared. The great cathedral of eastern Christendom, the patriarchal church of the bishop of Constantinople, was named Hagia Sophia, Holy Wisdom. The present magnificent structure, the third church to stand on the site, was constructed under the personal supervision of the emperor, Justinian I, and dedicated on 27 December, 537 AD. It is universally acknowledged to be one of the greatest buildings of the world and sometimes considered the eighth wonder of the world.

When Constantinople (now Istanbul) finally fell to the Turks in 1453 Hagia Sophia was turned into a mosque, and since 1935 it has been a museum. The name of the mother church of Byzantine Christendom honours Lady Wisdom, whom we meet in today's first reading from the book of Proverbs. And who is Lady Wisdom?

> She seems to be something of God, born of God, in God. Usually she is said to be a divine attribute, a personification of the wisdom with which God created the world.[425]

Lady Wisdom in the Hebrew scriptures 'oversees all of the mysteries of the universe; in her hands are the secrets of life. These are the delicacies with which she spreads her table; this is the fare that she offers her guests. No one can survive without Wisdom; the way of understanding is the way to life.'[426] Wisdom is about knowing, but as Luke Timothy Johnson points out, there are more ways of knowing reality than the simple one modernity imposes – 'Can it be empirically verified?'[427] The kind of philosophical absolutism that modernity implies is based in the natural sciences where theory can be tested and affirmed, or found wanting. The success of the empirical method relegated all other forms of knowledge to the margins as subjective.

Our English word technology comes from the Greek *techne*, which refers to the art, skill, craft, or the way, manner, or means by which a thing is gained. One could translate *techne* as know-how. *Techne* has become indispensable in our modern world, but the underlying mystery of existence cannot be reduced to simple propositions that yield scientifically verifiable answers. *Sophia* is a different kind of knowledge. Lady Wisdom seeks to know why rather than

---

425 Roland E. Murphy, 'Wisdom in the OT', in David Noel Freedman (ed.), *The Anchor Bible Dictionary, Volume 6*, Doubleday, New York, 1992, p. 927.
426 Dianne Bergant, with Richard Fragomeni, *Preaching the New Lectionary, Year B*, p. 329.
427 Luke Timothy Johnson, *The Creed*, Darton, Longman & Todd, London, 2003, p. 3.

how, meaning rather than technique. She is a trusted guide leading us on the way of perception, a hostess who bids us to 'eat my bread and drink the wine I have prepared!' Her task, therefore, is not simply to satisfy intellectual curiosity about metaphysical questions. The Buddha once told a parable about a man who had been wounded by a poisoned arrow. When a doctor arrived to tend his wound the man said, 'I will not allow you to remove the arrow until I have learned the caste, the age, the occupation, the birthplace and the motive of the person who wounded me.' We, too, can spend an inordinate amount of time asking the wrong questions.

In today's gospel Jesus tells the crowd that he is the living bread which has come down from heaven. Fr Raymond Brown points out that 'most of Jesus' sayings in John have some Old Testament or Jewish background that makes them partially intelligible to the audience portrayed in the scene.' The divine word and wisdom 'are often presented under the symbolism of food or bread in the Old Testament.' In the Bread of Life discourse

> Jesus is like Wisdom who in Proverbs 9:5 issues an invitation: 'Come, eat of my bread; drink of the wine I have mixed.'[428]

The rich imagery of bread and wine harks back to Wisdom's banquet, but it also evokes memories of the manna that Israel's ancestors ate in the desert, and Fr Raymond Brown says that 'manna was interpreted in some Jewish circles as signifying divine word or instruction.'[429]

---

428 Raymond E. Brown, *The Gospel According to John, I-XII*, p. 273.
429 Ibid., p. 272.

Releasing the Captive

All of this rich symbolism leads us to ask, 'Where do we find this manna and Wisdom, where do we find the divine word and instruction?' And the answer is: in Jesus, the true bread that has come down from heaven. But how and where do we encounter Jesus as the true bread? John's gospel provides the answer: 'one encounters the flesh and blood of Jesus Christ in the Eucharistic celebration.' For the Christian, 'the Eucharist is a place where one comes to eternal life.'[430] In other words, we receive Christ through eating – literally – the bread of the eucharist. The Greek word that John's gospel uses here emphasises that point. The usual word 'to eat' is *fagein*, but John's gospel uses *trōgein*, which can be translated into English by words such as 'munch', 'crunch' or 'chew'.[431] The church refers to this as the sacramental presence of Christ.

We are not speaking merely metaphorically. Fr Robert Barron tells a story about Mary Flannery O'Connor (1925–1964), whom he regards as the greatest Catholic fiction writer of the twentieth century. When she was a very young woman commencing her career she attended a high-powered literary dinner with Mary McCarthy (1912–1989) and some of her friends. The company intimidated O'Connor and she remained silent.

McCarthy, who had left the Catholic Church as a young woman, tried to reach out to the shy O'Connor, and knowing that she was a Catholic said, 'I think the Eucharist is wonderful; it's a very powerful symbol.' The first thing that O'Connor said that night was, in a shaky

---

430 Francis J. Maloney, *The Gospel of John*, The Liturgical Press, Collegeville, MN, 1998, pp. 223-4.
431 Ibid., p. 224; cf. also Tom Wright, *John for Everyone*, 2002, p. 86.

voice, 'Well, if it's only a symbol, I say to hell with it.'[432] In that blunt response we have the Catholic understanding of the Eucharist.

In the synagogue at Capernaum Jesus told his disciples that his flesh is real food and his blood is real drink, and whoever eats his flesh and blood lives in him, and he in them. He is the living bread which has come down from heaven. Many of his followers found this intolerable language and asked, 'How could anyone accept it?' And that same complaint has echoed down through the centuries.

For Berengar of Tours (c. 1010–88) it seemed natural to assume that things were what they seemed to be. It was obvious that the appearance of the bread and wine remained unchanged after the words of consecration. He therefore concluded that they must still be bread and wine. The presence of Christ in the eucharist must therefore be a spiritual, not a physical presence.[433]

Many of the Protestant reformers went much further and made a strict dichotomy between the signs of bread and wine and the presence of Christ. For John Calvin 'the reality is given to us along with the sign.'[434] Zwingli interpreted the words 'This is my Body' in a metaphorical sense. He argued that when Jesus said 'I am the door' or 'I am the vine' no one insisted that these statements should be understood literally. For him, the words 'This is my Body' must be understood to mean 'This is a sign of my body.' The bread and wine were, for Zwingli, only signs of a Christ present by faith.[435]

---

432 Robert E. Barron, *Eucharist*, DVD produced by Word on Fire.
433 Joseph Martos, *Doors to the Sacred*, SCM Press, London, 1981, p. 266.
434 Quoted in Diarmaid MacCulloch, *Christianity*, Viking, New York, 2009, p. 635.
435 Owen Chadwick, *The Reformation*, Penguin Books, Harmondsworth, Middlesex, repr. 1973, p. 79.

The Catholic tradition has always accepted the sacramental presence of Christ in the eucharist as a true and real presence. In the words of the Catechism of the Catholic Church,

> In the most blessed sacrament of the Eucharist 'the body and blood, together with the soul and divinity, of our Lord Jesus Christ and, therefore, the whole Christ is truly, really, and substantially contained.[436]

Jesus' body and blood are, in a mysterious way, offered to believers as food and drink. Cardinal Walter Kasper explains it thus:

> All that one can touch, see and taste externally by means of the senses is bread and wine; but through faith in Jesus' word we know that, thanks to the working of the Holy Spirit, the true reality which is not accessible to the senses (that which the Middle Ages called 'substance') is no longer bread and wine, but the body and blood of Christ ... Thus the forms of bread and wine which the senses can perceive become signs and real symbols of a new reality, that of the risen and exalted Lord; they are filled with this reality and make it present.[437]

---

[436] *Catechism of the Catholic Church*, n. 1374.
[437] Cardinal Walter Kasper, *Sacrament of Unity: The Eucharist and the Church*, trans. Brian McNeil (Crossroad, 2004), p. 51, quoted in Gerard Kelly, 'The Presence of Christ in the Eucharist and the Church', a talk given at the Sydney Clergy Forum (19 May 2005), p. 6.

TWENTY-FIRST SUNDAY IN ORDINARY TIME

(YEAR B)

You have the message of eternal life, and we believe. (Jn 6:68)

When Australian author James Cowan visited the Monastery of St Antony, located at the foot of Mt Colzim 334 kilometres southeast of Cairo in Egypt, he sought permission to visit the cave of St Antony of Egypt, the father of Christian monasticism. The cave where St Antony lived as a hermit is about two kilometres from the monastery. Cowan was advised that a monk had recently taken up residence on the mountain as a hermit, but the guest master gave him permission to climb up to the hermit's retreat, provided that he agreed to carry a week's supply of bread for the man. He was warned, though, that he would have to wait for the monk to give him a signal to continue his climb. 'If he thinks you are from Babylon, he may well decide not to wave you on up', Elias explained. 'And if he does, what city have I come from?' enquired Cowan. 'Why, Jerusalem, of course.' These were the two psychic poles of this anchorite's world – Babylon, the city of material entanglement, or Jerusalem, the celestial city.

Releasing the Captive

As Cowan climbed the mountain he saw a man dressed in the black habit and bonnet of a Coptic monk. The monk raised his hand and waved him to come on up. He had obviously passed the first test; Babylon was not his home. As Cowan introduced himself the monk replied in perfect English; he wasn't Egyptian at all, but Australian.[438]

Fr Lazarus had been a university lecturer in literature and philosophy, and he had been an atheist for about 40 years of his life. In a short film inspired by Cowan's book, *The Last Anchorite*, Fr Lazarus spoke about his spiritual journey:

> My name is particularly relevant to my life because it means the one who was resurrected – so I chose this name both for its power of resurrection, because I was not Christian all my life. I have become a monk and a Christian at the same time and changed my life completely. So, it was like I was dead and I came to life. Before, I was a man proud of himself. I was sure that I am the captain of my ship and the master of my fate. I was sure I am the one who determines my own destiny. Now I believe that I am in the hand of the Lord; I believe that I have changed completely from being the master of my own life to being the loving servant, the slave, of Jesus Christ.[439]

Lazarus, like St Antony of Egypt so many centuries earlier, had embarked on a voyage into the unknown with only Christ as his compass. Along with Simon Peter he was able to say, 'You have the words of eternal life, and I believe.'

---

[438] James Cowan, *Journey to the Inner Mountain*, Hodder & Stoughton, London, 2002, pp. 2-3.

[439] You can view the film, *The Last Anchorite*, at http://current.com/1m2a54c

Reflections for the year of Mark

In Peter's response we come to the heart of the Christian faith. Jesus is the Way, the Truth and the Life. No one can come to the Father except through him.

Jesus is not just one way among many others, nor is he one truth among other truths. Some people will respond to this claim in the same way that many of Jesus' followers reacted to his teaching: 'This is intolerable language.' And why? Well, it's not politically correct language in an age of interreligious dialogue. In an age of relativism the only absolute truth is that there are no absolute truths, and therefore no religion can claim to have a privileged insight into the reality of God. Christianity should not claim to be anything more than another brand-name product in the supermarket of 'spirituality'.

> George Weigel responds to this point of view by observing that in a culture that rates tolerance the highest virtue and imagines that tolerance means indifference to questions about the truth of things, the unambiguous claim that this is the truth, and that all other truths incline toward this truth as iron shavings incline to a magnet, is not just controversial. It's an outrage.[440]

This brings us back to the question Jesus himself posed to his disciples on the way to Caesarea Philippi: 'Who do you say that I am?' (Mt 16:15). The Christian response is that Jesus is 'the definitive, unique, unsurpassable revelation of God's purposes for the world and for history, the one in whom we find our way home.' The God of Abraham, Moses, Isaiah, and Jeremiah 'revealed himself definitively

---

[440] George Weigel, *The Truth of Catholicism*, Harper Perennial, New York, 2002, p. 6.

in Jesus Christ.'[441] It follows, therefore, that the Christian story is 'not merely an interesting story, perhaps even a noble story, but in fact the story of the human condition and of human history.'[442]

The theme of today's readings is that of decision. Just as Joshua challenges the people to choose whom they wish to serve, so Jesus turns to the Twelve and asks them to decide:

> Do you want to go away too? We, too, are brought to the threshold of decision: Will we choose Jesus, despite the incredible claims he makes? Or will we decide to stay where we are, satisfied with the lives we are living?[443]

Peter, answering for the Twelve, says 'You have the message of eternal life, and we believe ...' It's interesting that the Latin word *credo*, meaning 'I believe' – comes from the words *cor*, meaning 'heart', and *dare*, meaning 'to give'. Belief is not essentially about giving intellectual assent to a list of propositions, but rather that to which we give the heart.

Marcus Borg points out that prior to the seventeenth century, the English word 'believe' did not mean believing in the truth of statements or propositions.

> Grammatically, the object of believing was not statements, but a person. Moreover, the contexts in which it is used in premodern English make it clear that it meant: to hold dear; to prize; to give one's loyalty to; to give one's self to; to commit oneself.[444]

---

441 Ibid., p. 142.
442 Ibid., p. 13.
443 Dianne Bergant and Richard Fragomeni, *Preaching the New Lectionary*, Year B, p. 337.
444 Marcus J. Borg, *The Heart of Christianity*, p. 40.

Reflections for the year of Mark

This is what we mean when we say, together with Peter and the disciples, 'We believe.' Ultimately, the Christian life is not primarily about believing in the sense of giving intellectual assent to theological or dogmatic propositions. Marcus Borg once joked that if he were ever to write his spiritual autobiography, he would call it 'Beyond Belief', or the fuller title would be 'Beyond Belief to Relationship'. He writes that his own journey

> has led beyond belief (and beyond doubt and disbelief) to an understanding of the Christian life as a relationship to the Spirit of God – a relationship that involves one in a journey of transformation.[445]

Or to put it another way, Jesus' question in today's gospel invites us to move from second-hand religion to first-hand religion.[446] As the name suggests, second-hand religion

> is a way of being religious based on believing what one has heard from others ... Firsthand religion, on the other hand, consists of a relationship to ... that reality that we call God of the Spirit of God.[447]

That, surely, is one of the insights behind the story of a man who was asked by a friend what he was doing. 'I am contemplating the moon in a bowl of water.' Somewhat surprised his friend replied, 'Unless you have broken your neck, why don't you look at the moon in the sky?'

---

[445] Marcus J. Borg, *Meeting Jesus Again for the First Time*, HarperSanFrancisco, 1995, p. 16.
[446] The phrase 'second-hand religion' comes from William James, *The Varieties of Religious Experience*, ed. Martin Marty (Penguin, 1982; originally published in 1902), p. 6, quoted in Marcus Borg, *Meeting Jesus Again for the First Time*, p. 87.
[447] Marcus J. Borg, *Meeting Jesus Again for the First Time*, pp. 87-8.

TWENTY-SECOND SUNDAY IN ORDINARY TIME

(YEAR B)

You put aside the commandment of God to cling to human traditions.
(Mk 7:8)

The rather harsh words directed against the Pharisees and some of the scribes in today's gospel take us straight to the issue of Jesus' attitude to the Jewish Law. But first of all, let us clarify what we mean by the Jewish Law. The Hebrew word is *Torah*, but it's inadequately translated into English as 'law'. Torah in its most restrictive meaning refers to the first five books of the Bible – Genesis, Exodus, Leviticus, Numbers and Deuteronomy. It is the heart and soul of God's revelation of Israel, and a copy of the Torah is found in the ark of every synagogue, just as the blessed sacrament is reserved in the tabernacle in Catholic churches.

The first five books of the Bible, also known as the Pentateuch (coming from the Greek word *penta* which means five) certainly include a legal code, but the word *Torah* can't be reduced to a list of dos and don'ts. The commandments are intended to liberate rather than oppress. The Hebrew word *Torah* comes from root *yarah*, meaning 'to shoot', an image coming from archery. In other words, the Torah will help us to hit the bullseye, to find the right direction on life's journey. Having said that, the Torah does contain specific commandments, and many more than just ten.

The medieval rabbi Moses Maimonides (1135–1204) is responsible for compiling a list of all the commandments (*mitzvot*) in the Torah. There are 365 prohibitions and 248 prescriptions, covering almost every aspect of being human. However, if you read today's gospel carefully you'll notice that Jesus isn't condemning the Torah, but he does have some harsh words to say about people who put aside the commandment of God and cling to human traditions. What did Jesus mean? Alongside the Torah there was a large body of oral tradition, that is, additional laws that were passed on by word of mouth. This oral tradition, of human not divine origin, was eventually set down in writing about two hundred years after Jesus. It is known as the Mishnah and it contains six main divisions.

American journalist A.J. Jacobs grew up as a secular Jew in New York. His parents didn't badmouth religion, but spirituality was almost a taboo subject in the house. His only brushes with the Bible were brief and superficial. He was an agnostic before he even knew what the word meant. Jacobs is the type of journalist who likes to immerse himself in his topic, so he decided to follow the Bible as literally as possible for a year.

And why? Well, he had earlier written a book about reading the *Encyclopaedia Britannica*, all of it, from A to Z. Having completed that project, the only intellectual adventure that seemed a worthy follow-up was to explore the most influential book in the world, the all-time best seller, the Bible.[448]

The results of this experiment are recorded in the New York Times' best seller, *The Year of Living Biblically*. This project was also a way of exploring 'the huge and fascinating topic of biblical literalism'. It's interesting that 'millions of Americans say they take the Bible literally. According to a 2005 Gallup poll, the number hovers near 22 per cent; a 2004 Newsweek poll put it at 55 per cent. A literal interpretation of the Bible – both Jewish and Christian – shapes American policies on the Middle East, homosexuality, stem cell research, education, abortion – right on down to rules about buying beer on Sunday.'[449]

The first step in this project was to go carefully through the Bible, both the Old and New Testaments, finding 'every rule, every guideline, every suggestion, every nugget of advice' that he could find. He ended up with a very long list of 72 pages and more than 700 rules. 'All aspects of my life will be affected – the way I talk, walk, eat, bathe, dress, and hug my wife.'[450] And so, he avoided wearing clothes of mixed fibres, in accordance with Leviticus 19:19. To this end he employed the services of Mr Berkowitz, a shatnez tester. *Shatnez* is the Hebrew word for mixed fibres, and the tester comes to your home and inspects all of your clothing to make sure you have no hidden

---

448 A.J. Jacobs, *The Year of Living Biblically*, Simon & Schuster paperbacks, New York, 2007, p. 6.
449 Ibid.
450 Ibid., p. 8.

mixed fibres. Jacobs attached tassels to the corners of his garments (Num 15:38); he made no mention of other gods (Ex 23:13); and he adhered strictly to biblical rules banning many kinds of food. He didn't shave for the entire year because Leviticus 19:27 says that you cannot shave the corners of your beard. Not being entirely certain what was meant by the corners of the beard he decided not to shave at all. He even stoned an adulterer, as laid down by Leviticus 20:20.

Here's how it happened: A man in his mid-seventies challenged Jacobs about the way he was dressed. 'You're dressed queer.' Jacobs explained his project of trying to live the Bible literally, including stoning adulterers. 'I'm an adulterer,' the man admitted. 'You gonna stone me?' 'If I could, yes, that'd be great,' replied Jacobs. Note, by the way, that because the Bible doesn't specify the size of the stones he had filled a pocket with small white pebbles. 'I wouldn't stone you with big stones. Just these little guys.' As he opened his palm to show him the pebbles the man lunged at him, grabbing a pebble out of his hand and flinging it at his face. So, an eye for an eye! Jacobs took one of the remaining pebbles and threw it at the man's chest.[451] Mission accomplished!

Jacob's year-long project made it clear that it is impossible to observe the Bible literally, even if people think they do.

> Almost everyone's literalism consisted of picking and choosing. People plucked out the parts that fit their agenda, whether that agenda was to the right or left.[452]

---

451 Ibid., pp. 92-3.
452 Ibid., p. 6.

In other words, 'biblical literalism is necessarily a selective enterprise.'[453] As Jacobs acknowledges,

> You can commit idolatry on the Bible itself. You can start to worship the words instead of the spirit.[454]

Sadly, there is something of the legalist in all of us, a tendency to follow the letter of the law, to seek out loopholes. When a very overweight man decided to go on a diet he took it seriously, even changing his usual driving route to work so as to avoid passing his favourite bakery. One morning, though, he arrived at work carrying a calorie-laden coffee cake, for which he was teased by his colleagues. He only smiled, shrugged his shoulders and said,

> What could I do? By force of habit I accidentally drove towards my favourite bakery this morning and was severely tempted. But I thought, maybe this isn't an accident. Maybe God thinks I deserve a little treat because I've stuck to my diet so successfully. So I prayed, 'Lord, if you really want me to have one of those delicious coffee cakes, let me find a parking space right in front of the bakery.' And sure enough, on the ninth time around the block, there was the parking spot![455]

The Pharisees are called 'hypocrites' because they honoured God with their lips, but their hearts were far from God; their worship is worthless because they teach only 'human regulations', and they abandon God's commandments by holding to 'human tradition.' We then have one of the most radical sayings in the teaching of Jesus. He insists that 'Nothing that goes into a person from outside can make

---

453 Ibid., p. 289.
454 Ibid., p. 329.
455 Adapted from William J. Bausch, *The Yellow Brick Road*, p. 286-7.

them unclean.' This radically subverts Jewish purity laws, abolishing the distinction between clean (kosher) and unclean food. '

> Having declared all foods clean and thus having shown that there is no longer anything external to human beings that can defile them, the Markan Jesus goes on to identify the real source of defilement: the human heart itself.[456]

The heart, that is, the moral core of a person, is what is important in our relationship with God. Jesus is concerned about moral rather than ritual defilement. While purity laws make a person ritually unclean by eating or touching something outside, Jesus teaches that moral defilement

> begins and develops in the human heart, in the cultivation of evil thoughts, intentions, and imaginings. People work from the inside out; and if their minds are full of fornication, theft, murder, adultery, avarice, wickedness, deceit, licentiousness, envy, slander, pride, and folly, these become the drivers of actions.[457]

If our hearts are filled with the Spirit, the fruits are different indeed: Joy, peace, patience, kindness, goodness, trustfulness, gentleness and self-control (Gal 5:22).

---

[456] Joel Marcus, *Mark 1-8*, p. 458.
[457] John Shea, *Eating with the Bridegroom*, p. 215.

TWENTY-THIRD SUNDAY IN ORDINARY TIME

(YEAR B)

'Ephphatha,' that is, 'Be opened.' (Mk 7:34)

Ephphatha, be opened, is a healing word that we all need to hear, because we're all guilty of being selectively deaf. Charlie Brown tells Linus that there's nothing that his father doesn't know about cars. To illustrate his point he explains that only the previous day his father had heard a strange grinding noise coming from the engine. 'Don't tell me he stopped the car, and fixed it?' enquires Linus. 'No,' replies Charlie Brown, 'he just turned the radio up louder so he couldn't hear it!'[458]

Australian psychologist Peter O'Connor points out that in most situations people actually hear what is being said, but do not listen. '
> What is not being listened to are the feelings embedded in the words – the message about the message. But listening to the hidden subtext, sometimes referred to as listening with the third ear, can be difficult and requires that we take time and be receptive – attributes that are sometimes difficult to find in our manic and fact-obsessed world.[459]

---

[458] Charles M. Schulz, *The Complete Peanuts*, 1975 to 1976, Fantagraphics Books, Seattle, WA, 2010, p. 64.
[459] Peter A. O'Connor, *Looking Inwards*, Penguin Books, Camberwell, Vic., 2003, p. 168.

Reflections for the year of Mark

Morse code was devised by Samuel Morse in the early 1840s as a means of transmitting telegraphic information with short and long pulses or dots and dashes. The letter 'A' for example is a dot and a dash; 'B' is a dash and three dots. Morse code was in use until comparatively recent times. It was used for maritime communication until 1999, but now it is obsolete. However, when Morse Code was still a vital means of communication a young man answered a newspaper advertisement for a Morse Code operator.

He made his way to the receptionist's desk in a large international company and was given a form to complete. Having completed the form he joined a large number of applicants who were seated in the noisy waiting room. After about five minutes the young man got up and walked straight into the manager's office. All of the other applicants smiled smugly to themselves. 'Who does that upstart think he is, walking straight into the manager's office without being summoned? He'll get the flick straight away.'

About ten minutes later the young man returned to the waiting room accompanied by the manager who made the following announcement: 'Gentlemen, thank you for your applications, but the job has been filled.' One applicant angrily spoke up and said what was on everybody's mind: 'That's not fair. He arrived last, barged into your office without being summoned, and you give him the job. You haven't even interviewed us yet.' 'I'm sorry,' replied the manager, 'but all the time you've been sitting here in this noisy waiting room the telegraph has been ticking a message in Morse Code: 'If you understand this message, then come right in, the job is yours.' Apparently you neither heard nor understood the message. This man did, and the job is his.'

'*Ephphatha*', Jesus said to the deaf man, and his ears were opened. In a world crammed with a myriad of frantic frequencies, let us pray that the Lord will open our ears to hear God's life giving word. And from whom do we first hear that word? The National Church Life Survey is taken every five years in Australia. It is a joint project of the Uniting Church in Australia NSW Board of Mission, Anglicare, and the Australian Catholic Bishops Conference. The last survey, taken in 2006, involved about 6000 congregations and 400,000 people from 22 denominations. One of the questions asked in the survey was, 'Who were the most significant people to show you what the faith was about?' The responses are interesting. Mothers were top of the list (with 76 per cent), followed by fathers (53 per cent). In other words, our parents are the most significant people in our faith development. The parish priest scores a lowly 18 per cent.

We first encounter the Word of God, maybe not in words, but certainly as a lived reality in our families. The story is told of a young lion cub that wandered away from the pride and was lost. After some time he came across the flock of sheep, and before long he was accepted as one of them. He tried to imitate their bleating and to eat grass as they did. Before long he so identified with the flock that he thought that he was a little lamb. The flock was terrified one day when they heard the distant roar of a lion. They fled as quickly as they could, but something told the young lion cub that there was nothing to fear. He stood his ground and it wasn't long until a fierce

Reflections for the year of Mark

lion strode majestically towards him. He looked up at this king of the jungle and greeted him with the bleating of a lamb. The lion was aghast! He let out a tremendous roar, and then plucked up the cub by the scruff of his neck and carried him over to a puddle of water. He forced the youngster to look at his reflection in the mirror and then said, 'Now do you see who you are and whose you are?' So, in the homes of this parish – and the home has often been called the domestic church – may our children hear God's word telling them who they are and whose they are.

Our children need to hear that they are loved and appreciated. Mary Ann Bird was born with a cleft palate, and when she started school, her classmates made it clear how she looked to them: a little girl with a misshapen lip, crooked nose, lopsided teeth and garbled speech. When schoolmates asked what had happened to her lip she'd tell them that she'd fallen and cut it on a piece of glass. Somehow that seemed more acceptable than admitting that she'd been born that way. She was convinced that no one outside of her family could love her. But one person was to make a difference in her life, her second grade teacher Mrs Leonard. Each year the students had a hearing test, another source of embarrassment for Mary Ann because she was virtually deaf in one ear. Mrs Leonard was administering the test by asking each student individually to stand against the door, covering one ear and then the other. The teacher sitting at her desk would whisper something and the student had to repeat it back – things like 'the sky is blue' or 'do you have new shoes?' From previous years Mary Ann had learnt that if she did not press her hand tightly upon her good ear she could pass the test. The seven words that Mrs Leonard spoke changed Mary Ann's life. She said in her whisper, 'I wish you were my little girl.'[460]

Eric Butterworth tells the story of a sociology professor who had his students draw up case histories of 200 young boys who lived in the Baltimore slums. Their evaluation of each boy's future was bleak: 'He hasn't got a chance.' Twenty-five years later another sociology professor came across this earlier study and had his students follow up on the project to see what had happened to each of the boys. With the exception of 20 boys who had moved out of the area, or who had died, 176 of the remaining 180 students had achieved above average success as lawyers, doctors and businessmen.

The professor was astounded and decided to investigate further. Fortunately, most of the men still lived in the area and was happy to be interviewed. They were asked to account for their success when the evaluation of their prospects twenty-five years ago was so negative. In each case the reply came with feeling, 'There was a teacher.' The teacher was still alive, and the professor asked the old but still alert lady how she had achieved such success with these boys. The teacher's eyes sparkled and she smiled. 'It's really very simple,' she said. 'I loved those boys.'[461]

Finally, we all need to hear ourselves affirmed. Dante Gabriel Rossetti, the famous 19th-century English poet and artist was once

---

460 Adapted from William J. Bausch, *The Yellow Brick Road*, pp. 31-2.
461 Adapted from Eric Butterworth, 'Love: The One Creative Force', in Jack Canfield and Mark Victor Hansen, *Chicken Soup for the Soul*, Health Communications, Deerfield Beach, FL, 1993, pp. 3-4.

approached by an elderly man. The old fellow had some sketches and drawings that he wanted Rossetti to look at and to tell him if they were any good, or if they at least showed potential talent. Rossetti looked them over carefully. After the first few, he knew that they were worthless, showing not the least sign of artistic talent. But Rossetti was a kind man, and he told the elderly man as gently as possible that the pictures were without much value and showed little talent. He was sorry, but he could not lie to the man. The man was disappointed, but he seemed to expect Rossetti's judgment. He then apologised for taking up Rossetti's time, but would he just look at a few more drawings – those done by a young art student? Rossetti looked over the second batch of sketches and immediately became enthusiastic about the talent they revealed. 'These,' he said, 'Oh, these are good. This young student has great talent. He should be given every help and encouragement in his career as an artist. He has a great future if he will work hard and stick to it.' Rossetti could see that the old fellow was deeply moved. 'Who is this fine young artist?' he asked. 'Your son?' 'No,' said the old man sadly. 'It is me 60 years ago. If only I had heard your praise then! For you see, I got discouraged and gave up.'[462]

'Ephphetha!' May your ears be opened to hear life-giving words.

---

[462] William J. Bausch, *A World of Stories*, Twenty-Third Publications, Mystic, CT, 1998, pp. 301-02.

TWENTY-FOURTH SUNDAY IN ORDINARY TIME

(YEAR B)

For anyone who wants to save his life will lose it. (Mk 8:35)

In today's gospel Jesus tells us that we must lose our life to save it. That involves a letting go, which is a lesson that Peter has yet to learn. After acclaiming Jesus as the anointed one of God, it becomes clear that he is thinking of a Messiah surrounded with glory and triumph, not suffering and death.

Joel Marcus reminds us that we shall never understand this passage correctly if we do not realise how natural Peter's reaction is: 'Modern Christians, cushioned by two thousand years of church teaching, find the idea of a suffering Messiah unremarkable,' but that would certainly not have been the case in Jesus' day. 'Intrinsic to the OT/Jewish idea of the Messiah was the notion of triumph, not suffering and death.'[463]

The idea of a suffering Messiah was not prominent in pre-Christian Judaism and 'no early Jewish text speaks of such a figure.'[464]

---

463 Joel Marcus, *Mark 8-16*, Yale University Press, New Haven, 2009, p. 613.
464 Ibid., p. 1106.

Peter is simply reflecting an entrenched way of thinking which 'is not God's way but man's.' He is imprisoned in the tradition he has received as an Israelite. To follow Jesus means a cross, not comfort; foot-washing, not fame. In short, he must lose his life with all its preconceptions and certainties. Peter must learn to be at home in a strange new world.

On 4 July 1862 the Reverend Charles Lutwidge Dodgson and the Reverend Robinson Duckworth rowed a boat up the River Thames with the three young daughters of Henry Liddell, the Vice-Chancellor of Oxford University and Dean of Christ Church. The journey began at Folly Bridge near Oxford and ended some eight kilometres away at the village of Godstow. Perhaps sensing that the girls, Lorina, Alice and Edith, were becoming a little bored the Reverend Dodgson entertained them with a story about a bored little girl named Alice who goes searching for an adventure. The three sisters were intrigued by the story, and Alice Liddell asked Dodgson to write it down for her. He did, and we know the story today by the title *Alice's Adventures in Wonderland*, or more popularly as *Alice in Wonderland*, and the author, the Reverend Charles Dodgson, by his pseudonym Lewis Carroll.

The story begins on a hot day with Alice sitting alongside her sister on a river bank and having nothing to do. Once or twice she peeps into the book that her sister is reading, but she sees no sense in reading a book 'without pictures or conversations'. Perhaps she could make a daisy chain, but would it be worth the trouble of getting up and picking the daisies? And then a White Rabbit appears, and the adventure begins. This rather unusual rabbit, who is wearing a waistcoat, is obviously in a hurry, for he mutters to himself 'Oh dear! Oh dear! I shall be too late!' And when he checks the time from a watch that he takes from his waistcoat pocket, Alice is burning with curiosity. She runs across the field in pursuit of the rabbit, just in time to see him disappear down a large rabbit hole under the hedge. Without a second thought Alice goes down after him, and so enters Wonderland.[465]

Alice is bewildered in this strange world because all the certainties she took for granted disappeared. Animals could speak, her size changes, and she tries to recite some simple multiplications, but with odd results: 'Let me see: four times five is twelve, and four times six is thirteen, and four times seven is – oh dear!'[466]

One commentator has pointed out that this represents numbers using different bases. We commonly use base 10, but 4 x 5 = 12 uses a base of 18, and 4 x 6 = 13 uses a base of 21, on so on.[467] This is quite plausible because Charles Dodgson lectured in mathematics at Christ Church for 26 years.

At any rate, Alice finds herself lost in a topsy-turvy world. When she sees a Cheshire cat sitting on the bough of a nearby tree, she seeks directions: 'Cheshire Puss ... Would you tell me, please, which way I ought to go from here?' To which the cat replies, 'That depends a good deal on where you want to get to.' Alice doesn't seem to

---

[465] Lewis Carroll, *Alice in Wonderland* (illus. by Rodney Matthews), Hinkler Books, Heatherton, Vic., 2008, p. 9.
[466] Ibid., p. 15.
[467] http://en.wikipedia.org/wiki/Alice%27s_Adventures_in_Wonderland

care where she goes. 'Then it doesn't matter which way you go,' says the cat.[468]

Perhaps we can recognise something of ourselves in this fascinating story. Fr Ronan Kilgannon offers an interesting reflection on Alice's predicament:

> We will inevitably find ourselves at sometime or other wandering in a mist, lost in the dark, 'free falling' like Alice down a tunnel. This state of confusion may be caused by external or internal influences – illness, bereavement, temptation, trials of faith, inner purification. All the familiar certainties will disappear. At such times God may be asking us to surrender our illusory control and place our faith, trust and hope in Him alone. It takes great courage to do so in these circumstances.[469]

And such surrender can be like wrestling with God. The Spanish philosopher and poet Miguel de Unamuno (1864–1936) claimed that his vocation was to 'wrestle with God',[470] and the Australian writer Patrick White spoke about 'a daily wrestling match with an opponent whose limbs never become material.'[471]

This is an allusion to one of the most enigmatic episodes in scripture, recorded in Chapter 32 of the Book of Genesis. Jacob wrestles with a man until daybreak. And who was this aggressor? Another human being, an angel, or God himself? The text is ambiguous, but

---

468 Lewis Carroll, *Alice in Wonderland*, p. 45.
469 Ronan Kilgannon, 'Thus Grew the Tale of Wonderland', Unpublished homily, 2008.
470 Quoted in Tom Frame, *Losing My Religion*, University of New South Wales Press, Sydney, 2009, p. 302.
471 Ibid.

Jacob names the place of his encounter Penuel, literally 'the face of God'. Like Jacob, we wrestle with God because his way of thinking seems to be the reverse of ours. Those who wish to save their life must lose it; those who lose their life will save it.

The disciples of Jesus had to learn that following Jesus was not about positions of honour; he was not a Messiah about to restore Israel to the glories of the Davidic kingdom. Inner peace rarely comes from fame and fortune. Australian media personality Caroline Jones hosted the popular ABC radio programme *The Search for Meaning*.

The presumption behind the programme was that all people have within them an innate concern for meaning and coherence. In her introduction to the book that developed out of the series, Jones felt that it was only fair to talk about her own journey through the wilderness.

She was received into the Catholic Church on Easter Saturday 1985, but she admits that if someone had suggested this to her two years earlier she would have laughed in disbelief. She writes:

> By the end of 1981, I had been reporting politics and current affairs on television for many years, and had done five years of daily morning radio as well. I had enjoyed success and popularity and had been given several awards by my peers and the public. I had travelled widely, adventured enthusiastically, learned a great deal by hard experience, talked with some of the most interesting and influential people in our own country and from around the world.

But despite a successful career, Jones felt personally rather isolated. Her conversion was gradual. She joined the Rite of Christian

Reflections for the year of Mark

Initiation of Adults in her own parish, and she says that it 'began the healing of loneliness.' As she prepared to join a community of people who live with Jesus Christ as their basic inspiration she says

> it felt like coming home, after many years in a wilderness of excitement, of worldly achievement, but of spiritual loneliness. I did not need to be convinced intellectually of anything. Rather I was oriented to a new truth which made sense of life ... I turned the kaleidoscope and suddenly saw a beautiful new pattern. I experienced the deepest sigh of relief, like a lone sentry who had been left on guard, finally relieved of her lonely post. It was like falling in love – irrational but irresistible.[472]

Lose your life and you'll find it.

---

472 Caroline Jones, *The Search for Meaning*, Australian Broadcasting Corporation / Collins Dove, Sydney, repr. 1990, pp. 10-17.

TWENTY-FIFTH SUNDAY IN ORDINARY TIME

(YEAR B)

The Son of Man will be delivered into the hands of men; they will put him to death; and three days after he has been put to death he will rise again. (Mk 9:31)

Jesus and his disciples are travelling from Galilee in the north of Palestine towards Jerusalem in the south, a journey of about 120 kilometres as the crow flies. You could walk the distance in a few days. In Mark's gospel this geographical journey from north to south parallels an inner journey. As the disciples accompany Jesus on this fateful journey towards Jerusalem, they grow in understanding. But, it must be said, they are slow learners. On three occasions during the journey Jesus tells the disciples openly and unambiguously that he must suffer and die – recorded in Mark's gospel in three successive chapters: Chapters 8, 9 and 10. It's obvious, though, that the disciples could not conceive of a Messiah who would die an ignominious death, and so they turn a deaf ear to what Jesus is saying.

Reflections for the year of Mark

In Chapter 8 Jesus begins to teach the disciples, telling them quite openly that the Son of Man was destined to suffer grievously, and to be rejected by the elders and the chief priests and the scribes, and to be put to death, and after three days to rise again. The reaction? Peter takes Jesus aside and tries to rebuke him. In Chapter 9 – today's gospel reading – Jesus again forewarns the disciples, but we are told that they did not understand what he had said and were afraid to ask him. Not only had they failed to understand him, but they began arguing among themselves about which of them was the greatest. Finally, in Chapter 10 Jesus again tells them what was going to happen to him, and no sooner had he finished speaking than James and John come up to him asking for places on his right and left hand when he enters into his glory.

On each of these three occasions the disciples have failed to understand what Jesus said, almost certainly because their preconceived ideas of the Messiah didn't include suffering and death. Given that Messiah or Christ means 'anointed' it is clear that the Messiah was to be a figure anointed by God. Many of Jesus' contemporaries hailed him as a 'Son of David'. David was anointed king of Israel by the prophet Samuel, and during his reign – a thousand years before the birth of Jesus – Israel prospered. That obviously coloured popular perceptions of the Messiah – a Davidic figure who would restore the fortunes of Israel, or ensure that 'Israel's long history would at last reach its divinely ordained goal.'[473] The disciples, like so many

---

473 N.T. Wright, *Jesus and the Victory of God*, Fortress Press, Minneapolis, 1996, p. 482.

of their contemporaries, wanted 'a Messiah who would defeat the Romans, cleanse the land of paganism, and establish Israel as the top nation in the world.'[474] And, of course, the disciples expected to enjoy positions of honour and prestige. A Messiah who would have to suffer, still less to die, was beyond understanding.

> You might as well expect a footballer, planning the biggest game of the season, to explain to his friends that he was going to play with his legs tied together.[475]

And yet death and resurrection is the archetypal rhythm of our human journey. The word archetype, especially as it's used by the Swiss psychiatrist and psychoanalyst Carl Jung (1875–1961), refers to patterns of human behaviour that are repeated over and over again, in all cultures and throughout all ages. Archetypes are the templates of human nature. They are manifested in myth and in the great stories of humanity. And in the scriptures these archetypes find their most eloquent expression.

The psychologist James Hillman has pointed out that the ancients had no psychology, properly speaking, but they had myths. Myths are maps for the human journey. The Greek myth of Chiron, the wounded healer, is a story about the archetypal rhythm of death and resurrection. Chiron was born a centaur. Centaurs were creatures with a human head and torso and the body of a horse. Chiron was the offspring of a mortal nymph who was raped by one of the gods, disguised in the form of a horse. Consequently, Chiron was half-

---

474 N.T. Wright, *Following Jesus*, William B. Eerdmans Publishing Company, Grand Rapids, MI, 1994, p. 44.
475 Tom Wright, *Mark for Everyone*, p. 122.

horse, half-human; half-mortal, half-immortal. He was abandoned and rejected at birth, and adopted by the sun god Apollo. Apollo raised him and taught him all he knew. Chiron became a wise and respected teacher, renowned for his shrewd intelligence. He became the mentor to some of Greece's greatest heroes, including Hercules, Achilles and Jason.

Although Chiron was civilised and cultured, this couldn't be said for other centaurs, who were renowned for their tendency to go berserk after drinking wine. One day, at a wedding banquet, fighting broke out between an unruly group of centaurs who were drunk and the rest of the guests. Hercules was among the guests. In an attempt to quell the rioting, he fired a poisoned arrow at the centaurs. Chiron happened to be standing in their midst and the arrow struck him in the knee. As Chiron was half-immortal, the poisoned arrow did not kill him, but instead inflicted an agonising and unhealable wound.

The first half of Chiron's life had brought him success and acclaim among the kings and heroes of Greece. The latter part of his life saw him become a recluse. He withdrew into a cave, and in seclusion, tended his wound and began a desperate search for release from his suffering. The search was to last the rest of his life. He was unable to find a cure for his own wound, but he became wise in the use of all forms of healing herbs and compassionate to the suffering of others. Those who now came to visit him were not the rich and powerful, but the blind and the lame, and those in pain. He welcomed them and brought them comfort. They called him 'the wounded healer' and wondered why he couldn't heal himself.

Releasing the Captive

One day, Hercules visited Chiron. He explained that if Chiron were prepared to sacrifice his immortality, he would be freed of his suffering. He was to sacrifice his immortality on behalf of Prometheus, who was being punished for mocking the gods. Chiron agreed to the offer, and so he died and descended to the underworld. For nine days and nine nights he remained in the darkness of death. Then Zeus, father of the gods, recognised the generosity of Chiron's sacrifice and took pity on him and restored his immortality. He raised him to the heavens as a constellation of stars. And now you know the origin of the constellation we call Centaurus! But before Chiron was raised to the glory of the heavens he had first to descend to the depths of the underworld and enter Hades.

The seed must fall into the ground and die before it can yield an abundant harvest. The Chiron myth has been a source of enlightenment for Michael Kearney, a palliative care consultant now working in Dublin.[476] Many of Kearney's patients suffering from terminal diseases were in great pain. Just as Chiron searched relentlessly for a cure – but to no avail – some of Kearney's patients failed to respond to the standard regime of drugs administered to relieve their pain.

This led Kearney to seek other explanations, beyond the physical basis for pain. Using the analogy of an iceberg, he explains that the pain that the patient feels is like the tip of an iceberg visible above the surface of the water. Just as the greater mass of the iceberg remains submerged below the surface, so also do the root causes of

---

[476] Michael Kearney, *Mortally Wounded: Stories of Soul Pain, Death and Healing*, Mercier Press, Dublin, 1996.

the patient's pain. Some of these causes can be identified and treated, but other causes, such as trapped emotions, remain hidden. If these trapped emotions are not recognised, or repressed, their only means of expression is through physical pain, which acts like a megaphone.

Through various techniques Kearney attempts to encourage his patients to make the descent into what he calls the 'deep centre', just as Chiron had to relinquish his immortality and descend into the underworld. And there is often resistance to entering the 'deep centre'. Carl Jung once wrote:

> The dread and resistance which every human being experiences when it comes to delving too deeply into himself is, at bottom, the fear of the journey to Hades.[477]

But as Kearney has discovered, certain kinds of pain are healed only through 'the journey to Hades'. The truth of this ancient Greek myth finds its ultimate fulfillment in the death and resurrection of Jesus. The seed must fall into the ground and died before it yields a rich and abundant harvest. In his letter to the Romans St Paul reminds us that healing and new life come by entering the tomb and joining our Lord in death, and we do this at our baptism. We join him in death so that as Christ was raised from the dead by the Father's glory, we too might live a new life (Rom 6:3-5).

---

[477] Ibid., p. 58.

TWENTY-SIXTH SUNDAY IN ORDINARY TIME

(YEAR B)

Master, we saw a man who is not one of us casting out devils in your name; and because he was not one of us we tried to stop him.
(Mk 9:38)

Today's gospel is a little confusing because four quite independent and unrelated sayings of Jesus have been joined together as if they formed a single discourse. Firstly, there is the story of an outsider casting out devils in Jesus' name. Secondly, there is a saying that promises a reward for an act of kindness to a follower of Jesus. Thirdly, there is a warning about scandalising little ones. And finally, Jesus urges his disciples to discard whatever might prevent them from entering the kingdom of God. As you know, the first of the Sunday readings is chosen because in some way or another it complements the theme of the gospel. The lectionary's choice of a reading from the book of Numbers obviously takes up the first of the four sayings in today's gospel and parallels that story with a similar incident from that epic event that we know as the Exodus.

Reflections for the year of Mark

The Book of Numbers tells the story about Moses gathering seventy elders and stationing them around the Tent. The Tent, by the way, contained the Ark of the Covenant, or the Divine Presence. That's where our word tabernacle comes from; it's Latin for 'tent', and it refers to the Tent of Divine Presence. God's Spirit descends upon the seventy elders and they began to prophesy. However, two elders, Eldad and Medad, remained in the camp. Even though they had not gone to the tent, the Spirit came down upon them and they prophesied. But Joshua objected. He seems to be saying, 'The only people entitled to prophesy are the seventy elders Moses invited to the Tent. They're the only officially licensed prophets!' Moses is a little more broad-minded. 'If only all God's people were prophets; if only God were to give his Spirit to all his people.'

Something similar is happening in the gospel. Someone who is not a disciple of Jesus is casting out devils in Jesus' name, and the disciples are annoyed. Like Moses, Jesus is a little more broad-minded. 'Let him be. I'm not into power and control. Anyone who is not against us is for us.'

These two incidents – one from the Old Testament and the other from the gospel – warn us against thinking that we have a monopoly on the truth, or that God must act within strictly defined boundaries.

On 14 November 1996, Cardinal Joseph Bernardin, the archbishop of Chicago, died from pancreatic cancer at the age of sixty-eight. At a time of increasing polarisation between 'liberal' and 'conservative' within the American Catholic Church, Cardinal Bernardin's style of leadership was collaborative, consensus-building and conciliatory. He saw himself as a reconciler:

> I've been called a reconciler, and in all the places where I've administered ... God has used me to help create a climate that is more hospitable, a climate that tends to bring people together. And if I have succeeded in doing that, always as a ministry of the Lord's hand, then that's OK with me.[478]

Just a few months before his death Cardinal Bernardin held a press conference to announce that he was launching a 'Catholic Common Ground Project' aimed at reconciling differences among American Catholics by addressing a number of thorny issues, such as the role of women, the relationship between church and society, and sexual issues.

Through dialogue, conferences and publications the project aimed to establish common ground between the extremes that have divided the church, to bring liberal and conservative into the same room for dialogue. Cardinal Bernardin launched the Catholic Common Ground initiative with the statement *Called to Be Catholic: Church in a Time of Peril*. The statement outlined the concern driving the project:

> Will the Catholic Church in the United States enter the new millennium as a church of promise, augmented by the faith of rising generations and able to be a leavening force in our culture? Or will it become a church on the defensive, torn by dissension and weakened in its core structures? The outcome, we believe, depends on whether American Catholicism can confront an array of challenges with honesty and imagination and whether the church can reverse the polarization that inhibits discussion and cripples leadership.[479]

---

478 http://www.enquirer.com/bernardin/obitside.html
479 *Called to Be Catholic: Church in a Time of Peril*, http://www.nplc.org/common-ground/calledcatholic.htm

Cardinal Bernardin's Common Ground project did not dismiss the authentic tradition of the church; in fact it stated that accountability to the church's authentic tradition was fundamental to the whole project. But accountability must be correctly understood. It does not mean

> conceiving of faith as an ideology, an all-encompassing doctrinal system that produces ready explanations and practical prescriptions for every human question. At this time, as in previous ages, 'there has always been wide room for legitimate debate, discussion, and diversity.' Accountability demands 'serious engagement with the tradition and its authoritative representatives'. It rules out the pop scholarship, sound-bite theology, unhistorical assertions, and flippant dismissals that have become all too common on both the right and the left of the church. Authentic accountability rules out a fundamentalism that narrows the richness of the tradition to a text or a decree, and it rules out a narrow appeal to individual or contemporary experience that ignores the cloud of witnesses over the centuries or the living magisterium of the church exercised by the bishops and the Chair of Peter.[480]

Australian psychologist observes that the air is 'full at present with varying claims of "the truth".' Not just 'truth', mind you, but the truth. He is not just arguing about semantics when he points out that the regular and habitual use of the definite article 'the' is significant. Language, he points out,

> is more than just words and grammar; it is a vital means of communication that not only allows us to express thoughts and feelings directly, but can at the same time reveal underlying attitudes.

---

[480] *Called to Be Catholic: Church in a Time of Peril*, III, http://www.nplc.org/commonground/calledcatholic.htm

Fundamentalists of all persuasions are fond of using the definite article, thereby implying that they are the owners of the truth.

> If you don't accept their version, their language suggests, you are likely to be seen as either ignorant, unenlightened or downright dumb.[481]

The conclusions of *Called to Be Catholic: Church in a Time of Peril* are relevant far beyond the North American Church. The first conclusion states that

> We should recognize that no single group or viewpoint in the church has a complete monopoly on the truth. While the bishops united with the pope have been specially endowed by God with the power to preserve the true faith, they too exercise their office by taking counsel with one another and with the experience of the whole church, past and present. Solutions to the church's problems will almost inevitably emerge from a variety of sources.

The second conclusion echoes the concerns of today's readings:

> We should not envision ourselves or any one part of the church a saving remnant. No group within the church should judge itself alone to be possessed of enlightenment or spurn the mass of Catholics, their leaders, or their institutions as unfaithful.[482]

---

481 Peter A. O'Connor, *Looking Inwards*, Penguin Books, Camberwell, Vic., 2003, p. 175.
482 *Called to Be Catholic: Church in a Time of Peril*, IV.

TWENTY-SEVENTH SUNDAY IN ORDINARY TIME

(YEAR B)

Is it against the law for a man to divorce his wife? (Mk 10:2)

Today's first reading comes from the Book of Genesis. As the name suggests, this book is concerned with the genesis or origins of the world, of human beings, and of Israel and its ancestors. The Book of Genesis is not a science textbook that offers an eyewitness account of the events it describes. It is essentially a work of theology that explores major questions about God and humanity.

In Chapters 1 and 2 of the Book of Genesis there are two separate accounts of the creation of man and woman, and they offer distinct but complementary insights. The story in Chapter 1 tells us that God created the world in six days and rested on the seventh. The creation of man and woman on day six is therefore the peak of God's creative activity.

This story is a reworking of a common Mesopotamian story in which there was a rebellion in the heavens against the higher-class gods by the lower-class gods who resented the menial tasks that were allotted to them.[483] Human beings were created to do the tasks the rebels refused to do. The polemical intent of Genesis is clear. Human beings are not an afterthought created as domestic servants. They are, rather, masters of creation.

The second story of creation offers an insight into the relationship between man and woman. God plants a garden where he places the man he has created. God senses that the man is lonely and so fashions the wild animals, but none of them are a suitable companion. The Lord then makes the man fall into a deep sleep and takes one of his ribs, and fashions a woman from the rib he had taken from the man. When God brings her to the man he rejoices for she is 'bone of my bones and flesh of my flesh!'

The gospel text refers to the woman as a 'helper'. The Hebrew word is *ezer*, which is better translated as 'source of blessing'. Because the woman has been fashioned from his rib, he is no longer complete. When he and the woman become one he is once again made whole.[484]

The gospel confronts the question of divorce. The Law of Moses did not 'permit' divorce. It simply recognised it as a reality in human life and sought, through the practice of a bill of divorce, to regulate the harsh effects it could have upon women. Jesus' teaching on marriage and divorce was radical in the context of first-century Palestine.

---

483 Cf. Richard J. Clifford sj, 'Genesis' in Raymond E. Brown, Joseph A. Fitzmyer and Roland E. Murphy (eds), *The New Jerome Biblical Commentary*, Geoffrey Chapman, London, 1989, p. 8.
484 Cf. Dianne Bergant with Richard Fragomeni, *Preaching the New Lectionary, Year B*, p. 370.

Reflections for the year of Mark

Couples did not marry because they had fallen in love. In a patriarchal society marriages were generally arranged, and the arrangements were made between the bride's father and the groom (and his father). It was only after the engagement that the couple could meet and get to know one another, but always under supervision.

Divorce was not uncommon, and in Jesus' day most Jews took it for granted. A man divorced his wife simply by giving her a bill of divorce stating that she was no longer bound to him.

There were various interpretations about the basis for divorce reflected in the Mishnah. The school of Shammai recognised sexual misconduct on the woman's part as grounds for divorce, but the school of Hillel said, 'Even if she spoiled a dish for him,' and Rabbi Aqiba was even more lenient: 'Even if he found another more beautiful than she is.'[485]

The first-century Jewish historian Josephus gives us an insight into the predicament of women when he tells us that only the husband could initiate divorce, and a divorced woman could not marry again on her own initiative unless her former husband consents.'[486]

Jesus' absolute prohibition of divorce diverged from mainstream Judaism; it was a radical teaching that brought a measure of security to wives. He reclaims marriage 'from something where all the power and decision-making rest one-sidedly with one partner (the man) to something corresponding to the original design of the Creator, a lifelong, equal companionship of permanence and fidelity'.[487]

---

485 Donahue and Harrington, *The Gospel of Mark*, p. 296.
486 Ant. 15.259, quoted in Donahue and Harrington, p. 297.
487 Brendan Byrne, *Lifting the Burden*, St Pauls, Strathfield, NSW, 2004, pp. 60-1.

There are few families that are immune to the painful experience of divorce. When the daughter of an Australian prime minister married, *The Sydney Morning Herald* reflected on the changes that had occurred in Australian society between 2003 and 1971, the year in which the then prime minister, John Howard, had married. In 1971 there were 12,947 divorces; in 2003 that figure had soared to 55,000.[488] A 1995 Australian Bureau of Statistics study showed that 10 percent of all marriages are likely to end in divorce within six years, 20 per cent within 10 years, 30 per cent within 20 years, and 40 per cent within 30 years.[489]

We almost seem to take divorce for granted. As of 27 December 2000, prenuptial agreements became legally binding. Couples can now draw up a Binding Financial Agreement, which can include lifestyle causes, such as assignment of household chores, holiday destinations, sexual relations, the number of children and how they are to be educated.[490]

The Sydney Morning Herald featured a cartoon by Andrew Weldon in which there is a heated discussion between a man and a woman. He says, 'I want the house. You can have the cars and the kids.'

She replies, 'Bugger the cars! I want the house and the kids.'

He becomes quite angry. 'There's no way you're getting the house! You can have everything else, not the house!'

---

[488] David Dale, 'Dig deep, John, that special day has a hefty price tag', in *The Sydney Morning Herald*, 27-28 September 2003.
[489] Mark Riley, 'Until divorce do us part: a nation divided', in *The Sydney Morning Herald*, 12 September 1995.
[490] Ellen Connolly, 'The new marriage certificate that spells out who gets what', *The Sydney Morning Herald*, 27 December 2000.

Reflections for the year of Mark

She replies, 'I deserve that house, Michael. I deserve it! I don't even want the bloody kids.'

He is exasperated: 'Look! I told you. You can have the shares, the boat, everything. But the house is mine!'

A screaming match ensues: 'Mine!' 'Mine!' 'Mine!' 'Mine!'. They exchange insults: 'Bitch' ... 'Bastard.'

And finally, they come to a resolution: 'Look, if we can't even agree on the pre-nuptial agreement maybe we shouldn't be getting married!'[491]

What are we to make of Jesus' teaching about divorce? We live much longer now than when Jesus lived, and all commitments are tested by time. It's been estimated that the average lifespan in ancient Rome was only about 20 years. In Europe during the Middle Ages, it was about 33. In 1841, the average life expectation in England was 40 for a man and 42 for a woman. It is only during the last few decades that the bulk of the population has begun to reach the biblical limit of three score and 10 years.[492] Between 1970 and 1997, life expectancy for Australians rose by seven years to 81.1 for women and 75.5 for men.[493]

All commitments are tested by time, and we live much longer than our ancestors. Brendan Byrne also points out that the teaching of Jesus on divorce and remarriage must surely be influenced by the fact that

---

491 *The Sydney Morning Herald,* 29 September, 1995.
492 Cf. Darryl Reanney, *The Death of Forever*, Longman Cheshire, Melbourne, repr. 1993, p. 112.
493 Jason Koutsoukis, 'Huge wealth divide exposed by UN report', *The Age,* 13 July 1999.

> Jesus and the early community lived in the expectation that the world as then constituted was soon – perhaps in the very same generation – going to pass away (cf. Mk 9:1; 13:32)[494]

It is clear that the historical Jesus

> held that marriage was to be monogamous and indissoluble and that any divorce (with remarriage understood as the natural consequence) was equivalent to adultery.[495]

In Matthew's gospel the prohibition against divorce is repeated, except on one ground, that of adultery (or sexual misconduct in general).[496] So the Matthean Jesus does allow divorce in one specific instance. The early Christians also experienced some problems with the absolute prohibition against divorce, as instanced by Paul's advice to Christians who are married to an unbeliever who chooses to leave the marriage (1 Cor 7:15).

So, is the teaching of Jesus on divorce 'an ideal to strive for, a challenge to be faced, an extreme example, or divine law? And which part of the New Testament evidence is more important – Jesus' absolute prohibition of divorce or the exceptions introduced by Paul and Matthew?'[497]

The church will always experience a tension between its prophetic and pastoral roles. On the one hand the church proclaims

---

494 Brendan Byrne, *A Costly Freedom*, p. 159.
495 John P. Meier, *A Marginal Jew: Companions and Competitors, Volume III*, Doubleday, New York, 2001, p. 504.
496 Matthew uses the Greek word *porneia*, the meaning of which is disputed. Brendan Byrne says that in Matthew it more likely refers to 'adultery' or sexual misconduct in general (cf. *Lifting the Burden*, p. 60, n. 16).
497 Donahue and Harrington, *The Gospel of Mark*, p. 298.

the permanence and sanctity of married love, but on the other hand we are faced with the pastoral reality that an increasing number of Catholics are divorcing. In every congregation today there will be people in second marriages or people who have a family member in that situation. In many, if not most cases, that situation will have come about through circumstances beyond their control or from which they cannot now responsibly free themselves.[498]

How should the church today respond to the complexity of the New Testament evidence, keeping in mind that Paul and Matthew adopted a pastoral approach that went beyond the absolute prohibition laid down by Jesus?

In many areas of life we are forced to compromise between the lofty ideals that once inspired us and the murky reality of life. The church, too, is caught between the fine ideal that Jesus teaches and the fragility of human nature. The church's current position emphasises the prophetic role – proclaiming unambiguously what marriage should be. Perhaps we need to focus a little more on the ministry of Jesus the healer – he who heals the broken-hearted and binds up all their wounds.

---

498 Brendan Byrne, *A Costly Freedom*, p. 159.

TWENTY-EIGHTH SUNDAY IN ORDINARY TIME

(YEAR B)

Good Master, what must I do to inherit eternal life? (Mk 10:17)

Mark's gospel uses the coathanger of a journey to tell the story. We accompany Jesus from the Galilee region where he grew up, to Jerusalem, which is in the south. In comparison to Australia, Israel is tiny, and it doesn't take very long to travel from one end of the country to the other. But in the days when such journeys were undertaken on foot, the journey described in the gospel would have taken some time. Jesus used this time to instruct his disciples. And one important lesson is on the cost and the rewards of discipleship.

The rich man we encounter in today's gospel is keen to inherit eternal life, that is, to enter the kingdom of God. We're told that he runs up to Jesus and falls on his knees. Jesus doesn't answer his question immediately, 'but begins to explore the issue with him at a deeper level.'[499] His question to Jesus, 'What must I do to inherit eternal life?' was not a trick question, like many of the questions posed by the scribes and Pharisees elsewhere in the gospels. Jesus

---

499 Ibid., p. 161.

replies, 'Keep the commandments,' and he can truthfully reply that he has from his earliest days.

Jesus can see his sincerity and 'looked steadily at him and loved him.' He then extends an invitation: 'Go sell everything you own, give it to the poor, and come and follow me.' Jesus is inviting him to transfer his wealth 'into a far more secure "bank", a heavenly one, so that he will have "treasure in heaven".'[500] This invitation involves crossing a threshold: 'from a way of life centred on the Torah and its commandments to one centred totally on the Person of Jesus.'[501] Then come some of the saddest words in the New Testament. 'His face fell at these words and he want away sad, for he was a man of great wealth.'

The cost was too great. To give up his wealth was too high a price to pay. Why? Well, we can only speculate. His wealth was his security; perhaps his sense of identity and self-esteem were tied up with his wealth; maybe he enjoyed the power it gave him. But it is clear that he was unable to face the prospect of life without wealth. Perhaps he thought to himself, 'If I give my money to the poor and this doesn't work out, I can't get it back again.'

Jesus has some hard things to say about those who are wealthy. A lot of ink has been poured out trying to decipher the meaning of the sentence: 'It is easier for a camel to pass through the eye of a needle than for a rich person to enter the kingdom of God.' In some manuscripts, the word for camel (*kamelos* in the Greek) was

---

500 Ibid., p. 163.
501 Ibid.

replaced with *kamilos*, the Greek word for rope or cable.[502] Some medieval scribes found the image of a camel passing through the eye of a needle improbable, and so they corrupted the text with what they believed to be a more plausible substitution. It's still difficult to thread a needle with a piece of rope, but it is much easier than passing a camel through the eye of a needle. Other commentators have suggested that there may have been a very narrow gate in the walled city of Jerusalem known as the 'eye of the needle'. It would have been an extremely tight fit, but not impossible for a camel to pass through such a narrow gate. Alas, there isn't any convincing evidence that such a gate ever existed. Most biblical scholars today would simply point out that hyperbole, the deliberate exaggeration in Jesus' image, is a common Semitic idiom, expressing a truth in black and white for the sake of emphasis. In other words, wealth can often become an insurmountable barrier between ourselves and God. How difficult it is to detach ourselves from the seductive power of wealth.[503]

For most of us, though, the cost of discipleship is not wealth. We may wish that wealth was a hazard to our faith, but alas it isn't. Charles Schulz, the creator of the *Peanuts* cartoon strip, is a committed Christian and often uses this medium to preach a gospel message or re-tell a gospel story. His reflection on the parable of the Rich Young Man has young Linus pulling his sled up a snow-covered hillside. But he encounters a tree – dead in the centre of the path

---

[502] Joseph H. Thayer, *Thayer's Greek-English Lexicon of The New Testament*, Grand Rapids, Michigan, Baker Book House, 1977, p. 323.
[503] See William Barclay, *Gospel of Matthew, vol. 2*, Edinburgh, The Saint Andrew Press, 1969, pp. 239-40.

downwards. He sizes up the tree. He looks to the top of the mountain, speculating about the perfect ride from the top. But there is a risk – the risk of hitting the tree. Again he makes some calculations. The tree is big, but there is a narrow track either side that could be negotiated with difficulty. But alas! It is a risk that he's not prepared to take, and so he turns around where he is, halfway up the mountain, and settles for second best, the less than perfect trip.[504]

When the young man asks Jesus, 'What must I do to inherit eternal life?' he is sincere in his quest. Jesus, we are told, 'looked steadily at him and loved him.' But he is beset with fear. Who would he be without his wealth? What friends would he have were he to give away all his possessions? Linus' tree is the point at which one must either risk everything, or settle for mediocrity, like the rich young man, afraid to take the risk, afraid to let go of his wealth, afraid to surrender his power.

Christian life is about risk-taking. And some opportunities present themselves only once in life. Shakespeare reflects upon the tragedy of lost opportunities:

> There is a tide in the affairs of men
> Which, taken at the flood, leads on to fortune;
> Omitted, all the voyage of their life
> Is bound in shallows and miseries.[505]

It is for that reason that an ancient Latin saying has terrified more than one soul: *Time Jesum transeuntem et non reventem,* which

---

504 Charles M. Schulz, *The Complete Peanuts,* 1957 to 1958, Fantagraphics Books, Seattle, WA, p. 174.
505 William Shakespeare, *Julius Caesar,* Act IV, 3, 217-20.

translates as: 'Dread the passage of Jesus, for he does not return.'[506] This doesn't mean that God gives up on us; it merely states a sad but undeniable truth. Some moments of grace, such as the invitation in today's gospel, do not present themselves a second time.

And so we are invited today to reflect upon the tree in our life; that tree that threatens our perfect ride. It may be a weighty matter that we must tend to; it may be a minor trifle that holds us back. St Bernard once saw a small animal ensnared in a hunter's trap by the finest thread. He observed: 'It doesn't matter whether the animal is snared by a fine, slender thread, or by a heavy iron chain. Either way, the bird is still trapped.' We need to keep in mind the advice that Mother Teresa gave to Canadian businessman J.-Robert Ouimet over 25 years ago. When he asked her if he should give away everything he had, she replied, 'You can't give anything away. Nothing belongs to you. It has only been loaned to you.' Those words remained with him: 'Everything was in those words. "You can't give anything away; it's been loaned to you."'[507]

The rich man retained his wealth and the security it represented, 'but in place of the joy and freedom he might have known in loving companionship with Jesus he has the sadness of knowing he is trapped, controlled, prevented from gaining his deepest desire.'[508] He remains a captive who balked at the prospect of freedom.

---

506 Joseph Campbell, *The Hero with a Thousand Faces*, p. 59.
507 J.-Robert Ouimet, *Everything Has Been Loaned to You*, privately published, June 2010.
508 Brendan Byrne, p. 163.

TWENTY-NINTH SUNDAY IN ORDINARY TIME

(YEAR B)

Allow us to sit one at your right hand and the other at your left in your glory. (Mk 10:37)

Mark is the shortest of the four gospels, and six of its 16 chapters are devoted to the last week in Jesus' life (Chapters 11 to 16). Mark's gospel is the story of a journey from Galilee (in the country's north), to Jerusalem, where Jesus is to die and rise from the dead. Jesus and his disciples have begun the long journey from Galilee in the north towards Jerusalem in the south – a distance of some 120 kilometres as the crow flies, but considerably longer along the dusty roads of first-century Palestine. During this long journey Jesus has been attempting to forewarn his disciples about what awaited him in Jerusalem. Three times he has told them that he would suffer and die, but on each occasion they fail to understand (Chapters 8, 9 and 10). Peter at least has recognised that Jesus is the Christ (or Messiah) (8:29), but in Mark's gospel it's not evident that Peter really understands what that means. Peter and the disciples cannot reconcile these two truths: that Jesus is the Messiah, and that he is going to suffer and die.

What did it mean calling Jesus the Christ or the Messiah? Both words, Christ from the Greek and Messiah from the Hebrew, mean the anointed one. Kings and priests were anointed as part of their investiture, and holders of these offices were regularly referred to as 'anointed'.[509] Having been conquered time and again by foreign powers, the Jews of Jesus' day looked back a thousand years to the reign of King David and his son Solomon when the kingdom of Israel was at its most prosperous. They hoped that God would send another anointed one, like King David. The disciples shared the common idea of their day that the anointed one, the Messiah, would be a righteous, triumphant ruler who would restore Israel to the glories of the Davidic kingdom. James and John 'want to turn Jesus' messianic journey to Jerusalem into a march to glory – a glory in which they will sit on either side of him when he reigns as king.'[510]

In Chapters 8, 9 and 10 Jesus tells the disciples in plain language that he is destined to suffer and die, and on each occasion they fail to understand what he means. Today's gospel follows immediately after the third prophecy of the passion, and James and John seem incredibly insensitive.

Imagine returning home from a visit to the doctor and telling a family member or one of your closest friends that the diagnosis was not good. Your body is riddled with cancer and the doctor doesn't think you'll have more than a few weeks to live. How would you feel if their first reaction was to ask whether or not you've made a will,

---

[509] Marinus De Jonge, 'Christ', in David Noel Freedman (ed.), *The Anchor Bible Dictionary*, Doubleday, New York, 1992, vol. 1, p. 914.
[510] Tom Wright, *Mark for Everyone*, p. 140.

and who was getting your jewellery? James and John are about as sensitive as that!

Matthew wrote his gospel some 20 years after Mark, and he incorporated a good deal of Mark into his own gospel, making changes here and there. When Matthew came to this incident he was obviously embarrassed. How could James and John, two of Jesus' closest disciples, be so preoccupied with positions of power and so insensitive to what Jesus had just said? Matthew tries to protect the reputation of James and John by having their mother put the request to Jesus. Poor mum, blamed again! Luke omits the whole episode.

James and John are concerned about status and position, and their request sparks off a competitive race within the Twelve. When the other ten disciples heard about this, they began to feel indignant with James and John. 'Who are they to be requesting positions of honour at either side of Jesus?' Jesus takes this as an opportunity to teach the Twelve about discipleship. The disciple is not a person intent on positions of honour, but one who serves. And that is a hard lesson to learn.

Today's gospel also reminds us that serving others entails denying ourselves and taking up our cross. The sons of Zebedee, James and John, want the best seats in the house without knowing the price of admission. Jesus asks them, 'Can you drink the cup that I must drink, or be baptised with the baptism with which I must be baptised?' 'Baptism' in this context does not refer to the sacrament of baptism. The word 'baptism' comes from a Greek word that means literally to plunge or immerse. So, Jesus is asking, 'Are you willing to accompany me through the trials that lie ahead; are you ready to be immersed into the inescapable rhythm of Christian life – death and resurrection? Can you be plunged into the death experience that awaits me? Can you drink from that cup?' Impetuously, they say 'yes: without realising what they've said.

The Desert Fathers and Mothers sought refuge in the desert during the early centuries of Christianity. Here they learnt wisdom. Abbot John the Dwarf asked the Lord in prayer to take away all his passions. The prayer was answered, and in that condition he went to one of the elders of the community and said: 'You see before you a man who is completely at rest and has no more temptations.' The elder said by way of reply: 'Go and ask the Lord to command some struggle to be stirred up in you, for the soul is matured only in battles.' John heeded the advice, and when the temptations started up again, he did not pray that the struggle be taken away from him. He simply said, 'Lord, give me strength to get through the fight.'[511]

The cup that Jesus had to drink was that of suffering and death; for all of us it is the death of self – the self that is continually oriented towards domination, status, positions of honour and self-aggrandisement, the self that is consumed by a craving or grasping desire for possessions and status. Jesus tells us to seek first the kingdom of God, and everything else will fall into place.

The last of the four gospels to be written was that by John, some time towards the end of the first century. John obviously felt that the community for whom he wrote his gospel still hadn't learnt the

---

511 Thomas Merton, *The Wisdom of the Desert*, Sheldon Press, London, 1976, pp. 56-7.

lesson of service. Although John's gospel gives a lengthy account of the Last Supper – it devotes five chapters to that final meal Jesus shared with his disciples – not once is the institution of the eucharist mentioned. Instead, John – and John alone – tells us about the washing of the feet, a lowly task undertaken in that culture by a servant or slave. Having washed the feet of his disciples, Jesus says, 'If I, then, the Lord and Master, have washed your feet, you must wash each other's feet. I have given you an example so that you may copy what I have done.' By deliberately omitting an account of the institution of the eucharist and instead telling us of the washing of the feet, John is teaching his community a much needed lesson. Unless we wash each other's feet – truly serve each other – our celebration of the eucharist will be honouring God with our lips, but not with our hearts.

The German priest and artist Sieger Koder has painted an interesting and unusual portrait of Jesus washing the feet of Peter at the Last Supper. The painting is unusual because of its perspective. We view Jesus from behind, kneeling over Peter's feet which are immersed in a bowl of water. We cannot see the face of Jesus, seemingly resting against Peter's knees. But on closer inspection the face of Jesus is visible, reflected in the bowl of water used to wash Peter's feet. Where, today, do we see the face of Jesus?[512]

Here, in the bowl of water used to wash the feet of others.

---

[512] This image can be downloaded from a number of sites on the internet. One such site is http://servantleader.org/

THIRTIETH SUNDAY IN ORDINARY TIME

(YEAR B)

Master, let me see again. (Mk 10:51)

In last week's gospel James and John, the sons of Zebedee, wanted Jesus to do them a favour. 'What is it you want me to do for you?' Jesus asked. 'Allow us to sit one at your right hand and the other at your left in your glory.' Today, on the outskirts of Jericho, a blind beggar, the son of Timaeus, also seeks a favour. Jesus asks exactly the same question that he put to the sons of Zebedee: 'What do you want me to do for you?' The son of Timaeus is not after a position of honour; he simply asks, with a vigorous faith, that he might see again.

What a sharp contrast to the disciples who want power, prestige and glory. Bartimaeus is therefore a model to imitate. 'Unlike the disciples, who hadn't really understood what Jesus was about, he is already a man of faith, courage and true discipleship. He recognises who Jesus is ('son of David'); he clearly believes Jesus can help him ('your faith has saved you') … and he follows Jesus on the way ('the way' was the early Christian's word for what we call 'Christianity').[513]

---

513 Tom Wright, *Mark for Everyone*, p. 143.

Reflections for the year of Mark

The healing of Bartimaeus, just as Jesus is about to enter Jerusalem, is a sign 'that Jesus is trying to open his followers' eyes.'[514] That refers not only to the Twelve, but to us as well. In what ways might we be blind?

We can be blinded by our own pride or prejudice, as Hans Christian Andersen's fairy tale 'The Emperor's New Clothes' makes clear. The emperor of a prosperous city who cares more about clothes than military pursuits or entertainment is duped by two swindlers who promise him the finest suit of clothes from the most beautiful cloth. This cloth, they tell him, is invisible to anyone who is either stupid or unfit for his position. The emperor cannot see the (non-existent) cloth, but pretends that he can lest he appear to be stupid; his ministers do likewise. When the swindlers report that the suit is finished, they pretend to dress the emperor, who then processes through the capital showing off his new royal robes. During the course of the procession, a small child cries out, 'The emperor has no clothes!' It's as if the scales fall from everyone's eyes, and the crowd realises that the child is telling the truth. The emperor, however, holds his head high and continues the procession, refusing to open his eyes to what is now obvious to everyone. But that only happens in fairytales, or does it?

Clinging blindly to our own opinion can be a more effective block to direct contact with reality, and therefore to union with God, than vice itself. The majority of people who opposed Jesus were not evil people. They were 'right-thinking people; but they held uncriti-

---

[514] Ibid., p. 144.

cally to the accepted views about religion and closed their minds and hearts to the message of Jesus.

In the Buddhist tradition there is a story about a man who lived in a small village on the seacoast. He lived alone with his only son whom he loved dearly. While the father was abroad on business pirates came and plundered the village and burned it to the ground. Those villagers who couldn't flee the invaders were slaughtered and their bodies devoured by the flames that engulfed the village. The pirates took the man's son with him and later sold him as a slave. When the father returned from his travels he was confronted by the smouldering remains of the village. As he looked around he saw a charred body that he thought was his son. The body was cremated and the father took the ashes, placing them in a sack that he wore hanging from his neck. He then remained in his house and grieved unrestrainedly.

Some months later his son escaped from slavery and returned to the village. He knocked on the door of his father's house. 'Father, open the door; it's me, your son.'

The father yelled back, 'Go away. Who are you, some hooligan who has been sent to torment me? I carry my son in ashes around my neck. Who are you to do this to me?'

'No father,' said the voice. 'It is your son. Open the door for me.'

But the father replied, 'Go away! I cannot open the door for you. I carry my son in ashes around my neck.' And so, the son went away.

The Buddhist commentary on this story is instructive: Sometimes we cling so tightly to what we think is true that when the truth comes, which we deeply desire, and knocks upon our door, we refuse to open.[515]

We can turn a blind eye to the truth because of self-interest, and that is far more insidious. As Mark Twain once observed, 'What gets us into trouble is not what we don't know. It's what we know for sure that just ain't so.'[516] Upton Sinclair expressed the same idea in slightly different words when he said 'It is difficult to get a man to understand something when his salary depends upon his not understanding it.'[517]

Al Gore served as vice-president of the United States from 1993 to 2001. Following an unsuccessful bid for the presidency he has become a passionate spokesman for the environment, winning the Nobel Peace Prize in 2007. The 2006 documentary *An Inconvenient Truth* is about his campaign to educate people about global warming. It won the Academy Award for Best Documentary Feature. Gore attempts to respond to the view of skeptics and vested interest groups who seek to dismiss global warming as 'just a myth.' For example, 'the so-called global warming skeptics cite one article more than any other in arguing that global warming is just a myth: a statement of concern during the 1970s that the world might be in danger of entering a new ice age.

---

515 Adapted from John Shea, *Gospel Food for Hungry Christians: John – Images and Reflections from the Gospel*, CD produced by ACTA Publications, Skokie, IL, 2008.
516 Quoted by Al Gore in *An Inconvenient Truth*, Bloomsbury, London, 2006, pp. 20-1.
517 Ibid., pp. 266-7.

Releasing the Captive

But the article in which that scientist's comment appeared was published in *Newsweek* and never appeared in any peer-reviewed journal. Moreover, the scientist who made the statement corrected it shortly after with a clear explanation of why his offhand comment was erroneous.'[518]

Gore cites a study by Dr Naomi Oreskes, published in *Science* magazine, of every peer-reviewed science journal article on global warming from the previous ten years. She and her team selected a large random sample of 928 articles representing almost ten per cent of the total, and carefully analysed how many of the articles agreed or disagreed with the prevailing consensus view of global warming. Of the 928 articles examined, not a single one expressed doubt about the cause of global warming.

By way of contrast, another large study was conducted of all the articles on global warming during the previous fourteen years in the four newspapers considered by the authors of the study to be the most influential in the United States: *The New York Times*, the *Washington Post*, the *LA Times*, and the *Wall Street Journal*. A large random sample of almost 18 per cent of the articles came to an astonishingly different conclusion to that found in peer-reviewed scientific articles. They found that one-half gave equal weight to the consensus view on the one hand, and the scientifically discredited view that human beings play no role in global warming on the other. In other words, the American news media had been giving a totally distorted and unscientific view of the causes of global warming.[519]

---

518 Ibid., pp. 260-1.
519 Ibid., pp. 262-3.

Reflections for the year of Mark

Sowing seeds of doubt was a ploy adopted by the tobacco industry 40 years ago. During the 1960s, even though the surgeon general's report had made it abundantly clear that smoking can cause lung cancer, 'the tobacco companies were working overtime to encourage Americans not to believe the science – to create doubts about whether there was any real cause for concern.'[520] A tobacco company memo recently uncovered put it this way:

> Doubt is our product, since it is the best means of competing with the 'body of fact' that exists in the mind of the general public. It is also the means of establishing a controversy.[521]

Gore's family grew tobacco. Even after the surgeon general's report in 1964 they continued growing tobacco. It took a personal tragedy for the family to give up growing tobacco altogether. Gore's only sister, Nancy, started smoking when she was thirteen years old, and she never stopped. She died of lung cancer. Gore reflects on his sister's death:

> Believe me, lung cancer is one of the ways you don't want to die. Often, the victim actually drowns from the constant build-up of fluid in the lungs once the pathology overwhelms the body's natural healing processes. The suffering can be unspeakable.

Nancy was only 46 years of age.

Addiction, however can distort our perception. A recent international study published in the journal *Addiction* has found that 20 per cent of smokers believe that some brands of cigarettes are safer than

---

520 Ibid., p. 256.
521 Ibid., p. 263.

others, despite the fact that 'all conventional cigarette brands present the same level of risk to smokers, including so-called lower tar cigarettes.' The study surveyed more than 8000 current and former smokers, including more than 2000 Australians. Females were 'more likely to believe some brands may be less harmful while older people considered their brand was safer.'[522] An inconvenient truth!

The disciples of Jesus found it hard to let go of their idea of Jesus as a triumphant Messiah who is about to cast off the yoke of imperial Rome and inaugurate a reign of peace and prosperity for Israel, a reign in which they would enjoy positions of status and honour. Bartimaeus, the blind beggar, becomes a model of discipleship. He seeks neither status nor honour; he asks only that he might see.

---

[522] Nicky Phillips, 'One-in-five smokers swallow the line some cigarettes are safer', *The Sydney Morning Herald*, Thursday, 14 April, 2011.

Reflections for the year of Mark

THIRTY-FIRST SUNDAY IN ORDINARY TIME

(YEAR B)

Which is the first of all the commandments? (Mk 12:28)

Some time ago, there was a lively and amusing correspondence in the English Catholic magazine, *The Tablet*. This correspondence ignited, yet again, the ancient debate over which is the greatest of all the religious orders. The editor admitted that he was somewhat surprised at the enthusiasm of *The Tablet's* readers in sending in jokes about religious orders. Three orders seemed to feature most prominently – the Jesuits, the Dominicans and the Franciscans.

One such story is about a Jesuit, a Dominican and a Franciscan who found themselves together on a train. The Jesuit said to the Dominican: 'Father, what would you have been had you not been a Dominican?'

'Oh, Father, I would surely have been a Jesuit. And you, Father, had you not been a Jesuit, what would you have been?'

'I'd certainly have been a Dominican,' said the Jesuit. They both turned to the Franciscan. 'And you, Father, had you not been a Franciscan, what would have been?'

'If I'd not been a Franciscan ... I'd have been an utter fool!'

It would seem that the rabbis of Jesus' day were also good at arguing. In particular, they used to argue over which was the greatest commandment in the Jewish law, the Torah. And the Jewish law consists of much more than just the Ten Commandments that Moses received on Mt Sinai. If you go carefully through the five books of the Torah, you'll find not ten but 613 commandments. Rabbis speculated endlessly over which of the 613 commandments was the greatest.

It's not a silly question because there are times when we have to decide what is most important to us. Tom Wright gives the example of a house fire. What would you grab as you escaped from the flames? The children (if they can't walk), your computer, passport, personal documents, precious photographs, family heirlooms, letters ... In taking some things and leaving others we discover where our priorities really lie.

Today's question is like that. Of all these laws, which commandment really matters?[523] Jesus is asked for his opinion. In one sense, he sidestepped the question – refusing to label one of the 613 as the greatest. Instead, he summarised all of the commandments in a single sentence. He took one verse from the Book of Deuteronomy – we are to love God with our whole heart and soul. This 'first commandment' is a version of the prayer known to all Jews, the *Shema* (from the Hebrew word 'listen', as in 'Listen, Israel ...'). He joined that to a verse from the Book of Leviticus: Love your neighbour as you love yourself (Dt 6:5 and Lv 19:18).

---

523 Tom Wright, *Mark for Everyone*, pp. 169-70.

Jesus wasn't saying anything new. What he did emphasise, though, was the fact that the two parts of this commandment are inseparable: Love of God is impossible without love of neighbour. That truth is expressed forcefully in the first letter of St John:

> Anyone who says 'I love God' and hates his brother or sister, is a liar, since whoever does not love the brother or sister whom they can see cannot love God whom they have not seen (1 Jn 4:20).

This twofold commandment to love lays bare the path to human wholeness. A recent telephone poll of 1000 people conducted by Ipsos Mackay in 2006 revealed that personal relationships are the key to happiness. Almost 60 per cent of people polled nominated their relationship with their family, including partner or spouse, as the most important factor contributing to their happiness.[524]

When these relationships go awry we're in trouble. Interpersonal psychotherapy, a therapeutic strategy developed in the 1970s for the treatment of depression, has been employed successfully since then to assist patients recover from a number of other disorders, such as bulimia nervosa. In a nutshell, interpersonal psychotherapy focuses upon the patient's relationships with significant other people in his or her life as a means of resolving psychological symptoms. Troubled relationships often trigger disordered behaviour. An upheaval in personal relationships sometimes leads to feelings of rejection and hence of self-esteem. Some individuals whose self-evaluation is linked

---

[524] Adele Horin, 'We're richer than ever, but not happier', *The Sydney Morning Herald*, September 16-17, 2006.

to their physical appearance (shape and weight, for example) may resort to extreme forms of weight control to enhance self-esteem. Interpersonal psychotherapy doesn't claim to be a panacea for all eating disorders, but it highlights the nexus between dysfunctional relationships and certain psychological disorders.[525] Love is the path to healing and wholeness. St Paul reminds us that we are nothing without love (1 Cor 13:3).

John Shea tells of his old neighbourhood where there was a steady stream of mentally ill and handicapped people who begged. One man who had no legs below the knees lifted himself out of his wheelchair and sat on the ground, in winter as well as summer, with a large plastic cup positioned between the stubs of his knees.

As Shea walked past the man he always gave him some money, but one day he saw a woman squatting next to him and talking with great animation. He heard her say, 'So you haven't always lived in Chicago ...?' The woman was taking a personal interest in the man and in his predicament.

'My dollar or two tossed into his cup,' writes Shea, 'seemed impersonal, even demeaning.' He saw in this woman's generous form of presence a love of the transcendent God that makes us one with our neighbour.[526]

The love of which Jesus speaks, *agape* in the Greek text, is more than empty words. St Paul tells the Corinthians that it is always

---

[525] E. Rieger et al., 'Interpersonal Psychotherapy (IPT): Current Status and Future Directions', a paper delivered at the Twelfth Annual Meeting of the Eating Disorders Research Society, Port Douglas, 31 August 2006.
[526] John Shea, *Eating with the Bridegroom*, pp. 262-3.

ready 'to make allowances, to trust, to hope and to endure whatever comes (1 Cor 13:7). It endures in time of adversity.

A Jewish couple had been married for ten years without giving birth to a child. Following the law which governed such matters, they went to their rabbi to arrange for a divorce. The rabbi said to the couple, 'Just as you celebrated your marriage with a festive banquet, so you should not separate without also having a festive banquet.' The couple followed the rabbi's advice and prepared a great banquet. During the banquet the woman gave her husband more to drink than usual. When he was in high spirits, he said to his wife: 'My wife, when you leave my house to return to the house of your father, take with you whatever you like best'.

The husband then fell into a deep sleep. When he awoke he looked around in astonishment. 'Where am I?' he asked.

'You are in my father's house,' replied his wife. 'What business do I have in your father's house?' She replied, 'Don't you remember telling me last night that I may take with me whatever I like best when I return to my father's house? Nothing in the whole world do I like better than you!'[527]

---

[527] Adapted from William Bausch, *Storytelling: Imagination and Faith*, Twenty-Third Publications, Mystic, CT, 1984, pp. 79-80.

THIRTY-SECOND SUNDAY IN ORDINARY TIME

(YEAR B)

... but she from the little she had has put in everything she possessed, all she had to live on. (Mk 12:44)

Today's gospel, known traditionally as the widow's mite, is the lovely story of a woman who contributed to the treasury everything she possessed, all she had to live on. Being a widow, she had no inheritance rights in ancient Israel and was 'particularly fragile and open to physical, social, and financial abuse.'[528]

It is quite likely that this incident took place within the Temple precincts, in the court of the women. According to the Mishnah there were 13 receptacles for offerings located around the walls of that court, each of them labelled for different purposes,[529] and because they were trumpet-shaped they were known as 'the trumpets'. In contrast to the offerings of the rich, this widow contributed two lepta. The lepton (pl. lepta) means literally 'a tiny thing' (hence, 'mite' in English) and it was the smallest coin in circulation at that

---

[528] Francis J. Moloney, *The Gospel of Mark*, Hendrickson Publishers, Peabody, MA, 2002, p. 246.
[529] m. Sheqalim 6:5. Cf. Donahue and Harrington, *The Gospel of Mark*, p. 363.

Reflections for the year of Mark

time.[530] The contemporary Australian equivalent to the widow's offering would be two five cent coins. Almost nothing!

The story in today's first reading from the first book of Kings is also about a widow who gave all the food she had in order to prepare a meal for the prophet Elijah. Being a widow, she was one of the most vulnerable members of society, and she and her son were nearing starvation. Her generosity is repaid, for the meal was not spent, nor the jug of oil emptied.

We have before us today two examples of unselfish giving. Two widows, vulnerable and disadvantaged members of their society, held nothing back. Fr William Bausch suggests that 'the one single, most reliable, most accurate practical measure of our spiritual lives, how we stand with God, is our use of money.'[531] He points out that 16 out of 38 of Jesus' parables are concerned with how to handle money and possessions.

> In the gospels, an amazing one out of ten verses deals directly with the subject of money. The whole Bible offers 500 verses on prayer, fewer than 500 verses on faith, but more than 2000 verses on money and possessions.[532]

Money is such a dominant force in our lives and we spend most of our time and energy acquiring it. How we use it, or how it uses us, must therefore be the real litmus test of our spirituality.[533] Like

---

530 D.E. Nineham, *Saint Mark*, p. 335.
531 William J. Bausch, *60 More Seasonal Homilies*, Twenty-Third Publications, Mystic, CT, 2003, p. 177.
532 Ibid., p. 178.
533 Ibid., p. 179.

the scribes in today's gospel, we are easily beguiled by the trappings of privilege and affluence. Alain de Botton illustrates this point by recalling an incident from Marcel Proust's *In Search of Lost Time*. On a foggy evening in Paris at the end of the nineteenth century, the narrator travels to an expensive restaurant to dine with an aristocratic friend, the Marquis de Saint-Loup.

> He arrives early, Saint-Loup is late and the staff, judging their client on the basis of a shabby coat and an unfamiliar name, assume that a nobody has entered their establishment. They therefore patronise him, take him to a table around which an Arctic draught is blowing and are slow to offer him anything to drink or eat. But, a quarter of an hour later, the marquis arrives, identifies his friend and at a stroke transforms the narrator's value in the eyes of the staff. The manager bows deeply before him, draws out the menu, recites the specials of the day with evocative flourishes, compliments him on his clothes and, so as to prevent him thinking that these courtesies are in any way dependent on his link to an aristocrat, occasionally gives him a surreptitious little smile which seems to indicate a wholly personal affection.[534]

What has happened here? Has the manager had a change of heart? Sadly, no. As de Botton points out, he has not 'amended his snobbish value-system in any way. He has merely rewarded someone differently within its brutal confines …'[535]

Clive Hamilton and Richard Denniss use the coined word 'affluenza' to describe our addiction to possessions. Affluenza is the 'bloated, sluggish and unfulfilled feeling that results from efforts to

---

[534] Alain de Botton, *Status Anxiety*, Hamish Hamilton, Camberwell, Vic., 2004, p. 24.
[535] Ibid., pp. 24-5.

keep up with the Joneses.'[536] We are confused about what it takes to live a worthwhile life, and part of this confusion 'is a failure to distinguish between what we want and what we need.'

For example, only 20 per cent of Americans said a second car was a 'necessity' in 1973; by 1996 that figure had risen to 37 per cent. In Australia, items that were once considered as luxuries have become necessities – items such as flat-screen TVs, air conditioning, personal computers, second bathrooms and mobile phones, to name but a few.[537] Our expenditure on luxury items is rapidly increasing, 'reflected in booming sales of luxury travel, luxury cars, pleasure craft, cosmetic surgery, trophy homes, holiday homes and professional-quality home appliances.'[538]

We delude ourselves into thinking that we need all of these goods and services to be happy, and yet when we finally acquire them we don't feel happier, except perhaps fleetingly. Hamilton and Denniss argue that we should question the whole idea of seeking happiness through acquiring more stuff. Instead we engage in an internal dialogue that goes something like this:

> I hoped that getting to this income level would make me feel contented. I do have more stuff, but it doesn't seem to have done the trick. I obviously need to set my goals higher. I'm sure I'll be happy when I'm earning an extra $10,000 because then I'll be able to buy the other things I want.[539]

---

536 Clive Hamilton and Richard Denniss, *Affluenza*, Allen & Unwin, Crows Nest, NSW, 2005, p. 3.
537 Ibid., p. 7.
538 Ibid., pp. 9-10.
539 Ibid., pp. 5-6.

Releasing the Captive

There is a certain recklessness in the giving of both widows. They might have kept something for themselves, but they gave everything they had. William Barclay observes:

> There is a great symbolic truth here. It is our tragedy that there is so often some part of our lives, some part of our activities, some part of ourselves which we do not give to Christ. Somehow there is always something which we hold back. We rarely make the final sacrifice and the final surrender.[540]

That freedom to let go and hold nothing back is called detachment. The great Buddhist saint Nagarjuna moved around naked except for a loincloth and, incongruously, a golden begging bowl given to him as a gift by a wealthy disciple. One night as he lay down to sleep he noticed a man lurking nearby, a thief intent upon stealing the golden begging bowl.

'Here, take this,' said Nagarjuna, holding out the begging bowl. 'That way you won't disturb me once I have fallen asleep.'

The thief eagerly grabbed the bowl and made off, only to return the next morning with the bowl and a request. He said, 'When you gave away this bowl so freely last night, you made me feel very poor. Teach me how to acquire the riches that make this kind of light-hearted detachment possible.'[541]

---

540 William Barclay, *The Gospel of Mark*, pp. 316-7.
541 Adapted from Anthony de Mello, *The Heart of the Enlightened*, Fount Paperbacks, 1989, pp. 30-1.

THIRTY-THIRD SUNDAY IN ORDINARY TIME

(YEAR B)

And then they will see the Son of Man coming in the clouds with great power and glory. (Mk 13:26)

Chapter 13 of St Mark's gospel describes what is often called the Second Coming of Jesus and the end of the world. The sun will be darkened, the moon will lose it brightness, the stars will fall from heaven – and then we will see the Son of Man coming in the clouds with great power and glory. He will send the angels to gather his chosen from the four winds, from the ends of the world to the ends of heaven. The Second Coming! The end of the world!

Today, people either disregard it completely and never think about it, or they become obsessed by it. In March, 1997 – it was on Good Friday – thirty-nine people died in what appeared to be a mass suicide in San Diego, California. All of them, men and women, were members of the Heaven's Gate cult. Their leaders had urged followers, via the internet, to take their own lives before disaster befell the Earth. They believed that the Hale-Bopp comet, which was then streaking across the sky, was their ticket to heaven. Most of us shake our heads in disbelief. These were all intelligent and successful people. They worked with computers, designing web pages on the internet for respectable clients who spoke glowingly about them.

In today's gospel, Jesus warns us that no one but the Father knows the day or the hour when the end of the world as we know it will take place. And so it's very easy to dismiss the Second Coming and the end of the world as the preoccupation of the lunatic fringe. But the Second Coming is an inescapable reality for all of us. I am not referring to the coming of Jesus at the end of time. I am referring to the moment of our own death. That is a subject many of us wish to avoid because of a deeply ingrained terror of death. A Leunig cartoon has the following conversation between a man and an angel. The man says: 'I want certainty!' The angel replies: 'There is only one certainty: you are going to die.'

'I don't want to die!' the man yells back angrily.

The angel replies: 'That's the only certainty we've got and you're telling me you don't want it – what's the matter with you?'

'I'm not ready for it. I want happiness first.'

'No, no!' replies the angel. 'You get ready to die first, then you get happy. You've had it the wrong way around!'

The man looks perplexed, and then disgruntled. He yells out, as the angel flies off, 'You'll be hearing from my lawyer! I'll see you in court! ... How dare you threaten me ...'[542]

But therein lies a profound truth. Happiness does not come from running away from death; it comes rather from preparing for it.

---

542 *The Sydney Morning Herald*, 18 April 1997.

Reflections for the year of Mark

While Fr Ronald Rolheiser was giving a retreat at a Trappist monastery an old monk came to talk to him. He shared a great deal about the ups and downs of more than fifty years of monastic life. At the end of their chat he asked a question: 'Give me some hints on how I should prepare to die! What should I do to make myself more ready for death?' Rolheiser was humbled that a faith-filled man more than twice his age should him such a question and eagerly await an answer. 'I was not so naive as to offer him much by way of an answer … But his is a good question. Indeed, how can we prepare to die?'[543]

The theologian, doctor and Nobel Peace Prize winner Albert Schweitzer (1875–1965) once wrote: 'We must all become familiar with the thought of death if we want to grow into really good people. We need not think of it every day or every hour … When we are familiar with death, we accept each week, each day, as a gift.' St Benedict said in his Rule that 'a monk must have death daily before his eyes.'[544] Abbot Christopher Jamison observes how

> people diagnosed with a life-threatening illness often describe how the illness has led them to reassess their life and its priorities. This sometimes leads them to a better way of life that is simpler, giving time to what matters most in life.[545]

In the first Sunday of Lent reflection, I spoke about Eugene O'Kelly and how his life was transformed when he was diagnosed

---

543 Ronald Rolheiser, *Against an Infinite Horizon*, Hodder & Stoughton, London, 1995, pp. 76-7.
544 Quoted in Abbot Christopher Jamison, *Finding Happiness*, Weidenfeld & Nicolson, London, 2008, p. 25.
545 Ibid.

with late-stage brain cancer and told he had only three months to live. He was fifty-three years of age. His wife, Corinne, writes that the first lesson that her husband learnt was to face reality.

> When Gene was younger, he had an insatiable need for control. He needed to feel that he had authority over particular situations so he could execute them as successfully as possible. This is a common characteristic among CEOs and probably why Gene was an outstanding leader. However, when Gene found about his cancer, it was a major turning point in his life (for the obvious reasons) but also because there was nothing he could do to ride his body of the disease. He could fight for lofty radical treatments, keep himself in a state of denial, or just face reality. Facing reality is living precisely in this moment, right now, with as much awareness as we are capable of. And it means distinguishing between what we can exert influence over and what we can't.[546]

M. Scott Peck's *Further along the Road Less Travelled* reveals that, as a psychotherapist, he has had to push at least half of his patients to face the reality of their death. He argues that their reluctance to face the reality of death seems to be a part of their illness.[547] He believes that we live in a cowardly, death-denying culture. It is normal to be afraid of dying. Dying is a going into the unknown, and to a degree it is very healthy to be fearful of entering the unknown.

What is not healthy is to try to ignore it. As Leunig's angel says: 'There is only one certainty: you are going to die.' A merchant in

---

546 Eugene O'Kelly (with a new afterword by Corinne O'Kelly), *Chasing Daylight*, McGraw-Hill, New York, 2008, p. 183.
547 M. Scott Peck, *Further along the Road Less Travelled*, Simon & Schuster, New York, 1993, p. 52.

Reflections for the year of Mark

Florence sent his servant to the bazaar, but the man came back trembling and white with fear. 'Master,' he said. 'While I was in the market place, I bumped into a stranger. When I looked him in the face, I found that it was Death. 'He made a threatening gesture at me, and then walked away. Now I am afraid. Please give me a swift horse so that I can ride at once to Perugia and put as great a distance as possible between Death and myself.'

The merchant was anxious for his servant and gave him his swiftest steed. The servant galloped away with great haste. Later in the day, the merchant himself went down to the bazaar and saw Death loitering there in the crowd. So he went up to him and said, 'You made a threatening gesture at my poor servant this morning. What did it mean?'

Death replied, 'That was not a threatening gesture, sir. It was a gesture of surprise at seeing him here in Florence.'

'And why would he not be here in Florence? This is where the man lives.'

'Well', said Death. 'I had been led to understand that I was to meet him tonight in Perugia.'[548]

---

[548] Anthony de Mello, *The Heart of the Enlightened*, Fount Paperbacks, London, 1989, p. 169.

CHRIST THE KING

(YEAR B)

Mine is not a kingdom of this world. (Jn 18:36)

Today's first reading is taken from the prophet Daniel. Although the story of Daniel is set during the Babylonian exile in the sixth century before Christ, it was written during the reign of Antiochus IV Epiphanes, a tyrant who ruled over the Jewish people from 175 until 164 BC. The title *Epiphanes* means 'epiphany' or 'manifestation' (as a god). Because of his unstable character – instability verging on insanity – contemporary writers punned on his title, nicknaming him *Epimanes* ('utterly mad').

Antiochus sought to unify his diverse empire by imposing Greek culture and religion upon all his subjects. He forbade Jewish religious practices such as Sabbath observance, circumcision, and reading the Torah. The Temple was rededicated to Olympian Zeus and pagan sacrifices were offered to Zeus on an altar erected over the altar of burnt offering.[549] In the midst of this persecution, the Book of Daniel reminds the people that they had also been persecuted under the Babylonians hundreds of years earlier – Jerusalem had

---

[549] John Whitehorne, 'Antiochus', in David Noel Freedman (ed.), *The Anchor Bible Dictionary, vol. 1*, Doubleday, New York, 1992, pp. 270-1.

been destroyed, the Temple lay in ruins, and many of the people were led into exile where they languished 'by the rivers of Babylon' until Cyrus, King of Persia, defeated the Babylonians and allowed the Jews to return home.

Remember the past, the Book of Daniel tells the Jewish people in the midst of yet another persecution. God did not abandon his people then, nor will he now. The author of the book of Daniel was offering hope to an oppressed people. Just as a former foe was vanquished, this tyrant will meet a similar end.

Against this background it's interesting to reflect upon what was happening in the world when Pope Pius XI instituted the feast of Christ the King in 1925. Lenin had died a year earlier in 1924, but some seven years earlier in October 1917 the Bolsheviks under Lenin's leadership had seized power in Russia and established the Soviet Union. Under the leadership of Benito Mussolini the Fascists held power in Italy between 1922 until 1945, and in 1933 Adolf Hitler was appointed chancellor in Germany. These three movements – Communism, Fascism and Nazism – shaped the history of the twentieth century and were responsible for untold evil and loss of human life.

And what happened? Like Antiochus before them,[550] Hitler and Mussolini met ignominious deaths. Lenin's body is displayed in a mausoleum in Moscow, but the city named after him, Leningrad, has reverted to its former name, St Petersburg. One is reminded of a

---

550 Some lurid accounts of his death are given in 1 Macc 6:1-17, 2 Macc 1:13-17, 9:1-29.

ritual incorporated into the ceremony of papal coronation between 1409 until 1963. As the newly elected pope proceeded from the sacristy of St Peter's Basilica in his *sedia gestatoria* a smouldering flax was held before the pontiff, together with the admonition, '*Sancte Pater, sic transit gloria mundi!*' (Holy Father, thus passes the glory of this world).

Chapter 7 of the Book of Daniel is a dream-vision, a common literary device in apocalyptic writing. God (referred to as the Ancient of Days) is seated upon a throne, presiding over a divine court ready to render judgment upon all the major empires of the world, up to an including that of Antiochus. A mysterious figure called a 'son of man' appears, coming on the clouds of heaven. The Ancient of Days bestows upon him all the dominion formerly possessed by other kingdoms – empires that have oppressed God's people throughout the centuries.

Who is this son of man? He is not a single individual, but a collective entity. The son of man is the embodiment of those 'who even as the book (of Daniel) was being written were experiencing the pangs of persecution at the hands of the Syrian king (Antiochus). It is they who expect the reward of their devotion in the form of everlasting dominion.'[551]

The imagery of the Book of Daniel is taken over into today's second reading from the Apocalypse (or Book of Revelation). Christian eyes now see the 'one coming on the clouds' not as a corporate entity, but as Jesus himself. This reading is addressed to a Christian

---

551 W. Sibley Towner, *Daniel*, John Knox Press, Louisville, 1984, p. 106.

community oppressed by Roman imperial power. In the midst of persecution it urges them to stand firm, for they will soon share in the triumph of Christ who is the beginning (*alpha* – the first letter of the Greek alphabet) and end (*omega* – the last letter of the Greek alphabet) of all human history.

The centerpiece of the Passion story in John's gospel is the confrontation between Jesus and the Roman governor Pontius Pilate. It is a clash of kingdoms – the kingdom of God and the kingdom of Caesar. When Jesus tells Pilate that his kingdom is not of this world he isn't implying that his sphere of rule is other worldly, and that the earth can stew in its own juice. Jesus isn't talking about the kingdom's location, but about its character: this kingdom does not come by violence or imperial might.[552]

A painting by Holman Hunt entitled *The Light of the World* now hanging in St Paul's Cathedral, London, offers an instructive commentary on the kingship of Christ. The head of Jesus bears not only a traditional kingly crown, but also a crown of thorns. He stands at a door and knocks. He will not batter down the door to gain entry; he stands and awaits our response. If you look closely at the painting you will notice that there is no handle on the outside. The door can be opened only from the inside. As John Shea observes, 'Christ is not king because he can bend human will with his might. He is king because out of love he foregoes force and continues to talk. Peter may cut off ears, but Jesus restores them.'[553]

---

[552] N.T. Wright, *Twelve Months of Sundays: Year B*, SPCK, London, 2002, p. 127.
[553] John Shea, *Eating with the Bridegroom*, p. 278.

Releasing the Captive

The kingdom of God is not based on violence or maintained by force. A knight in medieval Japan deserted his liege lord after long inner struggles, for such an action was inconceivable according to the code of knighthood. He did it because he felt an overwhelming vocation for the Zen life. Having spent some twelve years in one of the mountain monasteries, he set out on pilgrimage.

Before long he encountered a knight on horseback who recognised him and made to strike him down but then decided against it as he was unwilling to sully his sword. So he just spat in the monk's face as he rode by. In the act of wiping away the spittle, the monk realised in a flash what in former days his reaction would have been to such an insult. Deeply moved, he turned round towards the mountain area where he had done his training, bowed, and composed a poem:

> The mountain is the mountain
> And the Way is the same as of old.
> Verily what has changed
> is my own heart.[554]

---

554 Irmgard Schloegl, *The Wisdom of the Zen Masters*, Sheldon Press, London, 1975, pp. 18-19.

BIBLIOGRAPHY

Armstrong, Karen, *A History of God*, Mandarin, London, 1993.

———, *The Spiral Staircase: A Memoir*, HarperCollins, London, 2004.

Barclay, William, *The Gospel of Mark*, The Saint Andrew Press, Edinburgh, repr. 1971.

Bausch, William J., *A World of Stories*, Twenty-Third Publications, Mystic CT, 1998

———, *More Telling Stories, Compelling Stories*, Twenty-Third Publications, Mystic CT, 1994.

———, *Once Upon a Gospel*, Twenty-Third Publications, Mystic, CT, 2008.

———, *Storytelling: Imagination and Faith*, Twenty-Third Publications, Mystic, CT, 1984.

———, *Storytelling the Word*, Mystic, Twenty-Third Publications, Mystic, CT, 1996.

———, *Telling Stories, Compelling Stories*, Twenty-Third Publications, Mystic, CT, 1992.

———, *The Total Parish Manual*, Twenty-Third Publications, Mystic, CT, 1994.

———, *The Yellow Brick Road*, Twenty-Third Publications, Mystic, CT, 1999.

———, *Timely Homilies*, Twenty-Third Publications, Mystic, CT, 1990.

———, *40 More Seasonal Homilies*, Twenty-Third Publications, Mystic, CT, 2005.

———, *60 More Seasonal Homilies*, Twenty-Third Publications, Mystic, CT, 2003.

Beck, Edward L., *God Underneath*, Image Books, New York, 2002.

———, *Soul Provider*, Image Books Doubleday, New York, 2007.

Bergant, Dianne and Richard Fragomeni, *Preaching the New Lectionary, Year B*, The Liturgical Press, Collegeville, MN, 1999.

Borg, Marcus J., *Meeting Jesus Again for the First Time*, HarperSanFrancisco, 1995.

———, *The Gospel of Mark*, Morehouse Publishing, Harrisburg, NY, 2009.

———, *The Heart of Christianity*, HarperSanFrancisco, 2003.

Brown, Raymond E., *The Birth of the Messiah*, An Image Book, New York, 1979.

———, *The Gospel According to John I-XII*, Doubleday & Company, New York, 1966.

———, *Responses to 101 Questions on the Bible*, Paulist Press, New York, 1990.

———, Joseph A. Fitzmyer and Roland E. Murphy (eds), *The New Jerome Biblical Commentary*, Geoffrey Chapman, London, 1989.

Byrne, Brendan, *A Costly Freedom*, St Paul's, Strathfield, NSW, 2008.

Campbell, Joseph, *The Hero with a Thousand Faces*, Fontana Press, London, 1993.

Brian Cavanaugh, *The Sower's Seeds*, Paulist Press, Mahwah, NJ, 1990

Covey, Stephen R., *The 7 Habits of Highly Effective People*, The Business Library, Melbourne, 1989.

Cowan, James, *Journey to the Inner Mountain*, Hodder & Stoughton, London, 2002.

Cross, F.L. and E.A. Livingstone, *The Oxford Dictionary of the Christian Church*, Oxford University Press, Oxford, repr. 1997.

Crossan, John Dominic, *Jesus: A Revolutionary Biography*, HarperSanFrancisco, 1994.

de Botton, Alain, *Status Anxiety*, Hamish Hamilton, Camberwell, Vic., 2004.

de Mello, Anthony, *The Heart of the Enlightened*, Fount Paperbacks, 1989.

———, *The Prayer of the Frog, vol. 1*, Gujarat Sahitya Prakash, Anand, India, 1989.

———, *The Song of the Bird*, Gujarat Sahitya Prakash, Anand, India, 1985.

Donahue, John R. and Daniel J. Harrington, *The Gospel of Mark*, The Liturgical Press, Collegeville, MN, 2002.

Fitzmyer, Joseph A., *A Christological Catechism*, Paulist Press, New York, 1981.

———, *The Gospel According to Luke I-IX*, The Anchor Bible, New York, 1970.

Frame, Tom, *Losing My Religion*, University of New South Wales Press, Sydney, 2009.

Freeman, Laurence, *Jesus: The Teacher Within*, Continuum, New York, 2000.

Gore, Al, *An Inconvenient Truth*, Bloomsbury, London, 2006.

Hamilton, Clive and Richard Denniss, *Affluenza*, Allen & Unwin, Crows Nest, NSW, 2005.

Hendra, Tony, *Father Joe*, Hamish Hamilton, Camberwell, Vic, 2004.

Holloway, Richard, *Between the Monster and the Saint*, Canongate, Edinburgh, 2008.

———, *Doubts and Loves*, Canongate, Edinburgh, 2005.

———, *How to Read the Bible*, W.W. Norton & Company, New York, 2007.

Jamison, Christopher, *Finding Happiness*, Weidenfeld & Nicolson, London, 2008.

Jacobs, A.J., *The Year of Living Biblically*, Simon & Schuster Paperbacks, New York, 2007.

Jones, Alan, *Living the Truth*, Cowley Publications, 2000.

———, *Passion for Pilgrimage*, Morehouse Publishing, Harrisburg, PA, 1989.

———, *Soulmaking: The Desert Way of Spirituality*, HarperSanFrancisco, 1989.

———, *The Soul's Journey*, Cowley Publications, Cambridge, MA, 2001.

Jones, Caroline, *An Authentic Life*, ABC Books, Sydney, 1998.

———, *The Search for Meaning*, Australian Broadcasting Corporation / Collins Dove, Sydney, repr. 1990.

Kearney, Michael, *Mortally Wounded: Stories of Soul Pain, Death and Healing*, Mercier Press, Dublin, 1996.

Kornfield, Jack, *After the Ecstasy, the Laundry*, Bantam Books, New York, 2000.

Kushner, Harold S., *When Bad Things Happen to Good People*, Pan Books, London, 1981.

Kysar, Robert, *Preaching John*, Fortress Press, Minneapolis, 2002.

McGinn, Bernard, *The Foundations of Mysticism*, Crossroad, New York, 1991.

Marcus, Joel, *Mark 1-8*, Doubleday, New York, 2000.

———, *Mark 8-16*, Yale University Press, New Haven, 2009.

Meier, John P., *A Marginal Jew: The Roots of the Problem and the Person, Volume 1*, Doubleday, New York, 1991.

———, *A Marginal Jew: Rethinking the Historical Jesus: Mentor, Message, and Miracles, Volume II*, Doubleday, New York, 1994.

———, *A Marginal Jew: Companions and Competitors, Volume III*, Doubleday, New York, 2001.

———, *A Marginal Jew: Law and Love, Volume IV*, Yale University Press, New Haven, 2009.

Merton, Thomas, *New Seeds of Contemplation*, Burns & Oates, London, repr. 2003.

———, *The Wisdom of the Desert*, Sheldon Press, London, 1976.

Moloney, Francis J., *The Gospel of John*, The Liturgical Press, Collegeville, MN, 1998.

———, *The Gospel of Mark*, Hendrickson Publishers, Peabody, MA, 2002.

Moore, Thomas, *Care of the Soul*, HarperPerennial, New York, 1994.

Moses, John, *The Desert: An Anthology for Lent*, Canterbury Press, Norwich, 1977.

Murphy-O'Connor, Jerome, *The Holy Land*, new edn, Oxford University Press, Oxford, 1992.

Nineham, D.E., *Saint Mark*, Penguin Books, Harmondsworth, 1963..

Nouwen, Henri, *Making All Things New: An Introduction to the Spiritual Life*, Doubleday, New York, 1981.

O'Collins, Gerald, *Experiencing Jesus*, E.J. Dwyer, Sydney, 1994.

——— and Mario Farrugia, *Catholicism: The Story of Catholic Christianity*, Oxford University Press, Oxford, 2003.

O'Connor, Peter A., *Looking Inwards*, Penguin Books, Camberwell, Vic, 2003.

O'Kelly, Eugene, *Chasing Daylight*, McGraw-Hill (with a new afterword by Corinne O'Kelly), New York, 2008.

Peck, M. Scott, *Further along the Road Less Travelled*, Simon & Schuster, New York, 1993.

———, *The Road Less Travelled*, Arrow Books, London, repr. 1999.

Ratzinger, Joseph, *Introduction to Christianity*, Search Press, London, 1968.

———, (Pope Benedict XVI), *Jesus of Nazareth*, Doubleday, New York, 2007.

Rolheiser, Ronald, *Against an Infinite Horizon*, Hodder & Stoughton, London, 1995.

———, *Forgotten Among the Lilies*, Doubleday, New York, 2005.

———, *The Shattered Lantern*, Hodder & Stoughton, London, 1994.

Sacks, Jonathan, *To Heal a Fractured World*, Continuum, London, 2005.

Schloegl, Irmgard, *The Wisdom of the Zen Masters*, Sheldon Press, London, 1975.

Shea, John, *Eating with the Bridegroom: Year B*, Liturgical Press, Collegeville, MN, 2005.

———, *Stories of God*, The Thomas More Press, Chicago, IL, 1978.

Thayer, Joseph H., *Thayer's Greek-English Lexicon of The New Testament*, Grand Rapids, Michigan, Baker Book House, 1977.

Tredinnick, Mark (ed.), *A Place on Earth*, University of New South Wales Press, Sydney, 2003.

Tyndale, Philippa, *Don't Look Back*, Allen & Unwin, Sydney, 2000.

Ward, Benedicta, *The Desert Fathers: Sayings of the Early Christian Monks*, Penguin Books, London, 2003.

Weigel, George, *Letters to a Young Catholic*, Basic Books, New York, 2004.

———, *The Cube and the Cathedral*, Basic Books, New York, 2005.

———, *The Truth of Catholicism*, Harper Perennial, New York, 2002.

Williams, Rowan, *Silence and Honey Cakes*, A Lion Book, Oxford, 2003.

Wright, N.T., *Following Jesus*, William B. Eerdmans Publishing Company, Grand Rapids, MI, 1994.

———, *For All the Saints?* Morehouse Publishing, Harrisburg, PA, 2003.

———, *Jesus and the Victory of God*, Fortress Press, Minneapolis, 1996.

———, *The Challenge of Jesus*, InterVarsity Press, Downers Grove, IL, 1999.

———, *Twelve Months of Sundays: Year B*, SPCK, London, 2002.

Wright, Tom, *John for Everyone, Part 1*, SPCK, London, 2002.

———, *Mark for Everyone*, SPCK, London, 2001.

Releasing the Captive

Reflections for the year of Mark

Releasing the Captive

www.ingramcontent.com/pod-product-compliance
Lightning Source LLC
Chambersburg PA
CBHW070748230426
43665CB00017B/2285